I0750532

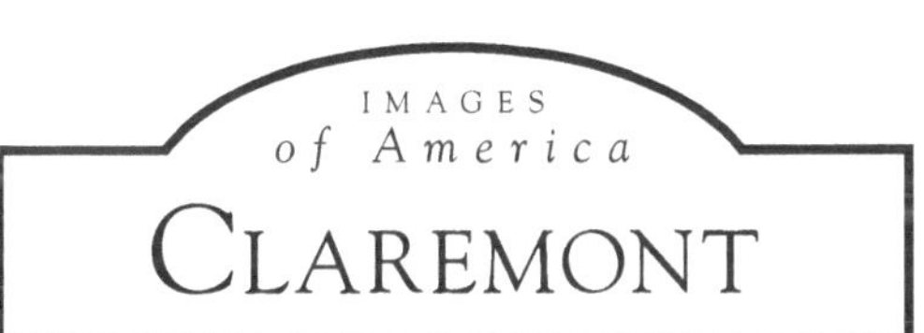
IMAGES
of America
CLAREMONT

On the Cover: This view of Pleasant Street looks north toward the square around 1895. The Hotel Claremont, now known as the Moody Building, is in the background, with its original center facade above the marquee. (Claremont Historical Society.)

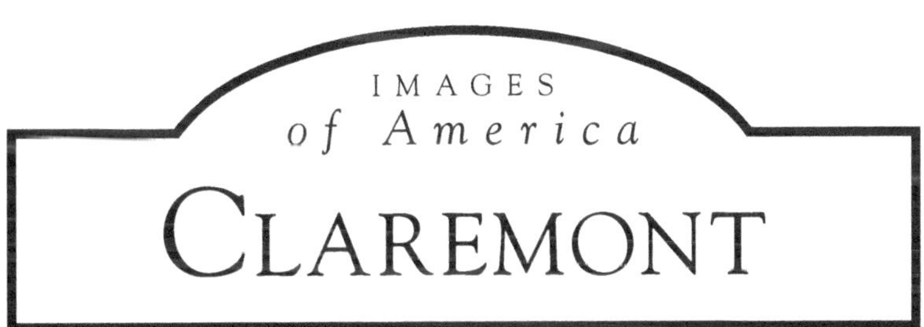

Wayne L. McElreavy

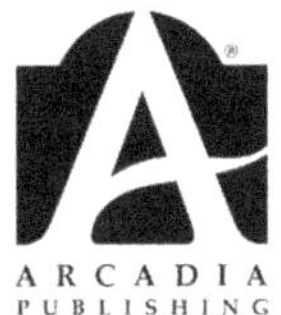

ISBN 978-0-7385-9297-8

Published by Arcadia Publishing
Charleston, South Carolina

Library of Congress Control Number: 2012935538

For all general information, please contact Arcadia Publishing:
Telephone 843-853-2070
Fax 843-853-0044
E-mail sales@arcadiapublishing.com
For customer service and orders:
Toll-Free 1-888-313-2665

Visit us on the Internet at www.arcadiapublishing.com

For my son, Ryan W. McElreavy

Contents

Acknowledgments

The photographs in this book came from two sources: those designated CHS are courtesy of the Claremont Historical Society and those designated WLM are from the author's personal collection.

A number of people have been helpful over the years in my quest for historical information. Among them are John Bennett, longtime Claremont educator; Colin Sanborn, of Claremont's Fiske Free Library and my predecessor as president of the Claremont Historical Society; and Arthur Dion, longtime resident and former coworker whose office I often visited for answers to my historical questions.

INTRODUCTION

Other than Native Americans, the first known settlement in Claremont occurred in 1762 when Moses Spafford and David Lynde cleared land and built cabins. Two years later, on October 26, 1764, Gov. Benning Wentworth issued land grants to 70 people, most of whom were from Connecticut. Claremont was named after the Surrey, England, estate of the Earl of Clare, which was built by Thomas Pelham-Holles, a cousin of Wentworth.

Settlement was minimal in the first few years, with the grantees finally taking steps to settle or dispose of their shares in 1767, partially due to the realization that more squatters were settling upon the land. Only three of the original grantees ever inhabited the town.

The lifting of trade embargoes at the end of the War of 1812 enabled the diversification of industry, with numerous factories sprouting up along the Sugar River, which is fed by Lake Sunapee and has a series of falls totaling about 250 feet as it twists through Claremont. The 1820 creation of the Sunapee Dam Company, which controls water flow from Lake Sunapee into the Sugar River, further enabled an industrial boom in Claremont. With the growth of industry in the 1830s, Claremont's population outpaced that of its neighbors and Claremont emerged to prominence and became a prosperous mill town for about 150 years.

Claremont owes some of its industrial prosperity to inventions made by its own people. John Tyler developed the iron turbine waterwheel, which was a major advance in the harnessing of waterpower. The most notable figure in Claremont's industrial development was Albert Ball. Among more than 130 patents, Ball's most notable invention was the diamond core drill. This and other inventions of his revolutionized the mining industry and led to the formation of what was Claremont's largest employer for decades.

Despite the construction of the Sullivan Railroad on the western edge of town in 1849, which connected Claremont to points north and south, the town was lacking rail service to the state's larger cities to the east. This changed when the steep Newbury Cut was finally completed in 1871, allowing tracks to connect Concord and Claremont a year later. This gave Claremont another boost as it increased trade and tourism to the area.

The influx of industry brought with it retail success, as Pleasant Street developed into a thriving shopping district to go along with the lower village on Main Street. Claremont became known as "The Shoppers Town" in this period and was the industrial, commercial, and social center of western New Hampshire.

Though it took years for the full effects to be realized, Claremont was the big loser in the New Hampshire Interstate system. Preliminary plans for Interstate 89, which would connect Concord and Montreal, called for the road to pass close to Claremont, which, at the time, was considered too important to bypass. Similarly, Interstate 91 was originally slated for New Hampshire and would have passed between Claremont and Newport.

Despite Interstate 91 being built in Vermont just across the Connecticut River—still close enough to Claremont—Interstate 89 ended up 25 miles to the north. Claremont's city government was under the thumb of its largest employer, who did not want to increase wages to compete for workers with the new companies they figured the interstate would bring. The general thinking was that everything was great in Claremont, so why tinker with it?

What appeared to be shortsightedness to the rest of the state was actually the result of small-town political maneuvering to keep Interstate 89 away from Claremont. It happened that our governor at the time was a Lebanon resident, and one of our senators was a Hanover resident. They were more than happy to use their political clout to capitalize on Claremont's folly. The recent economic woes of Claremont should be measured not only by the industry that has left the city—including that influential large employer—but also by the industries that never came because their competition was unwanted.

As a result, the Lebanon area saw a major increase in industry and retail establishments, while those in Claremont dwindled. Claremont was no longer the shoppers' town, as people from surrounding towns as well as Claremonters began traveling to West Lebanon for shopping. In the early 1980s, this pattern caused one Claremont merchant to lament, "Claremonters don't support Claremont businesses."

Claremont also bears the stigma of the Claremont Lawsuit. In 1991, the Claremont school district joined in a coalition with the school districts of Allenstown, Pittsfield, Franklin, and Lisbon in a suit against the state regarding the funding of education. At the time, towns needed to fund any educational expenses not covered by the state through property taxes. The lawsuit argued this was unconstitutional on the part of the state, and the system placed a hardship on property-poor towns such as Claremont.

The towns ultimately prevailed in their suit, which resulted in property-rich towns becoming donor towns to the educational funding system. While this helped the city monetarily, it was a major black eye to the city's image. Despite being a latecomer to the issue—the other towns had taken part in the Jessemen and Augenblick suits against the state in the 1980s—the lawsuit became commonly known as the "Claremont Lawsuit." Once one of the most prosperous communities in the state, Claremont's image as a poor town was firmly cemented, while the other towns in the lawsuit have been relatively untarnished.

Today, Claremont is taking steps to revitalize itself. It became a Main Street Community, and the group involved with that later morphed into the Heart of Claremont Association. After sitting empty for years and thought by many to be a lost cause, empty mill buildings came to life with the Monadnock Mills Revitalization Project, which brought the Common Man Inn & Restaurant and Red River Computer Company to Claremont. Among the city's excellent parks system, improvements to Monadnock Park have made it one of the best athletic facilities in the state. As this is being written, a new community center is under construction. Despite a vote for a new high school being narrowly defeated in 2010, Claremont is a city on the move as it continues to take steps to return to prosperity.

One

Around Town

This chapter features various photographs from around town, from street scenes to mountain scenes. The changing landscape of the downtown area includes some of the large homes that once lined Pleasant and Broad Streets.

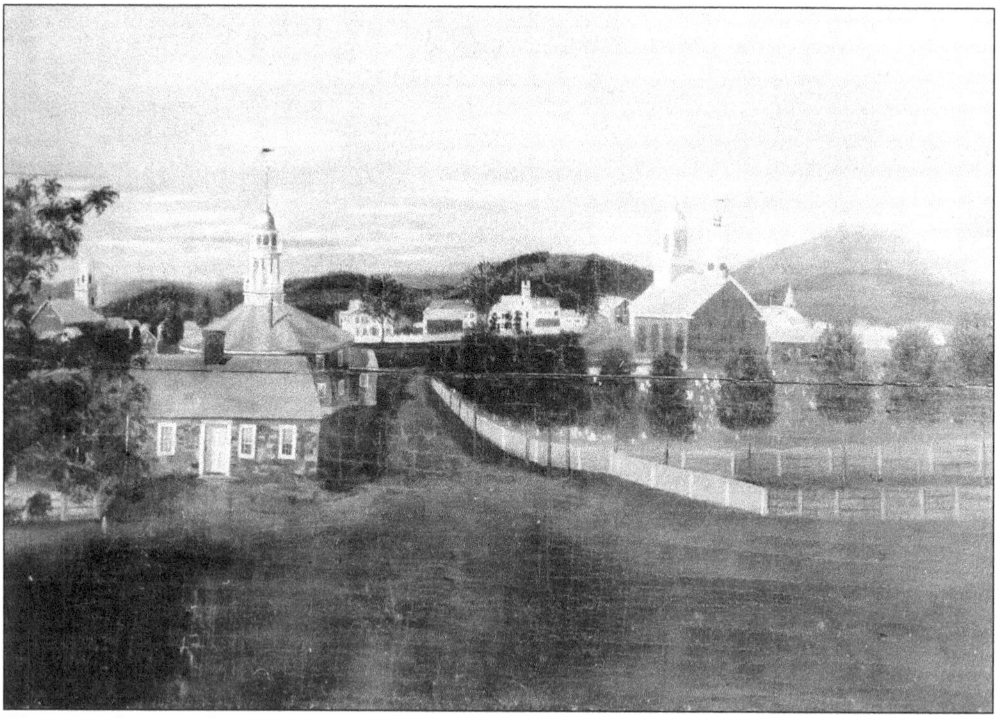

This is a photograph of an 1846 painting hanging in the Fiske Free Library. The scene shows Broad Street from High Street. On the site of the Trinity Episcopal Church, there is now an octagonal Universalist church. (CHS.)

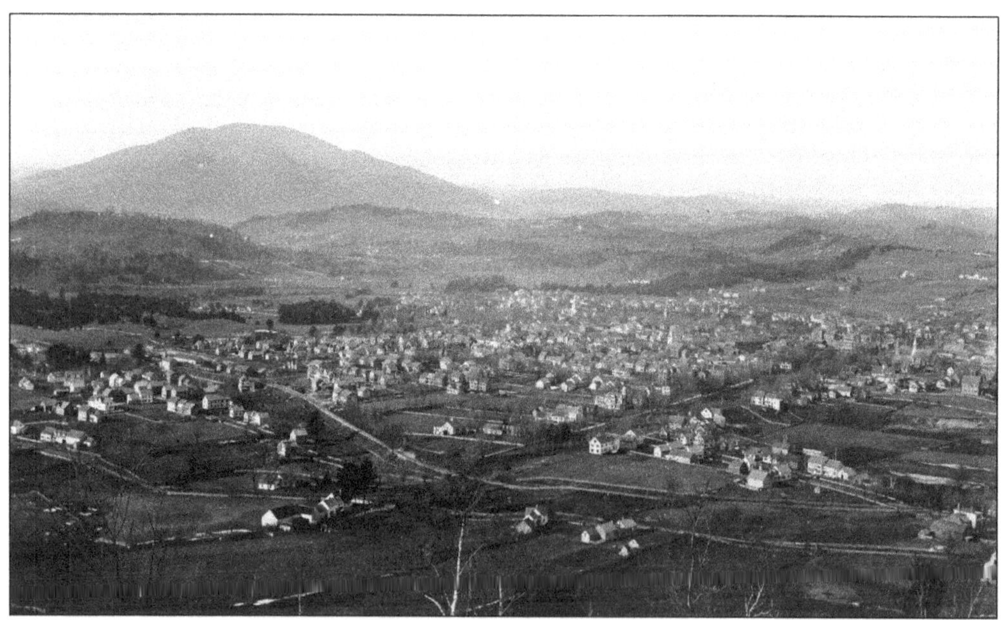

This bird's-eye view, from Flat Rock around 1880, shows a view that is impossible today, due to the growth of trees at the summit of Mount Arrowhead. (WLM.)

Green Mountain is seen here from the Broad Street Bridge around 1910. (WLM.)

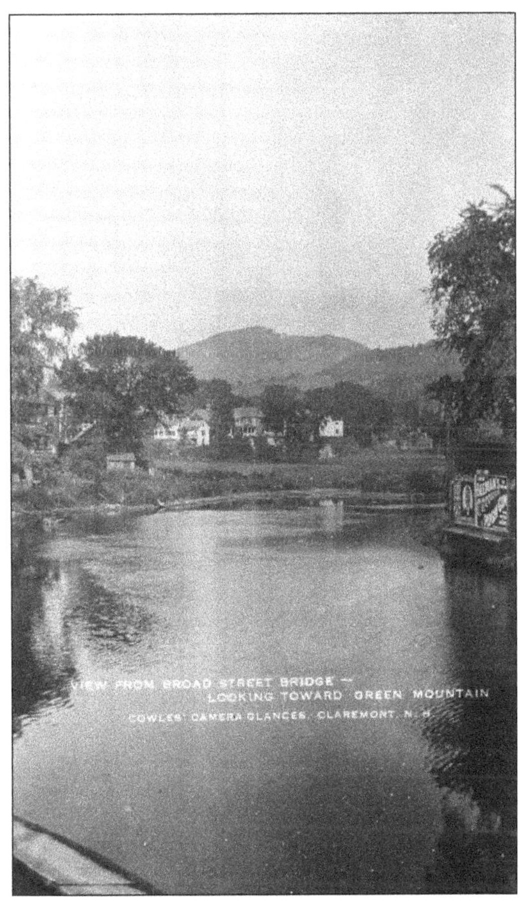

The intersection of North and Hanover Streets is seen here around 1890. (CHS.)

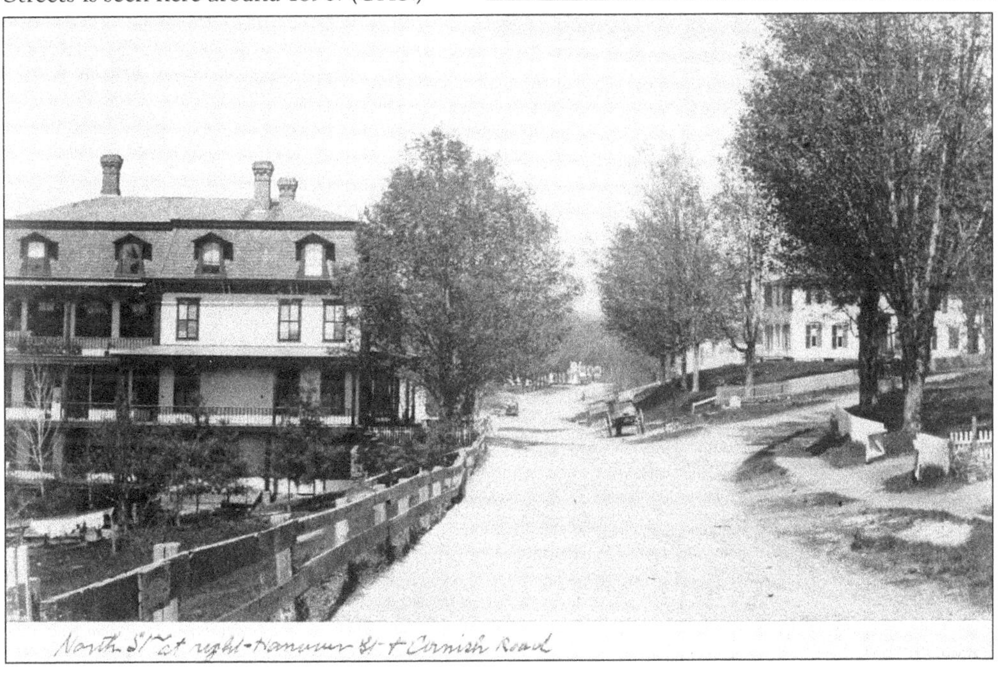

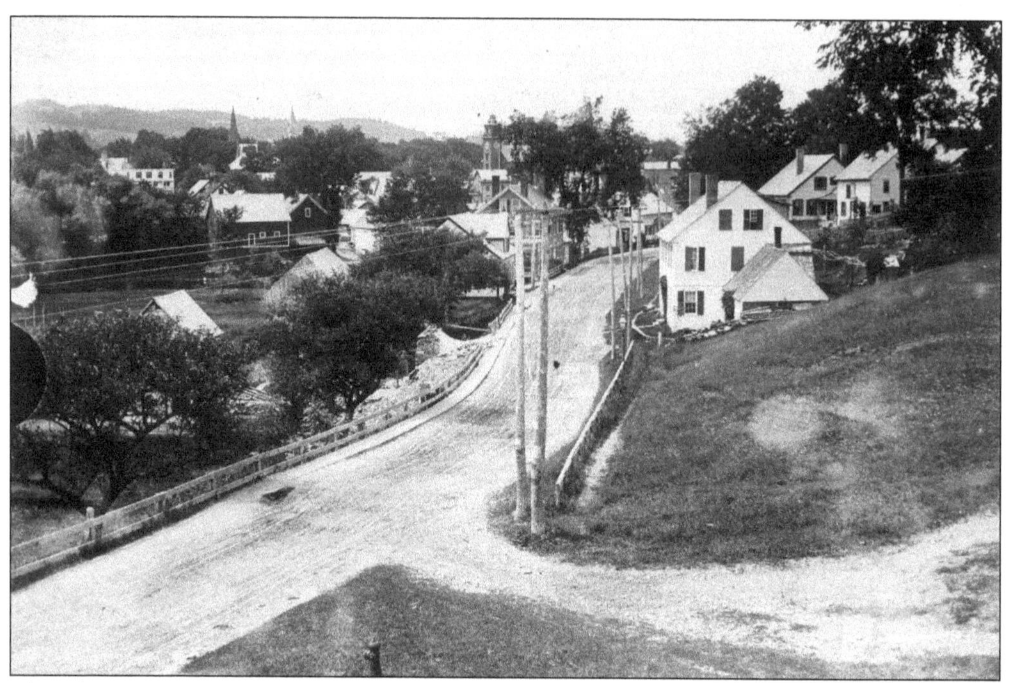

This photograph shows the intersection of Washington and Winter Streets. Note the wooden sidewalks. The house on the right, 38 Washington Street, was the home of Abraham Fisher and still stands. Miranda Steele's homestead, with the distinctive upstairs porch, is in the background to the right. (CHS.)

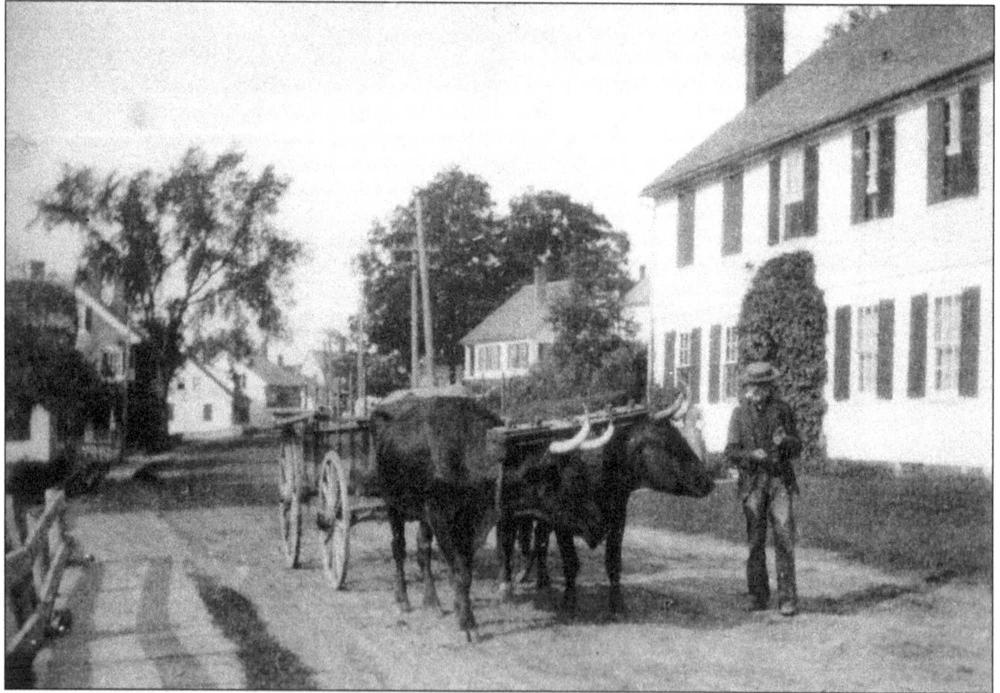

This is another view of 38 Washington Street taken around 1898. The wooden sidewalk is more distinguishable in this photograph. (CHS.)

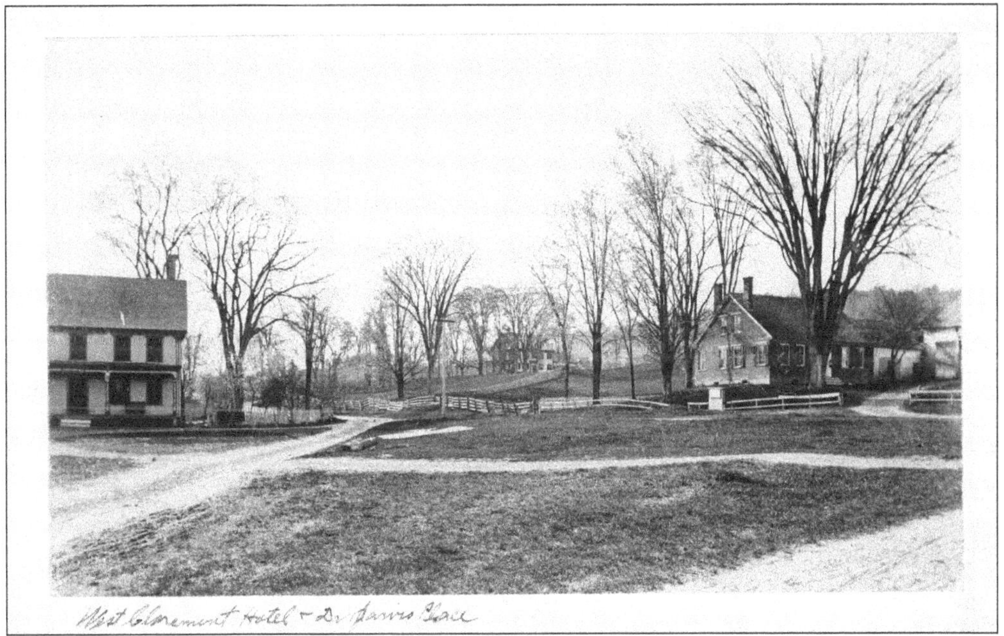

This image shows the spot where Plains Road and Clay Hill Road meet Main Street. West Claremont Hotel is on the left, and the home of Dr. Leonard Jarvis is on the right. (WLM.)

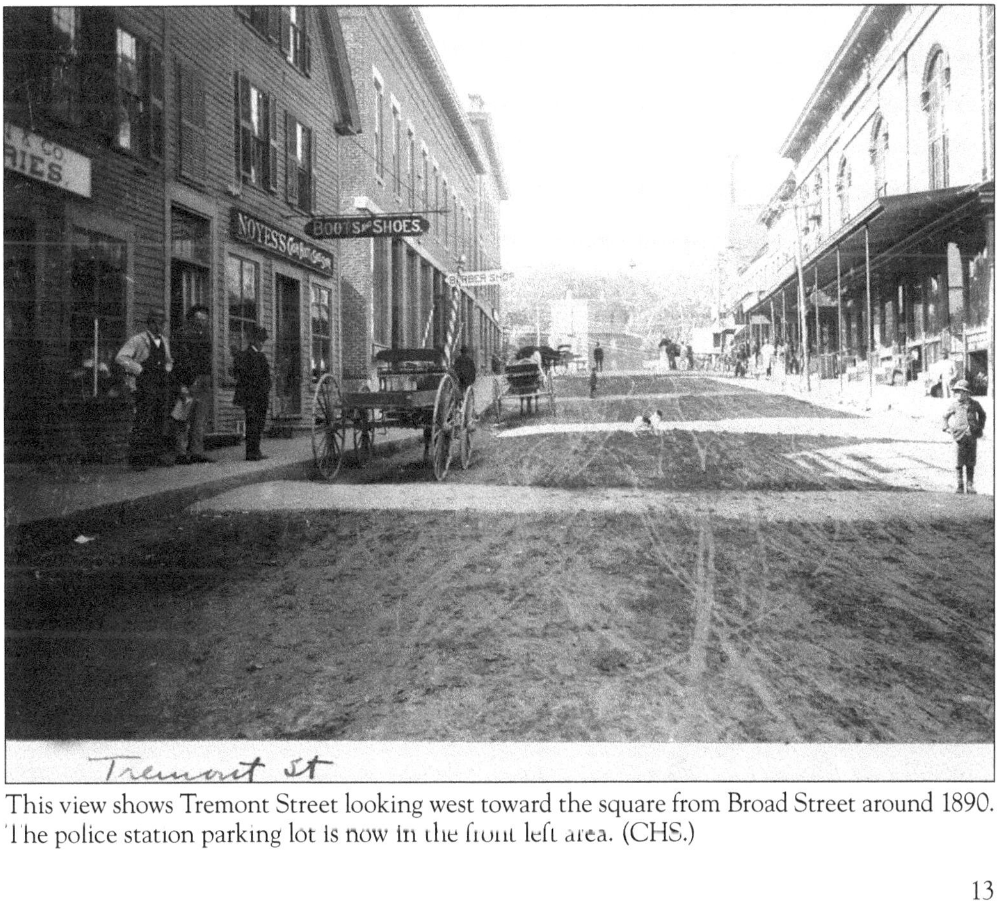

This view shows Tremont Street looking west toward the square from Broad Street around 1890. The police station parking lot is now in the front left area. (CHS.)

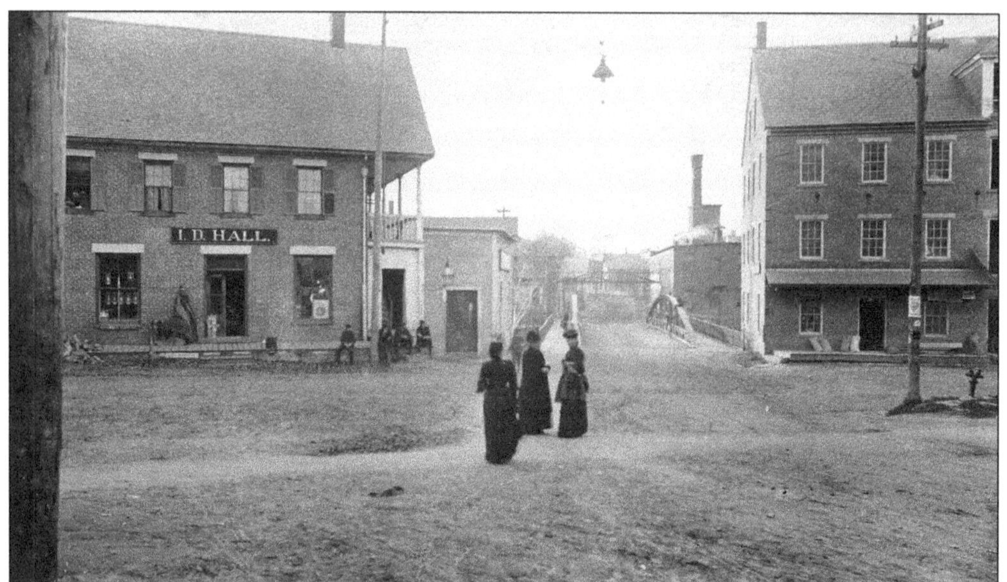

The lower village just east of the Main Street Bridge is seen here. The I.D. Hall store occupies the building known to recent generations of Claremonters as the longtime home of Eserskey's Hardware. The old gristmill is still in use today as part of the housing complex of Sugar River Mills. (CHS.)

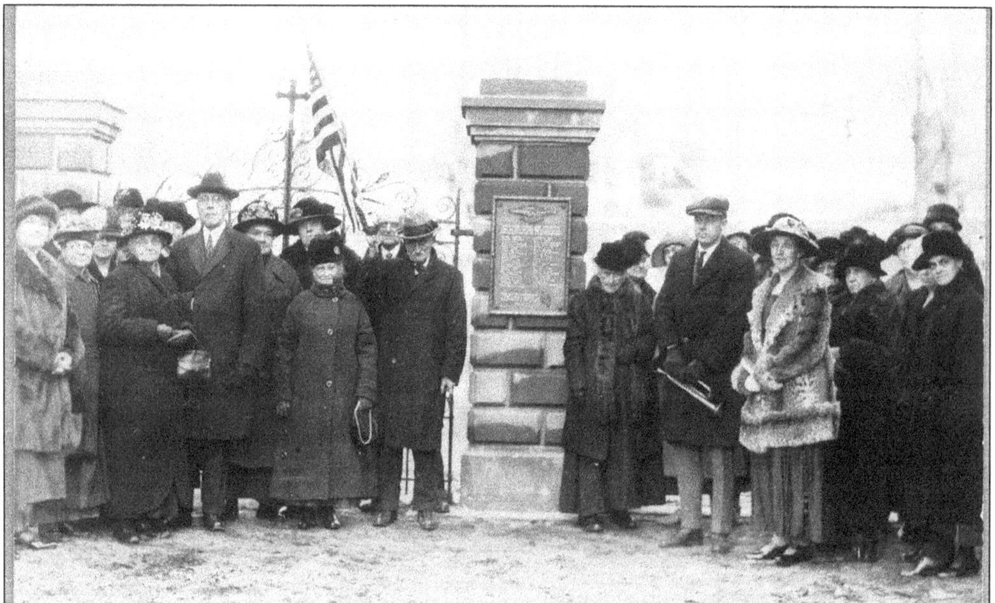

At dedication of D.A.R. Tablet at entrance to Broad St. Cemetary on Dec. 7, 1923. Group includes Rev. Ferrin,

This photograph shows Rev. Allan C. Ferrin (tall man with hat at left) and others at the dedication of the Daughters of the American Revolution tablet at the Broad Street Cemetery on December 7, 1923. (CHS.)

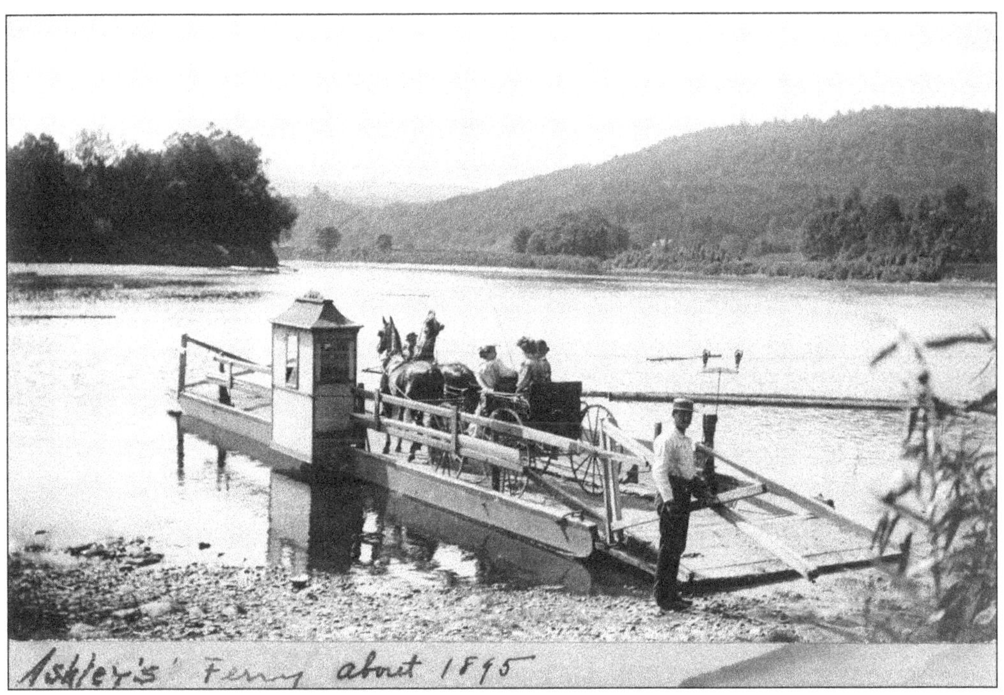

Ashley's Ferry is seen here about 1895. Oliver Ashley was granted a charter for a ferry service in 1784 and this ferry operated until 1927, taking passengers across the Connecticut River to Weathersfield-Bow, Vermont. The ferryboat sat on the east bank of the river and was washed away in the 1936 flood. (CHS.)

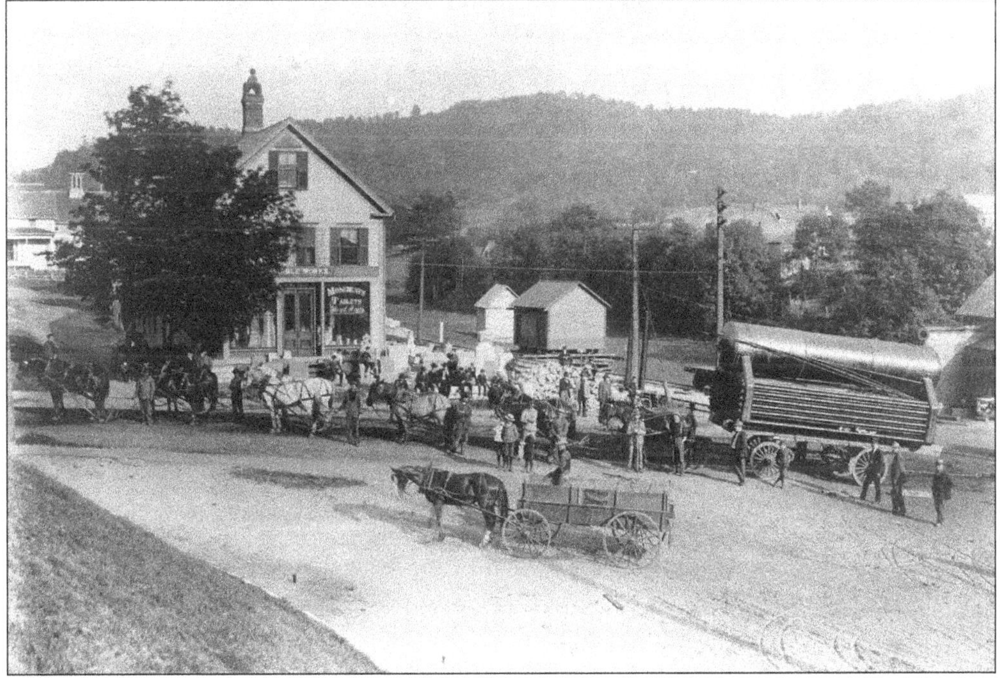

This cart pulls a wagon in front of Claremont Marble Works on Pleasant Street, the longtime home of American Plate Glass and Claremont Custom Framing. (CHS.)

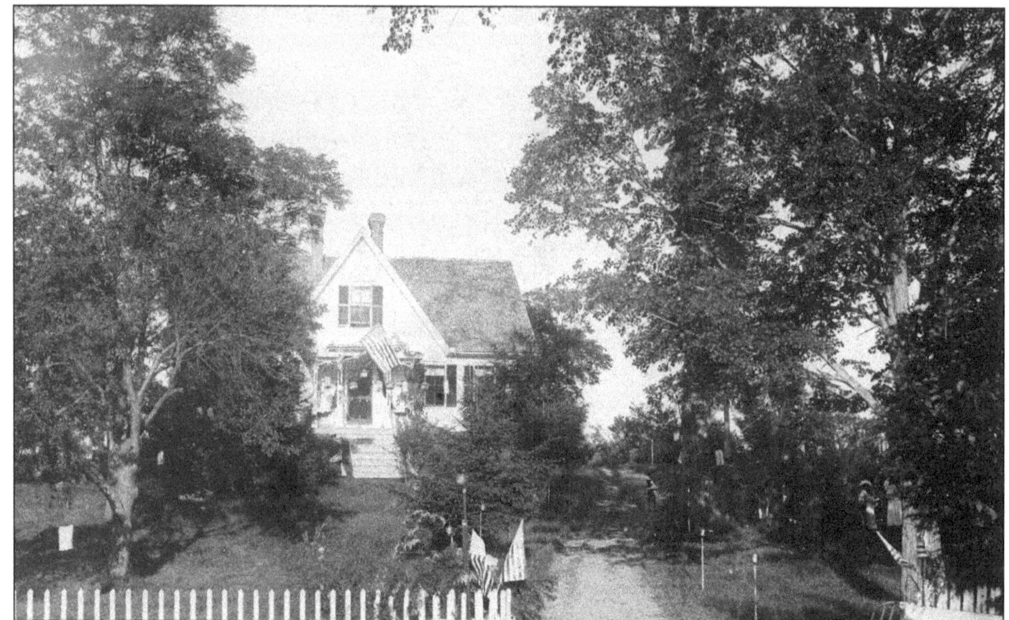

The original Cottage Hospital is seen here in 1893. The grounds on and around Dunning Street evolved over the years to become Claremont General Hospital and then Valley Regional Hospital. (CHS.)

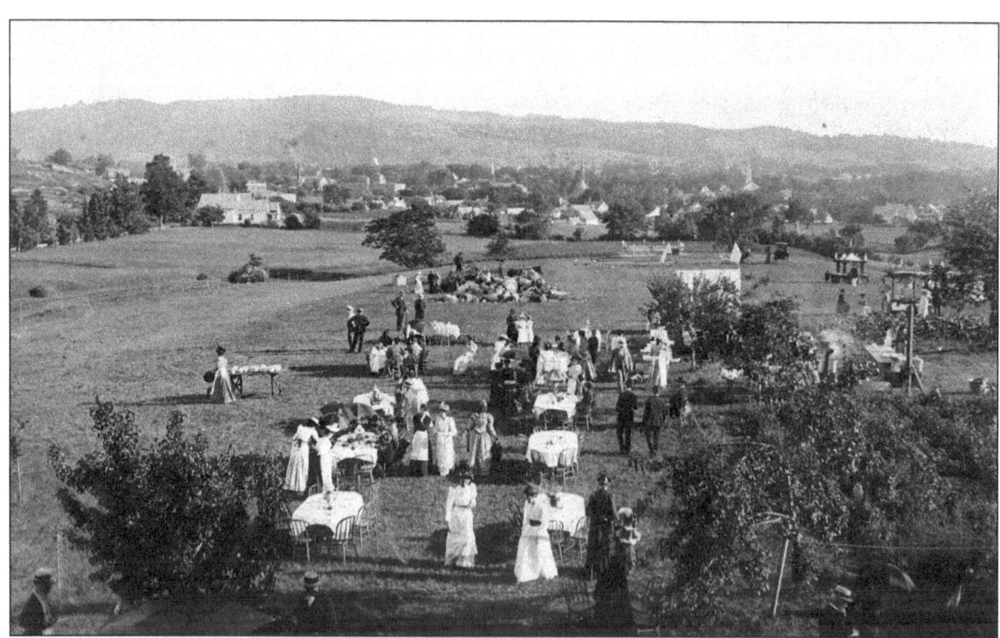

This photograph shows the festivities celebrating the dedication of Cottage Hospital on July 13, 1893, off what is now Dunning Street. (CHS.)

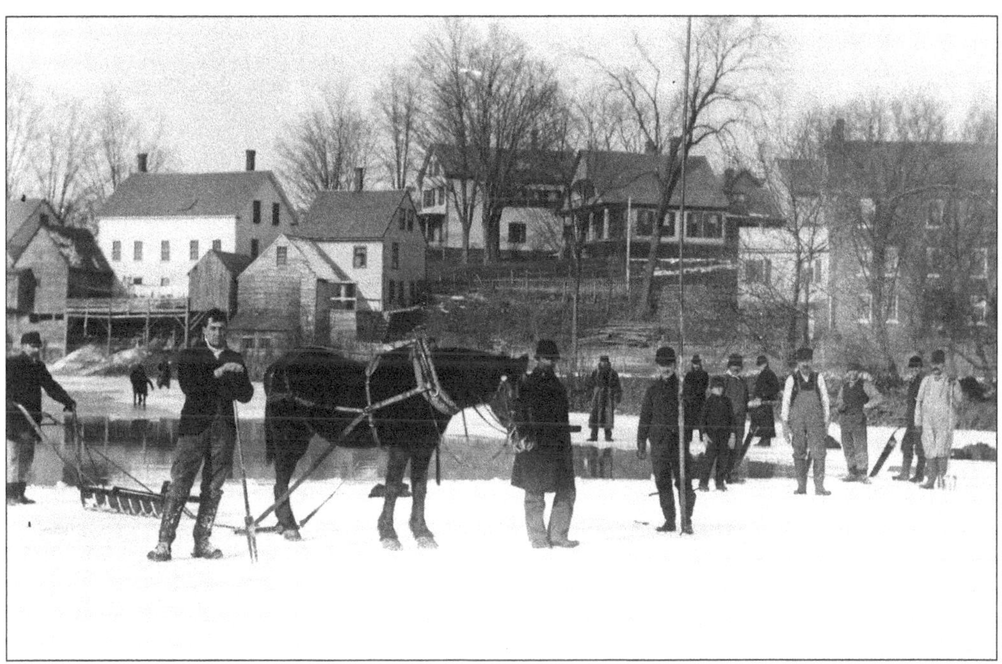

This ice-harvesting crew works on the Sugar River just east of the Broad Street Bridge around 1895. Note the horse-drawn saw. (CHS.)

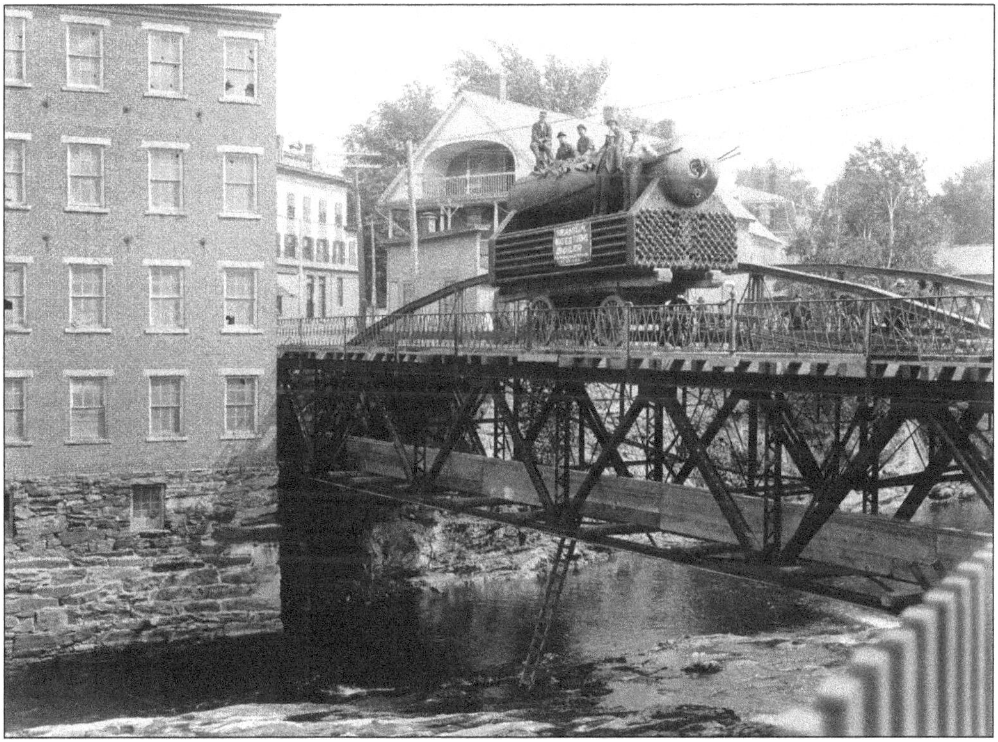

A Franklin water tube boiler crosses the Main Street Bridge around 1900. (CHS.)

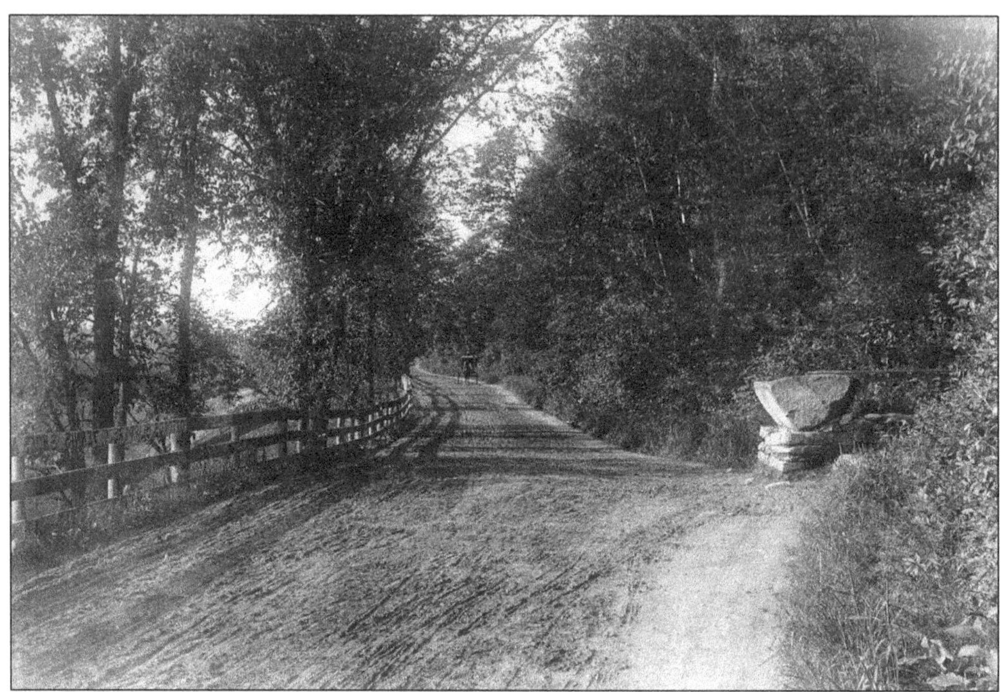

This stone watering trough was cut by Eli Stevens and put in place on West Claremont Road by Austin Tyler in 1840. It was on the way to West Claremont, on the right side of the road a short ways before the Beauregard Village Bridge. It was removed for road widening in the 1990s and now sits on the property of the Claremont History Museum on Mulberry Street. (CHS.)

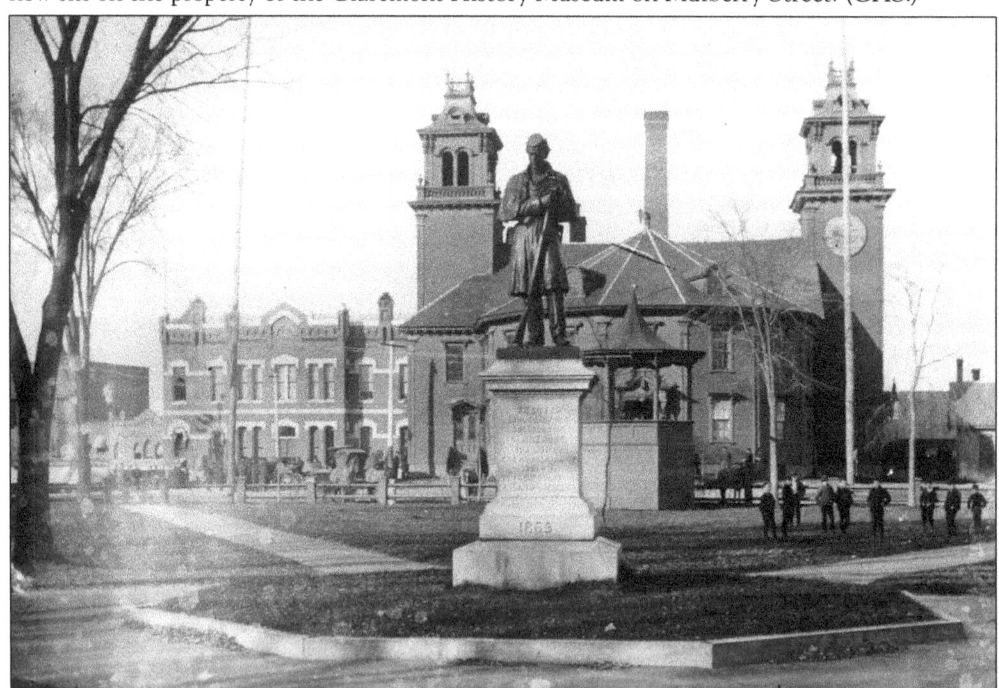

Noted sculptor Martin Milmore was commissioned to make this Civil War monument, which was erected in Broad Street Park in 1869. (CHS.)

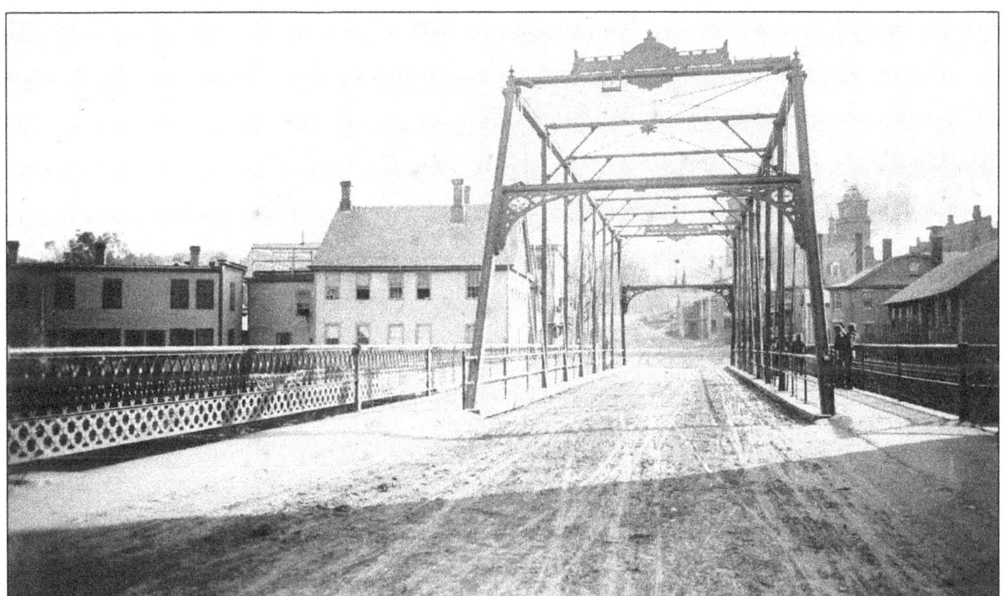

This view of Broad Street Bridge, taken before 1897, shows the two towers on the old town hall. (CHS.)

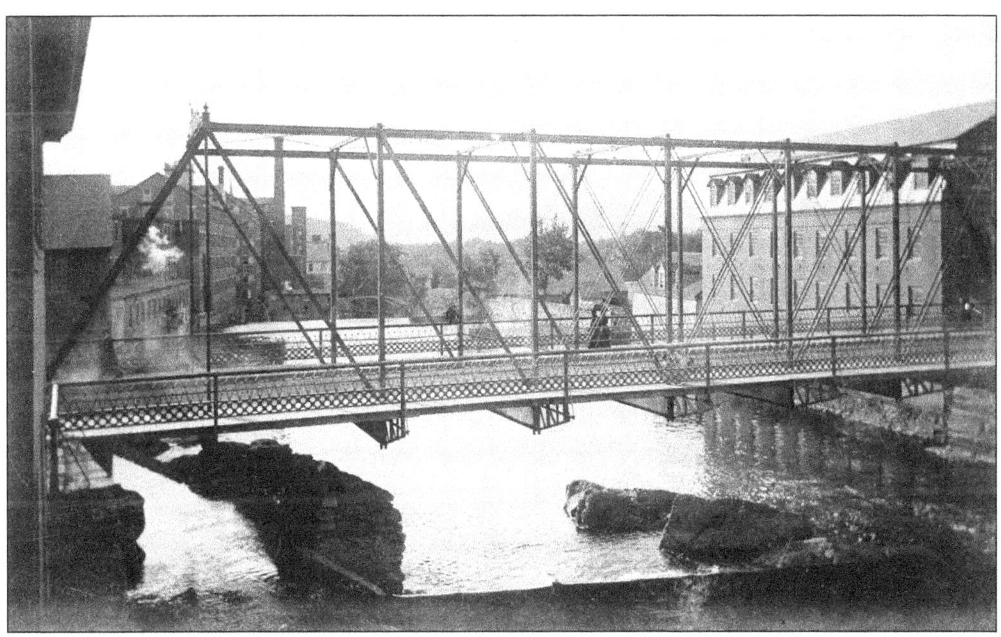

This view looks downstream at the Broad Street Bridge. The building on the right is 57 Broad Street, which was built in 1900 and was Store House No. 3 of the Monadnock Mills complex. (CHS.)

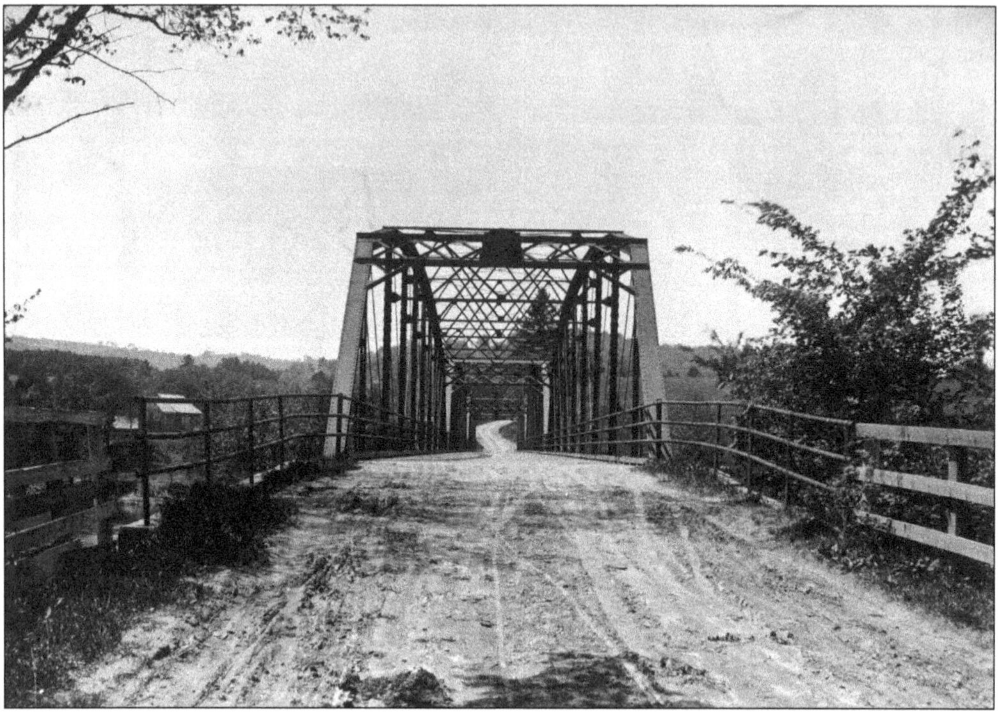

This photograph from around 1910 shows the Ascutneyville Bridge, which replaced a wooden structure that had washed away several years earlier. (CHS.)

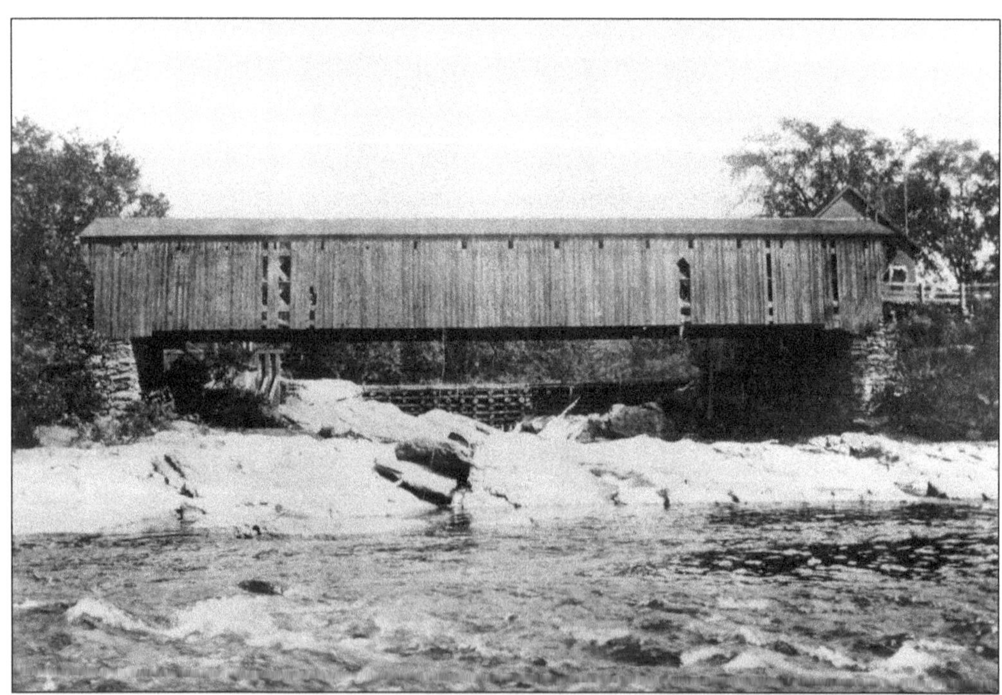

This view shows the old covered bridge next to the falls by the Coy Paper Mill on Plains Road. (CHS.)

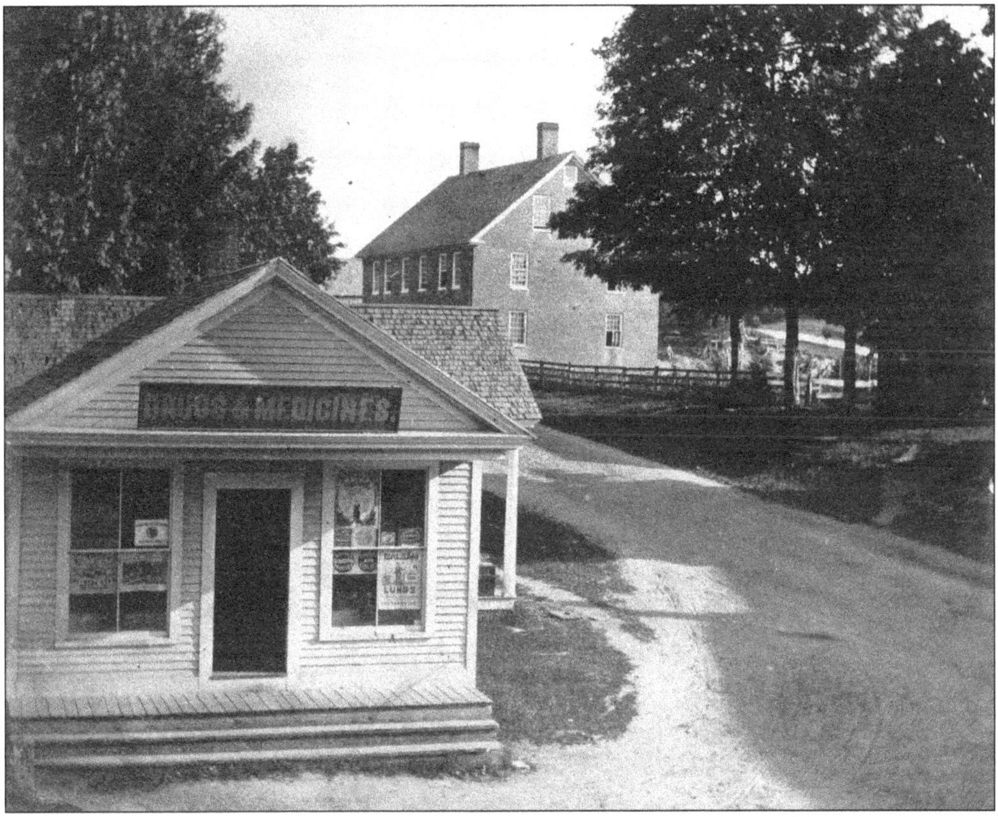

The corner of Union and Main Streets is seen here in the 1860s, when a small drugstore (pictured above) sat on the site. The Polish-American Club now sits on that corner. (CHS.)

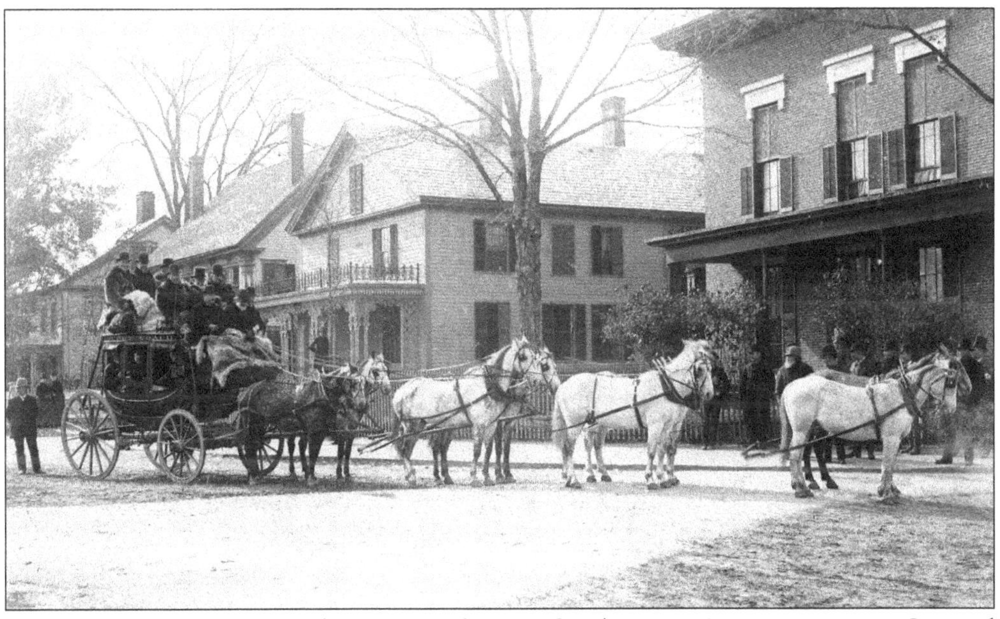

Oscar Brown, an active stage driver, is seen here on October 22, 1888, setting out in a Concord coach for dinner in Windsor, Vermont, to celebrate his 80th birthday. (CHS.)

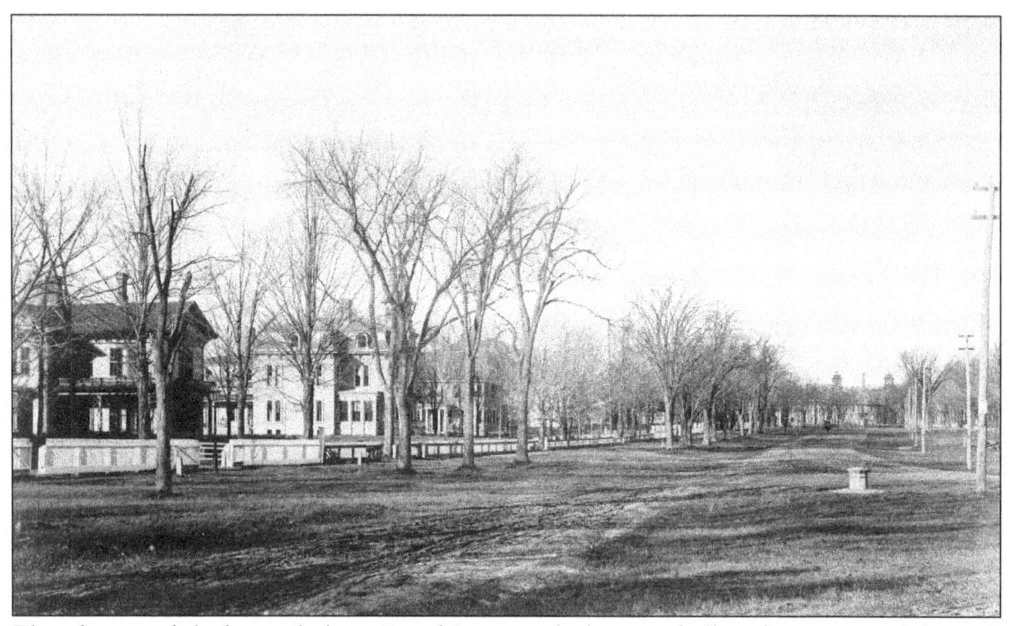

This photograph looks north down Broad Street with the town hall in the center and the park on the right. (CHS.)

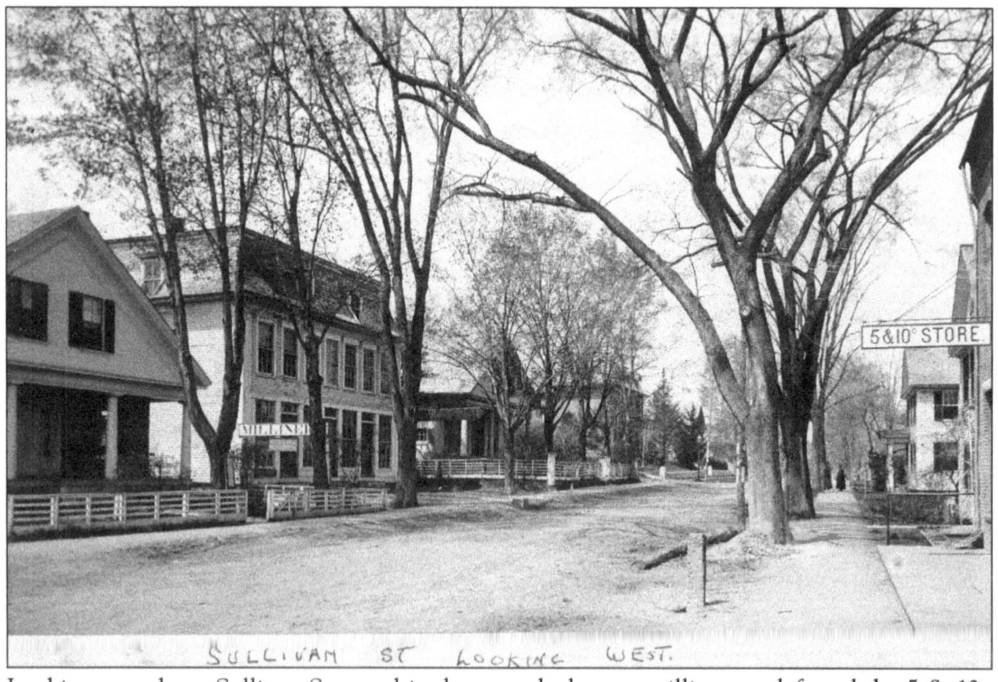

Looking west down Sullivan Street, this photograph shows a millinery at left and the 5 & 10¢ Store at right. (CHS.)

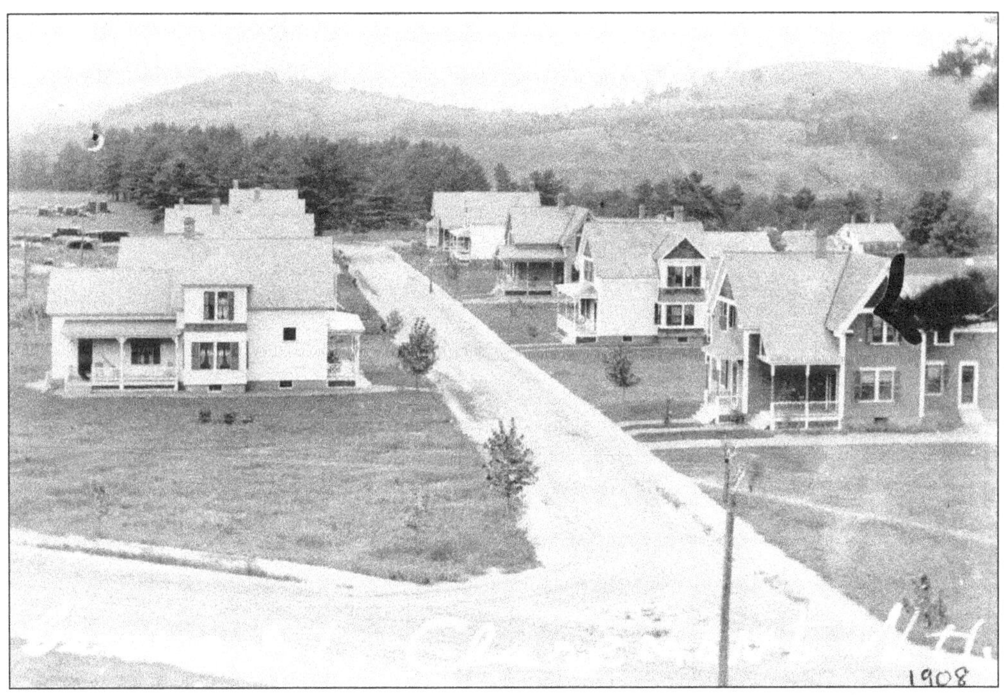

The land in the Bluff area was divided into lots in 1905. The intersection of Summit and Grove Streets, seen here around 1908, shows some of the first houses built in the neighborhood. (WLM.)

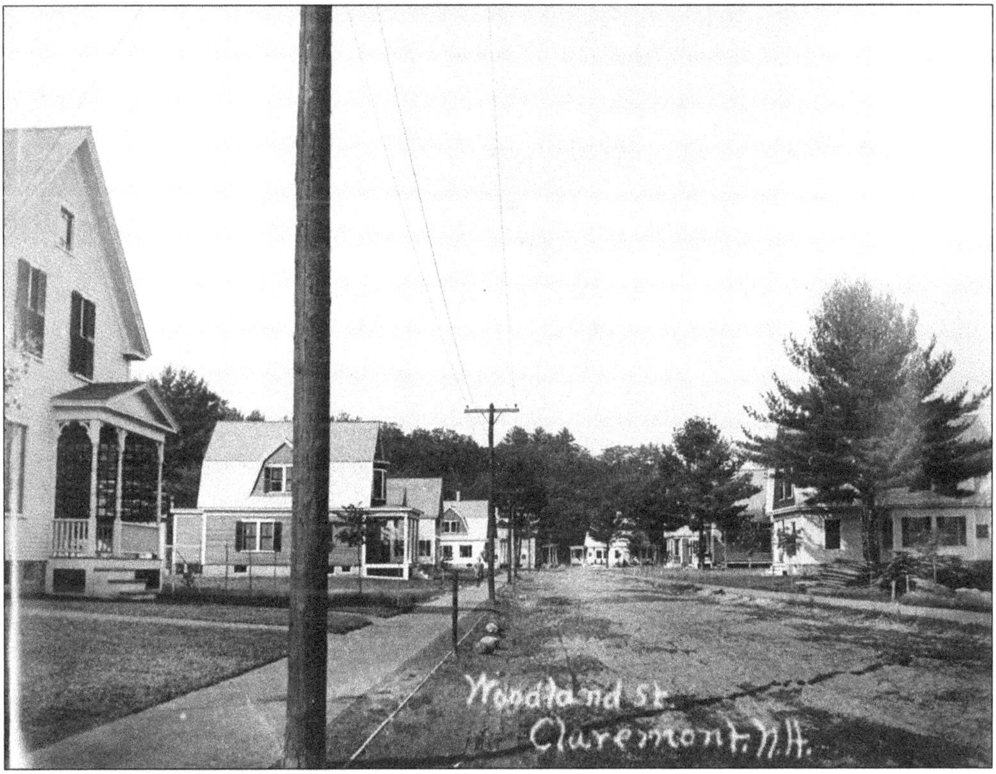

This photograph shows Woodland Street from Myrtle Street. (WLM.)

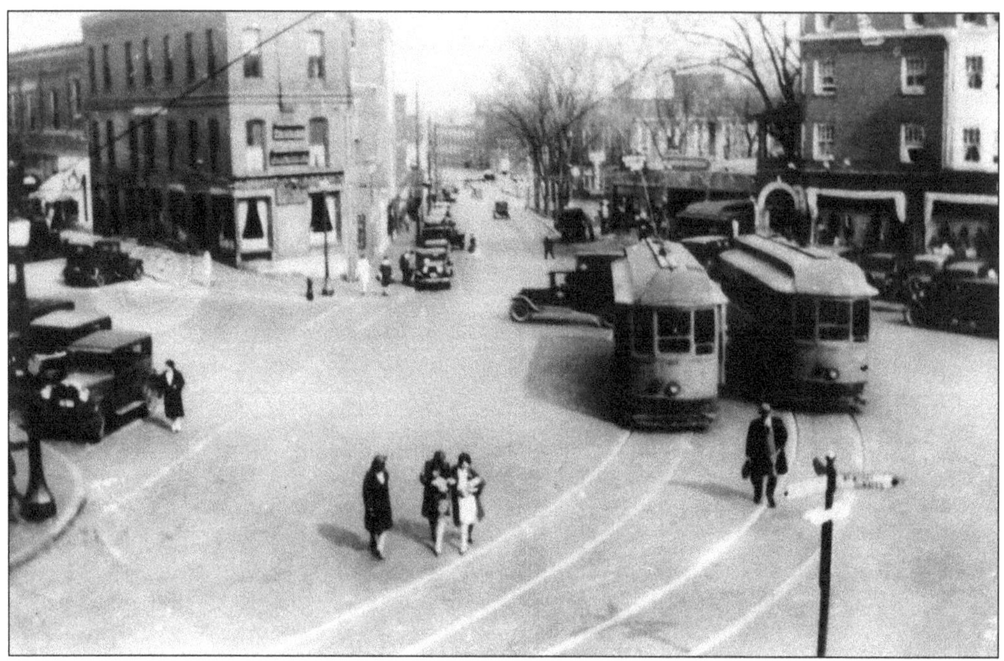

The Claremont Electric Railway operated from 1902 to 1930. The trolleys were housed on Lafayette Street and ran up Main Street, across Pleasant Street, and down Maple Avenue to the junction. These two trolleys make the final run in 1930. (WLM.)

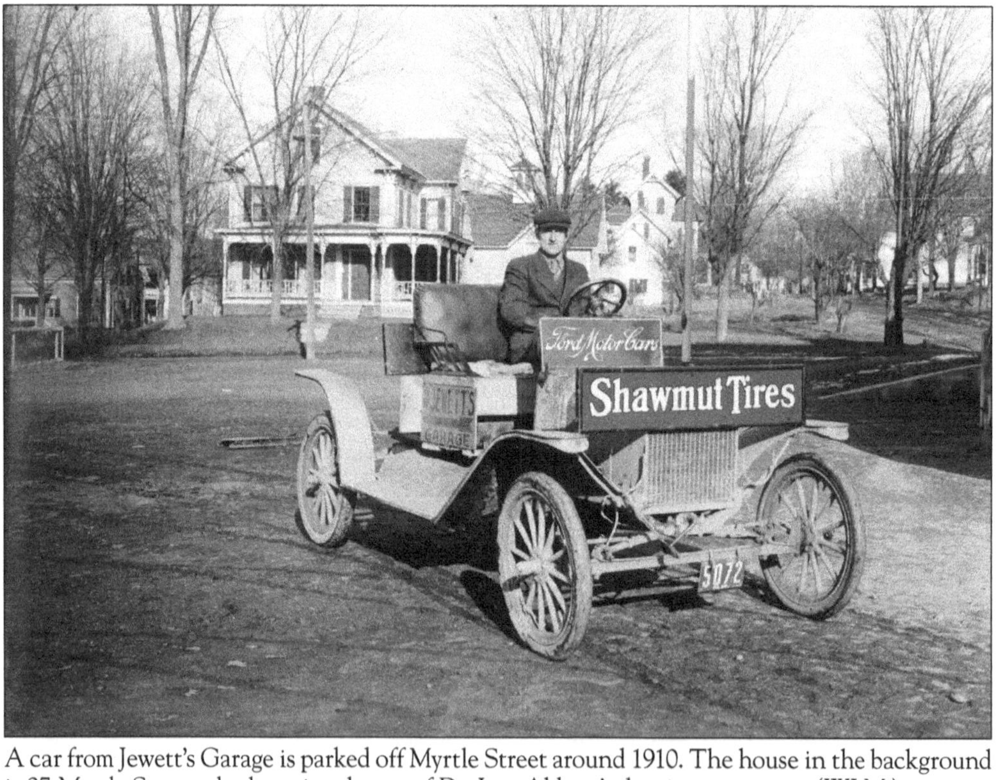

A car from Jewett's Garage is parked off Myrtle Street around 1910. The house in the background is 27 Myrtle Street, the longtime home of Dr. Leo Abbott's dentistry practice. (WLM.)

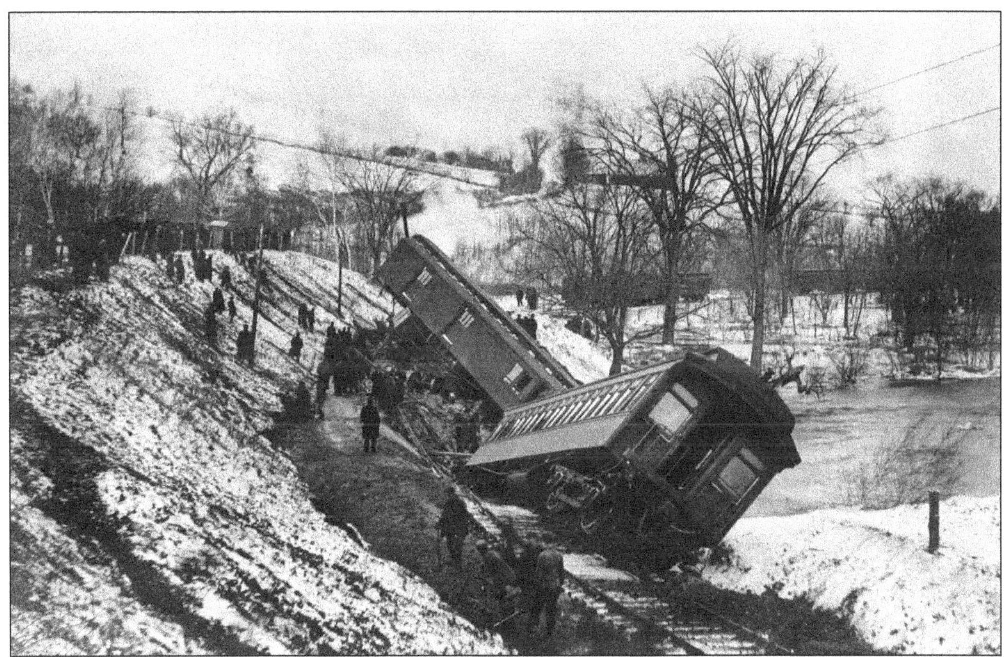

This train tilted off the track when making the curve off Washington Street opposite the Rush Chellis farm near Roberts Hill Road on February 26, 1915. The 30 passengers were unhurt, but conductor Daniel Chandler died of a skull fracture the following day. (WLM.)

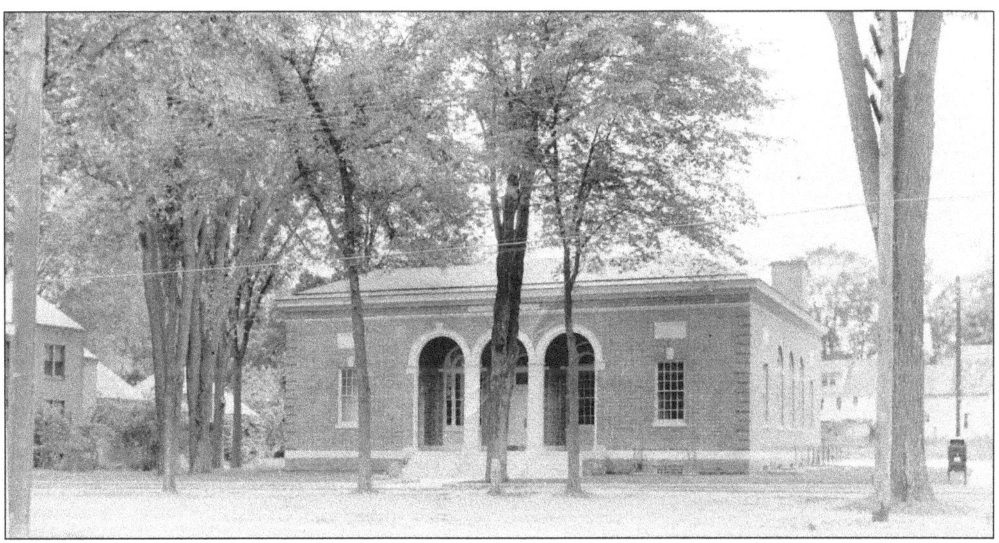

The post office on Broad Street is seen here upon its completion in 1932. (WLM.)

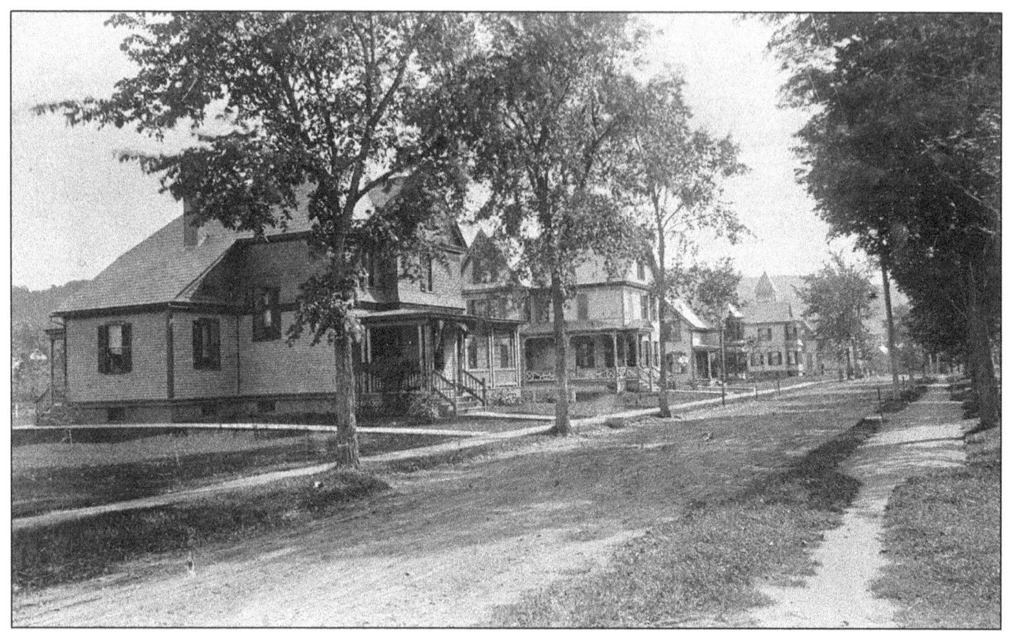

The homes on Bond Street are seen here around 1900. (CHS.)

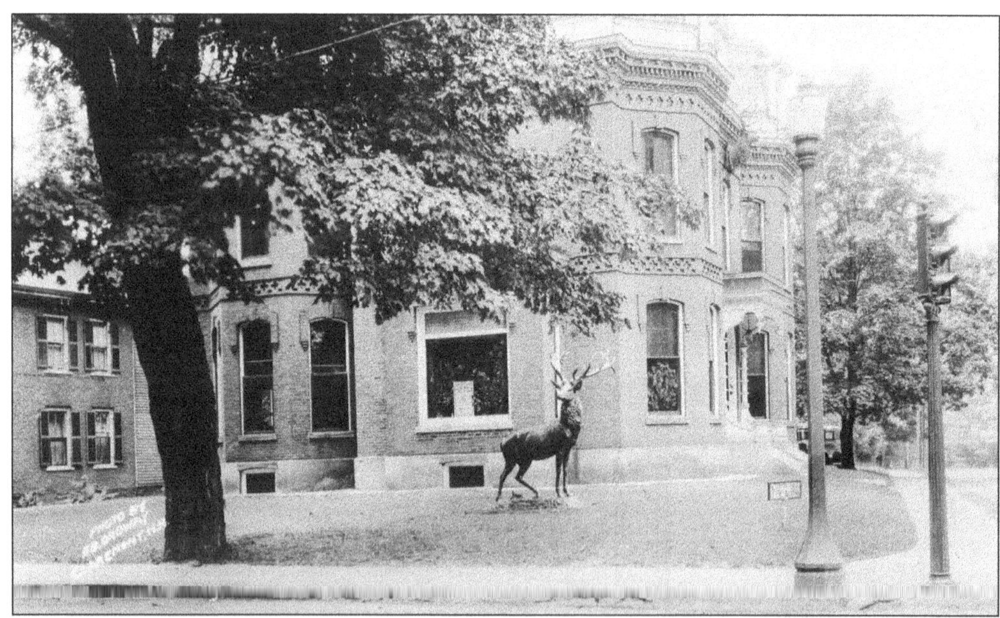

Built in 1859, this was the residence of John Tyler II. Later, it became the home of Claremont Elks Lodge No. 879. (WLM.)

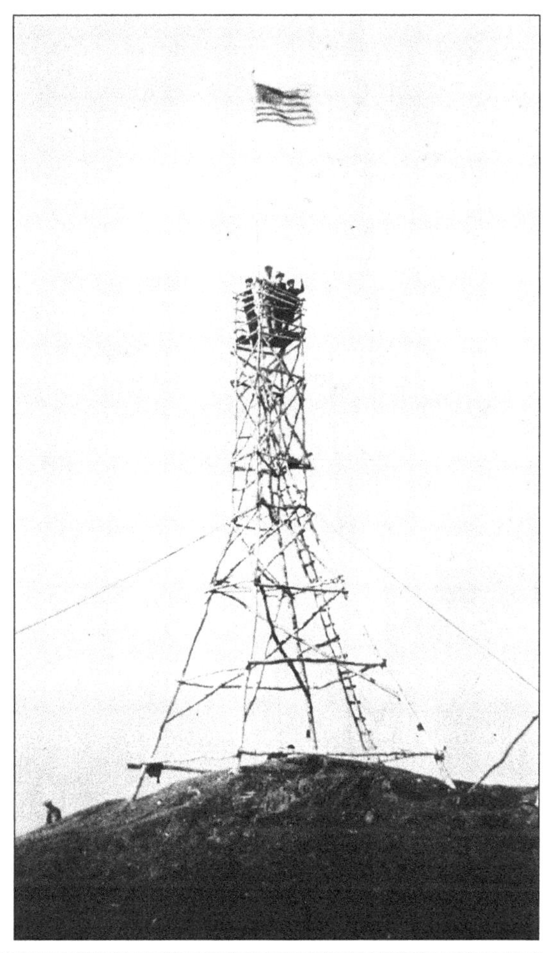

This white birch tower was built in the summer of 1922 on Mount Arrowhead's Flat Rock by F.A. Billings for public use. By the end of the first fall, over 1,500 people had signed the register in the tower. (WLM.)

This winter scene looks toward Tremont Street from the square in March 1888. (CHS.)

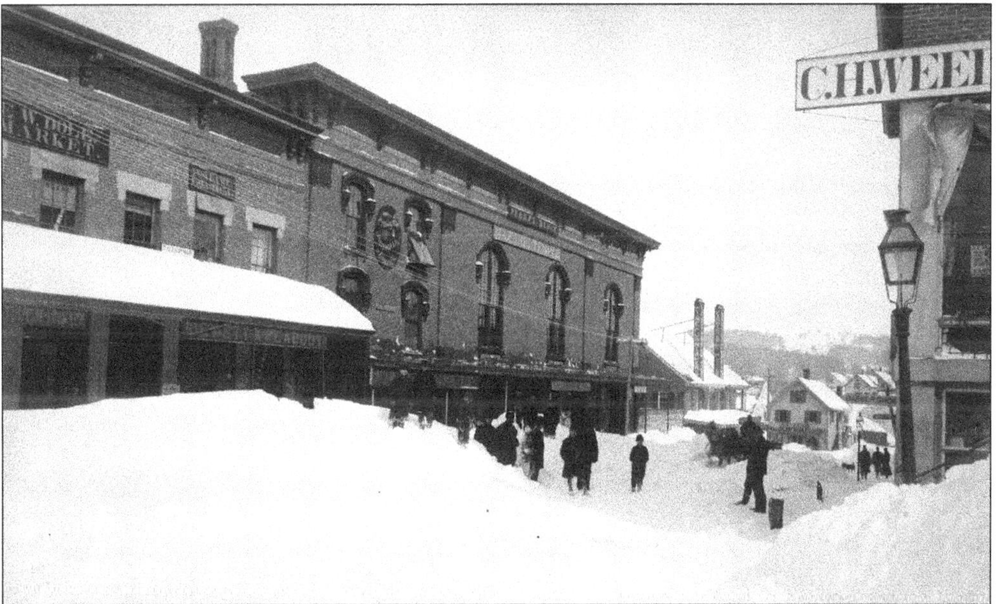

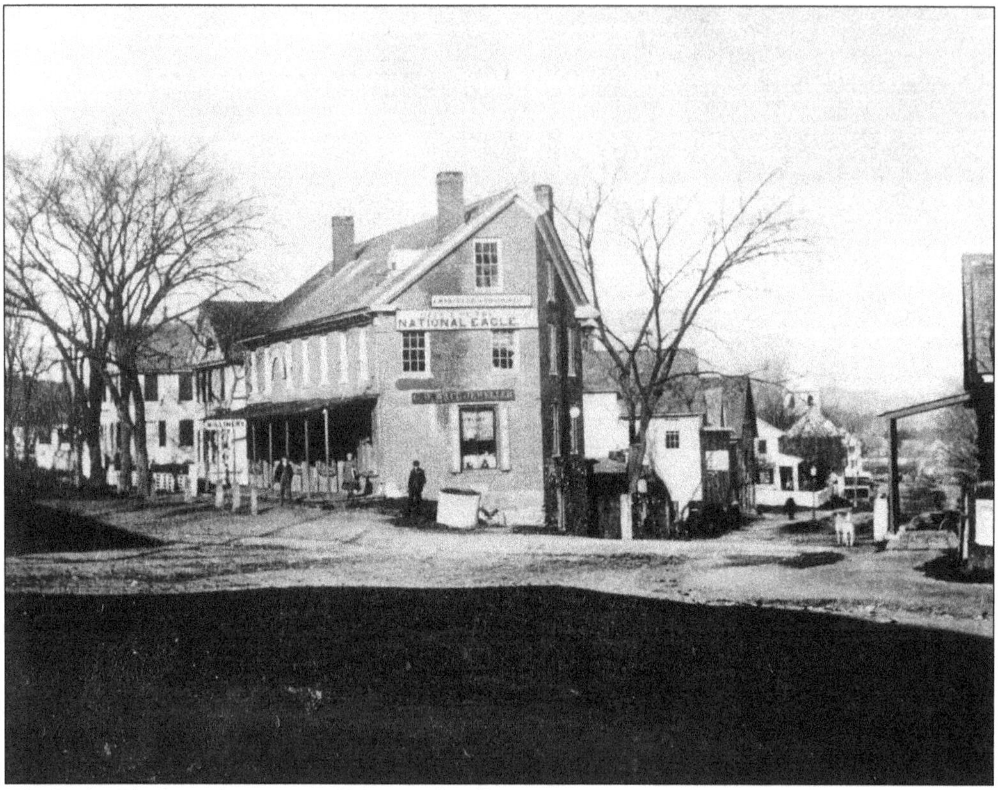

The Bailey Block, at the corner of Main and Sullivan Streets, is seen here around 1880. Ebenezer E. Bailey, who ran a silversmith business in West Unity, purchased the land in 1836 and constructed this building so he could move his business to Claremont. (CHS.)

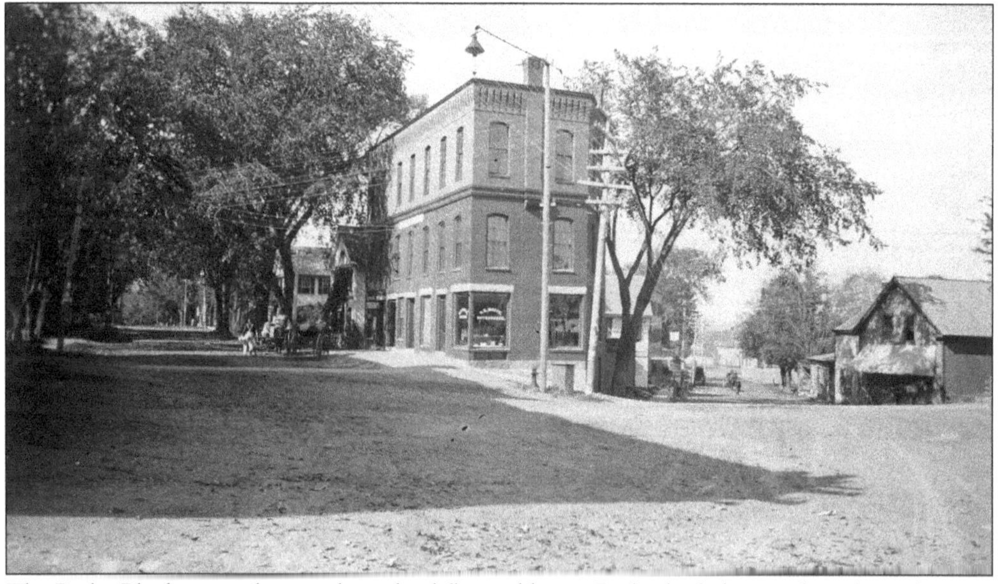

The Bailey Block is seen here with its third-floor addition. Bailey had also purchased an adjoining lot and put an addition on the building, which housed the Fiske Free Library from 1877 until the library moved to its present location in 1903. (CHS.)

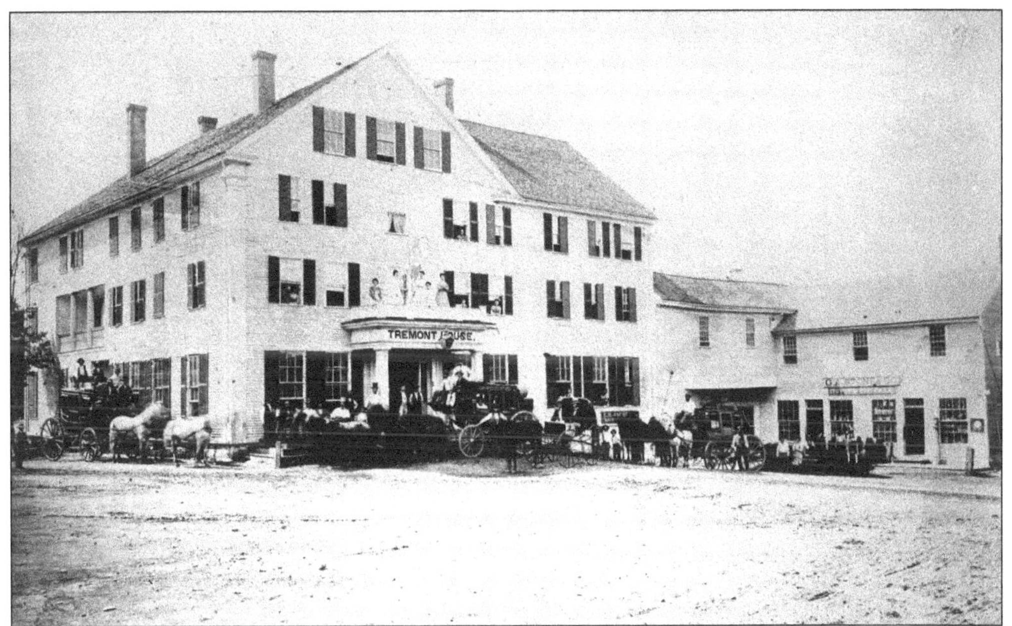

The Tremont House hotel occupied a large section of what became Tremont Square (now Opera House Square). It was built in 1800 by Josiah Stevens, the father of Paran Stevens, who later became the sole proprietor and eventually sold it in 1838. (CHS.)

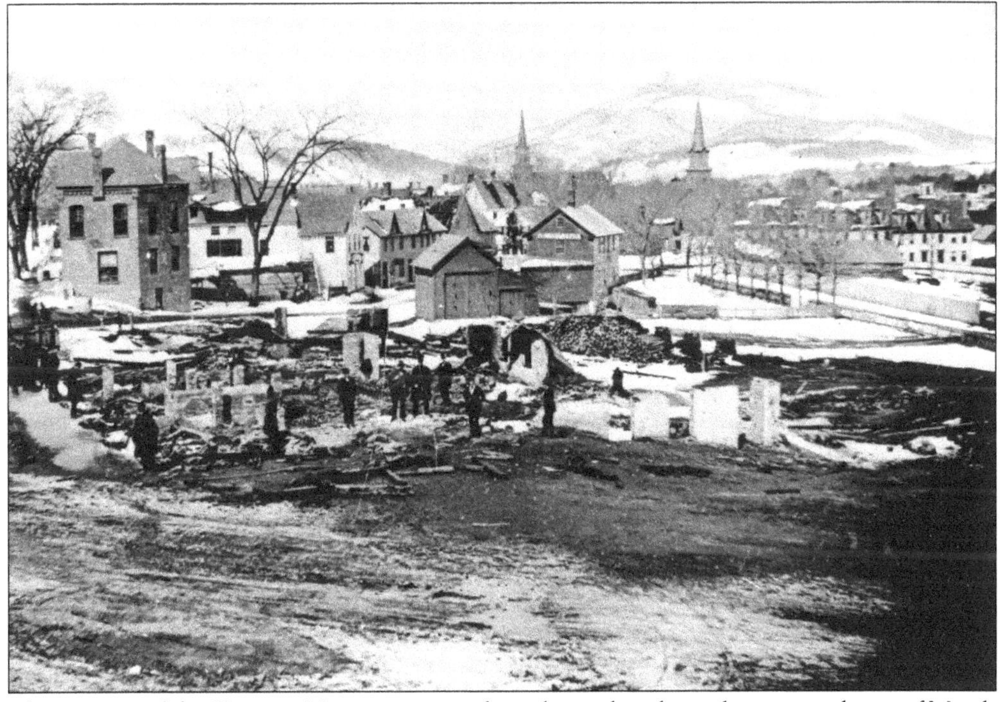

The remains of the Tremont House are seen after it burned in the early morning hours of March 29, 1879, with three confirmed deaths and one missing person. (CHS.)

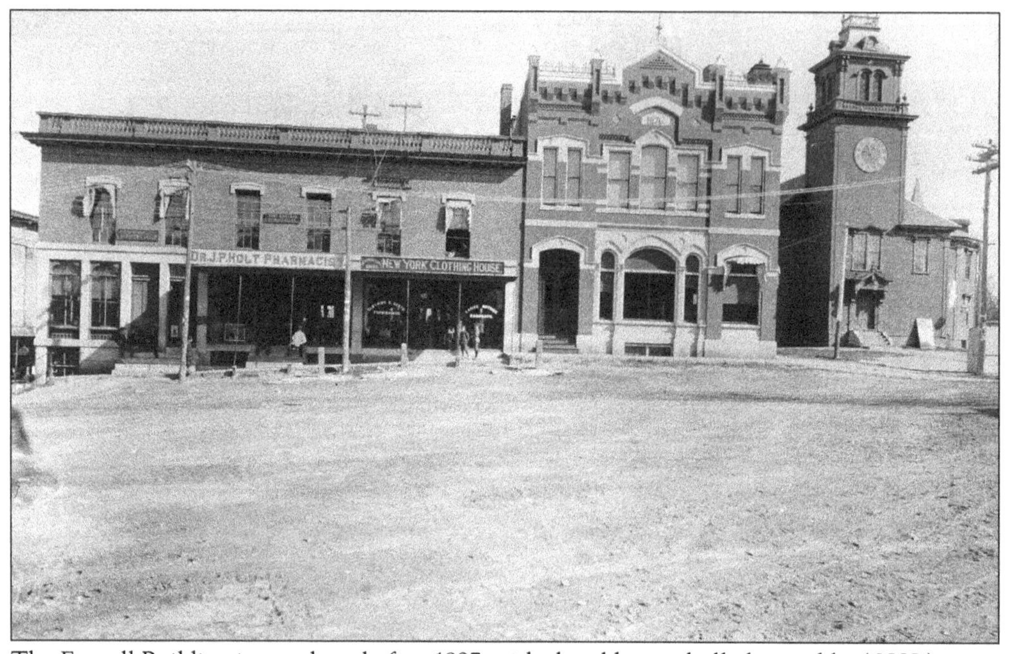

The Farwell Building is seen here before 1897, with the old town hall also visible. (CHS.)

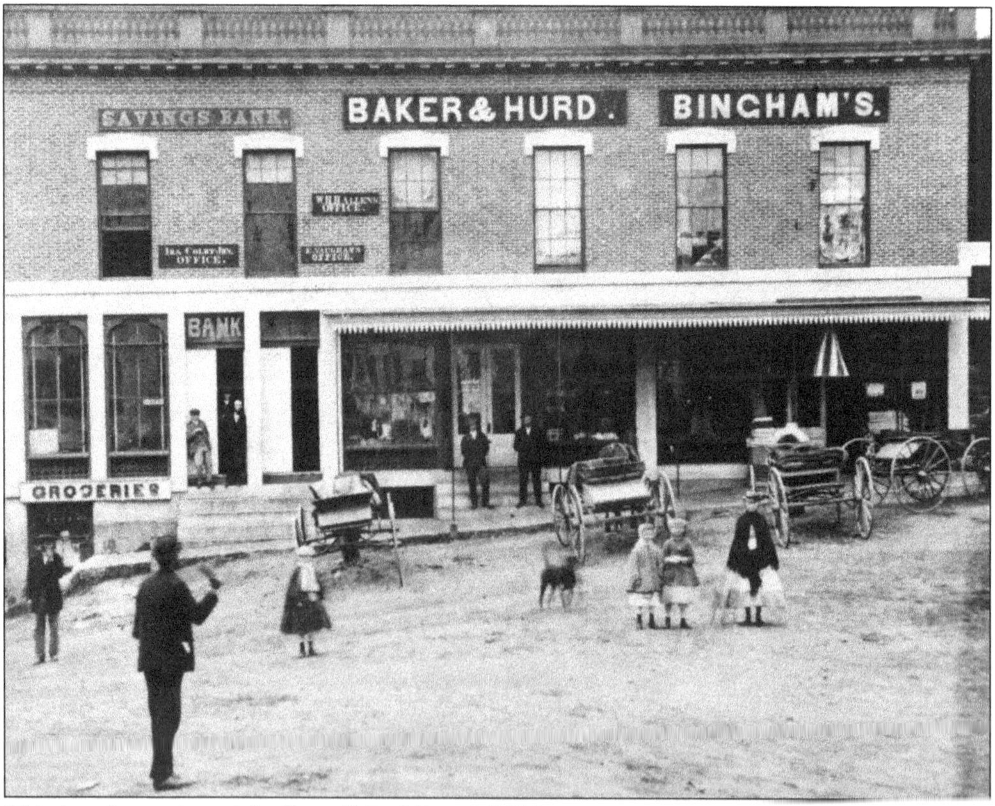

This is a closer view of the Farwell Building. (CHS.)

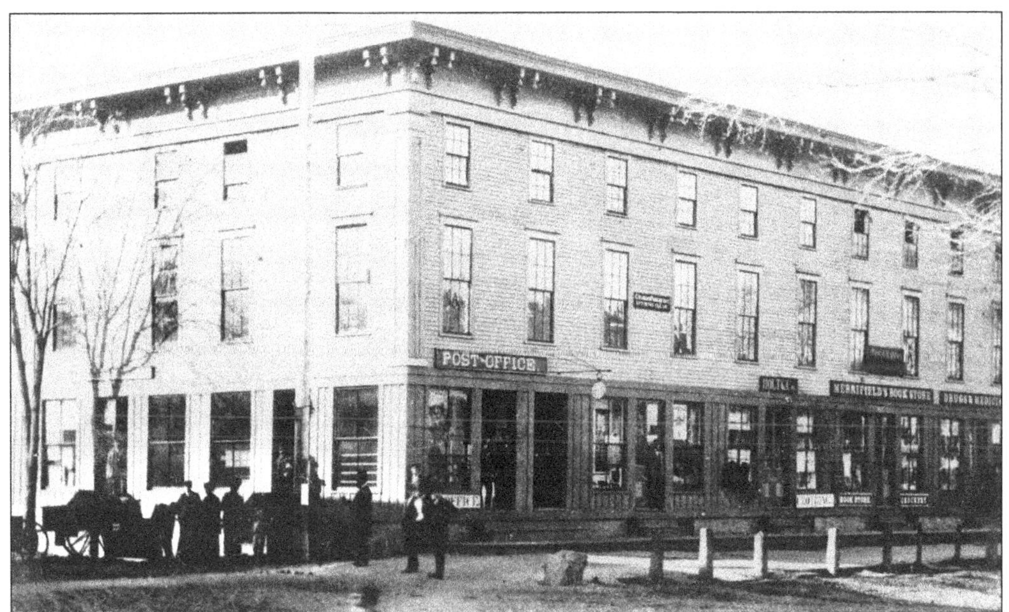

This is Oscar Brown's wooden block on the corner of Pleasant and Sullivan Streets. It was built in 1850, and two floors were added in 1854. This building burned down along with an adjoining structure on March 25, 1887. (CHS.)

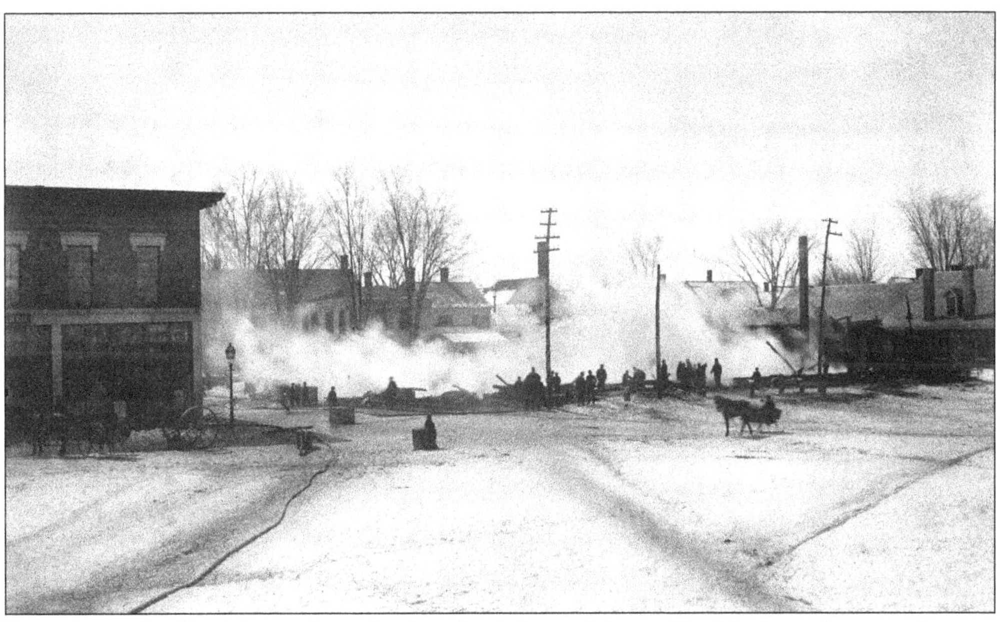

Brown's wooden block is seen here the day after it burned down. The block was home to the post office, the express office, stores on the first floor, a meat market in the basement, and offices and halls on the top floors. Most of the post office and express office contents were saved, but the other businesses suffered nearly total losses. (CHS.)

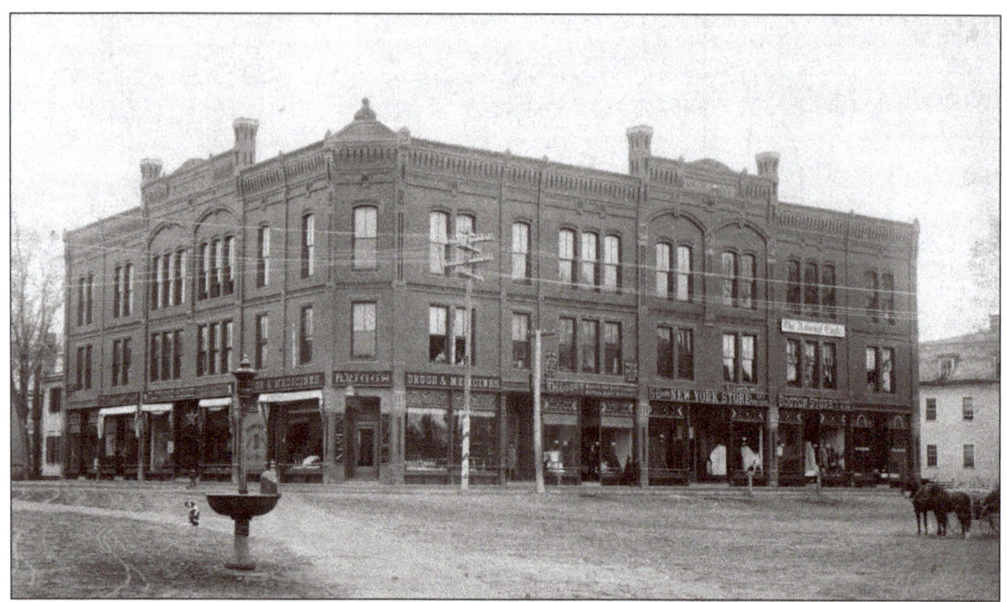

The brick Union Block was built in 1892 on the site of Brown's wooden block at the corner of Pleasant and Sullivan Streets. (WLM)

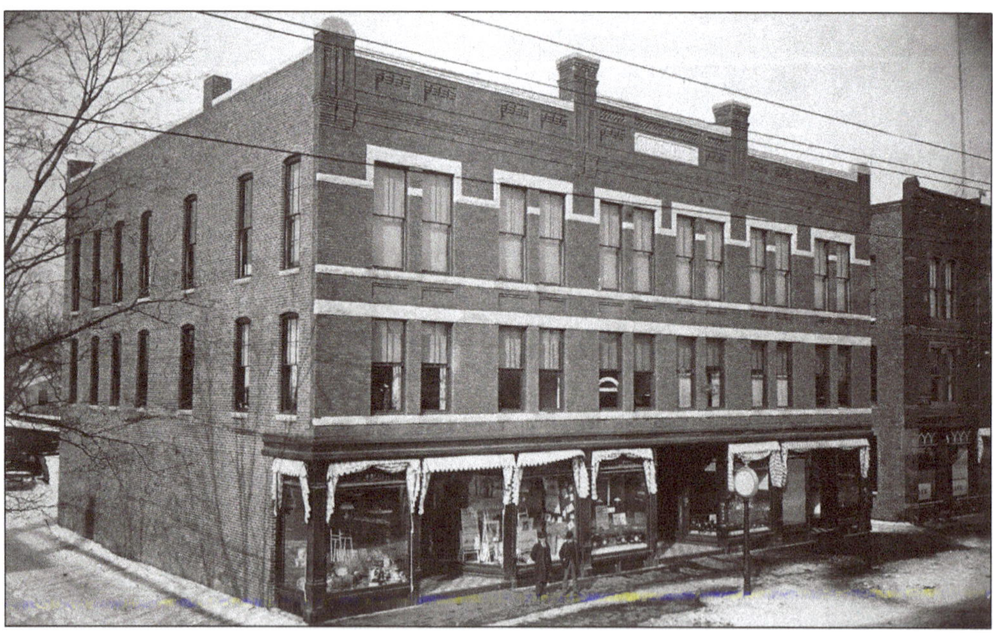

This photograph shows the Hunton Block, built in 1900. It was the site of a J.J. Newberry store for a number of years and is now Twisted Fitness. (CHS.)

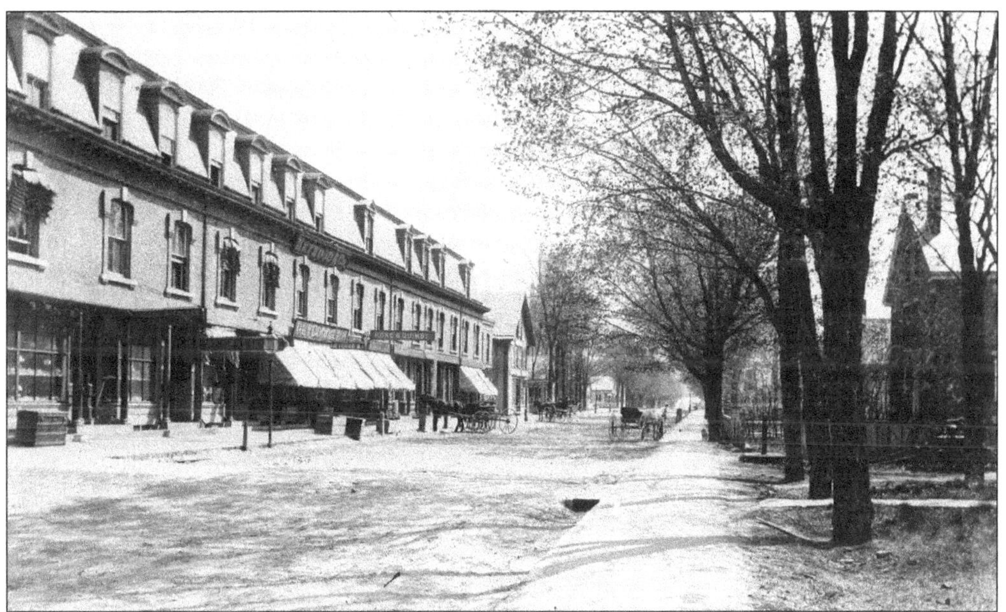

This south-facing view shows Pleasant Street and various businesses. The long building on the left was later reduced in size after a fire. (CHS.)

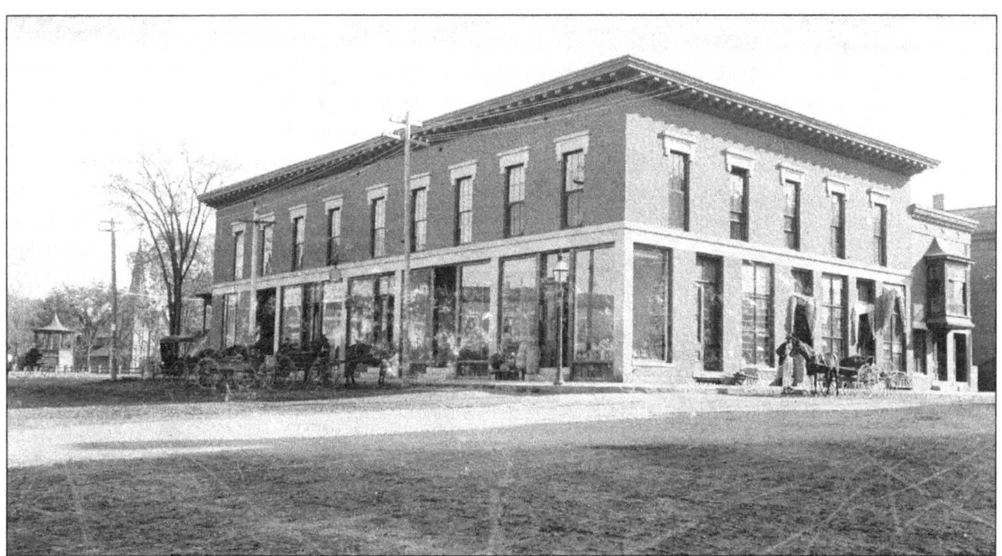

The northeast corner of Pleasant Street is seen here where it meets the square. Brown's brick block, which was built in 1860, is on the corner. Broad Street Park is on the left. (CHS.)

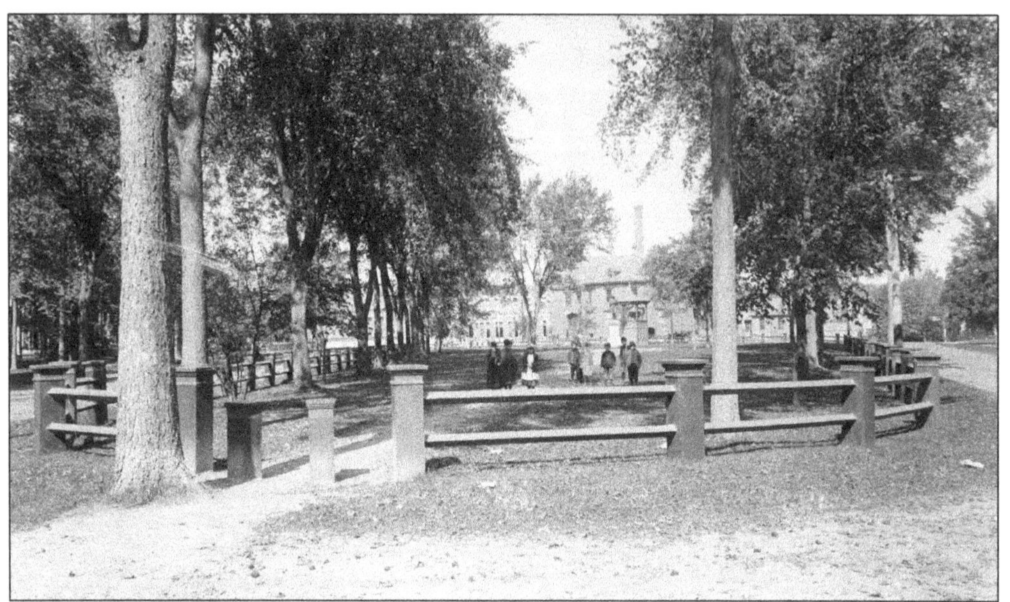

Broad Street Park is pictured here around 1893. (CHS.)

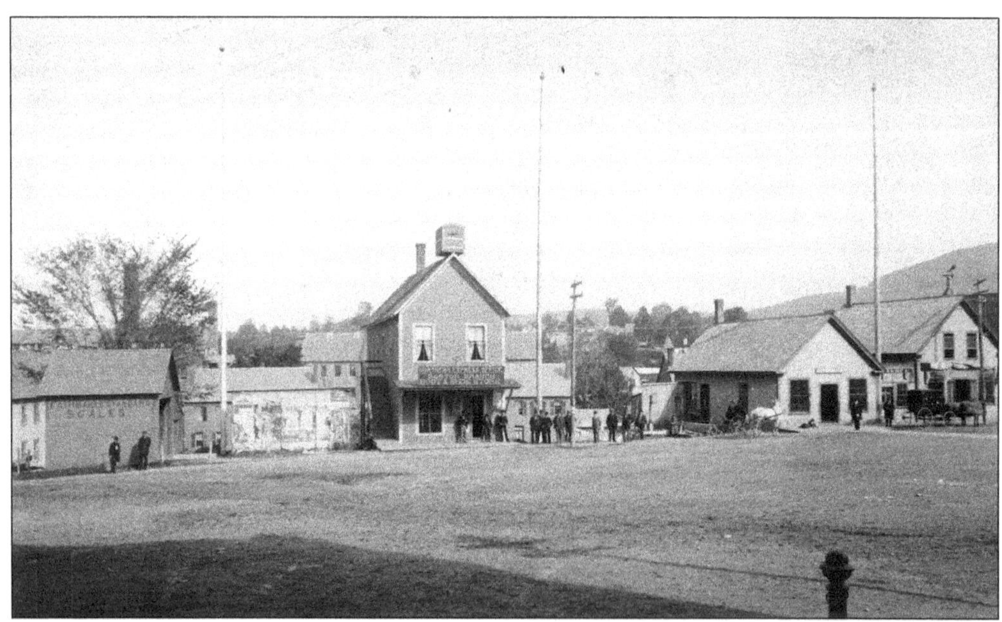

The northern side of the square is seen here in 1891, prior to the construction of the Hotel Claremont but after the burning of Brown's wooden block. Unable to secure financing from a banker on the east side of the square, a local businessman secured a trunk to his roof to block the banker's view of Mount Ascutney. The buildings in the background on Crescent Street, which still stand, were quarters for the foremen at Monadnock Mills. (CHS.)

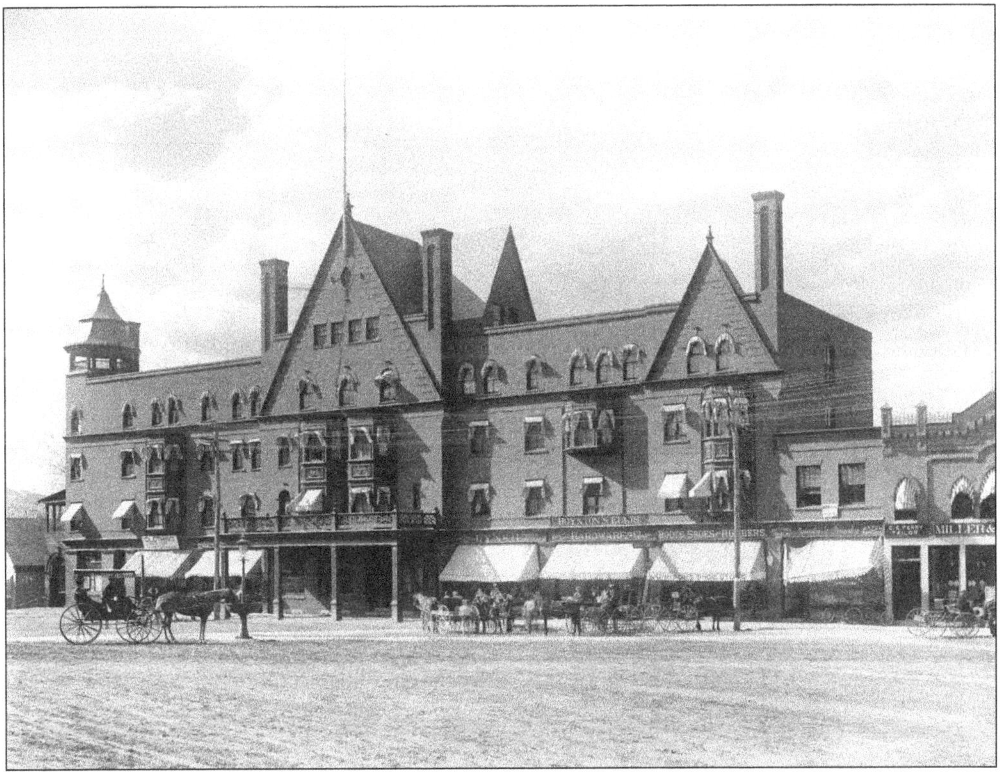

Hotel Claremont, later the Moody Building, is seen here with its original triangular facade in 1895. (CHS.)

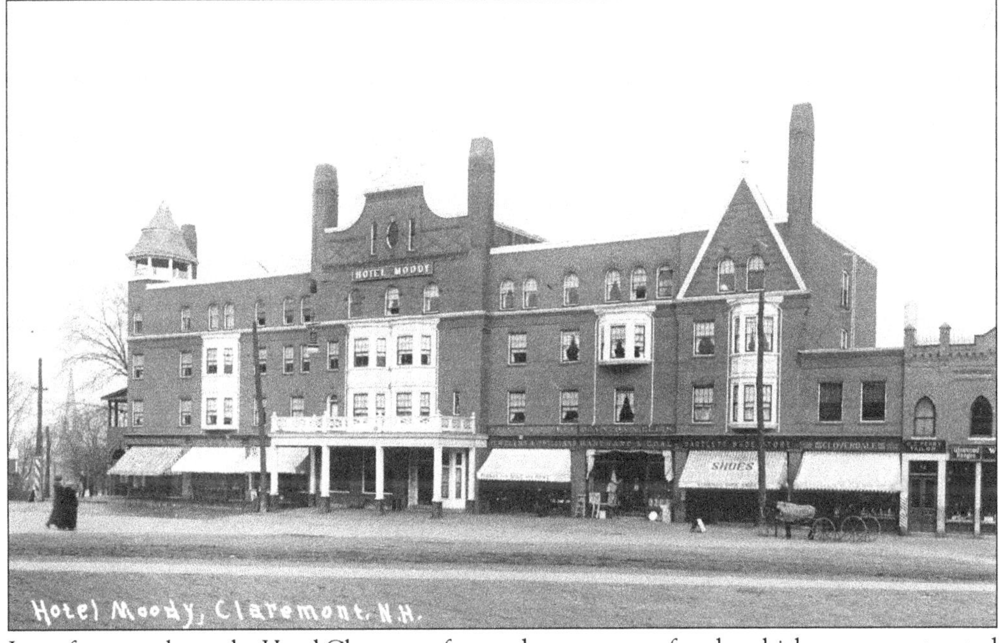

Just a few years later, the Hotel Claremont featured a new center facade, which was reconstructed following a fire. It is seen here around 1900. (CHS.)

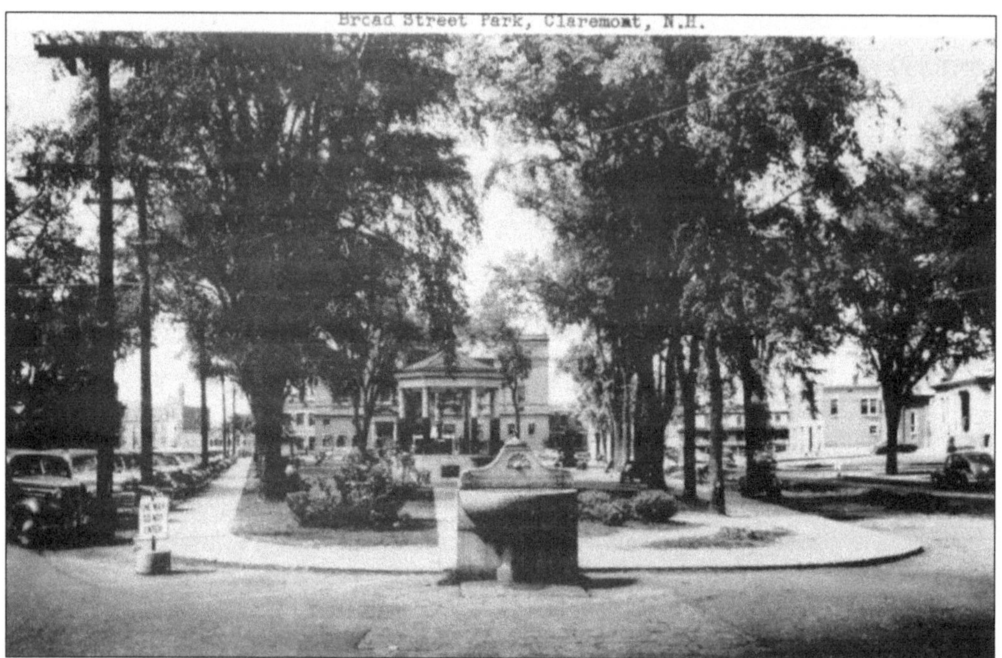

Broad Street Park is seen here around 1930. The fountain was later moved near the entrance to Mountain View Cemetery off Main Street. (WLM.)

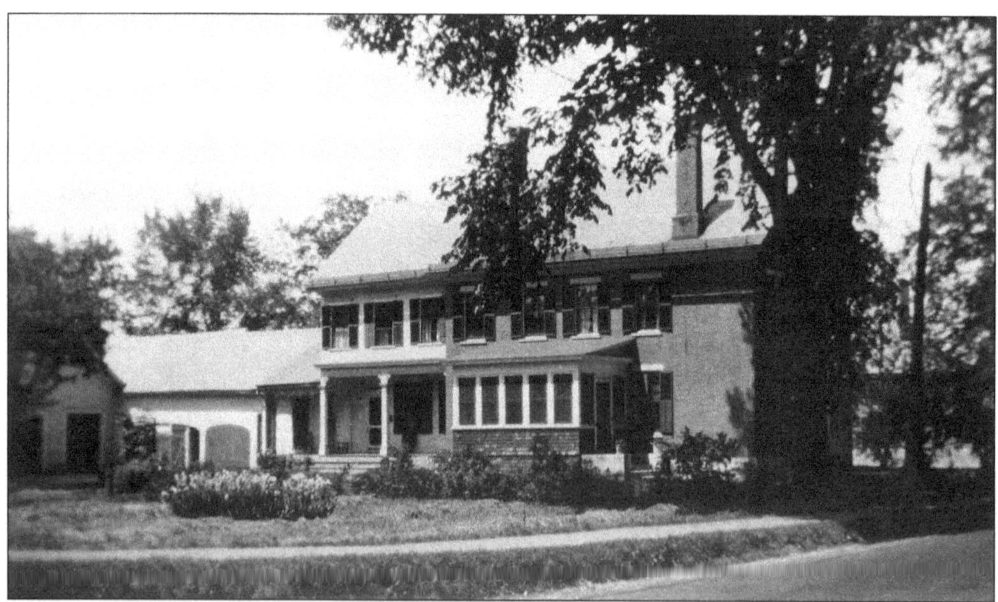

The Francis J. Tolles home, at 44 Sullivan Street, is seen here around 1925. It was built in 1880 and bequeathed to the town in 1922 to be used as a housing facility for elderly ladies. (WLM.)

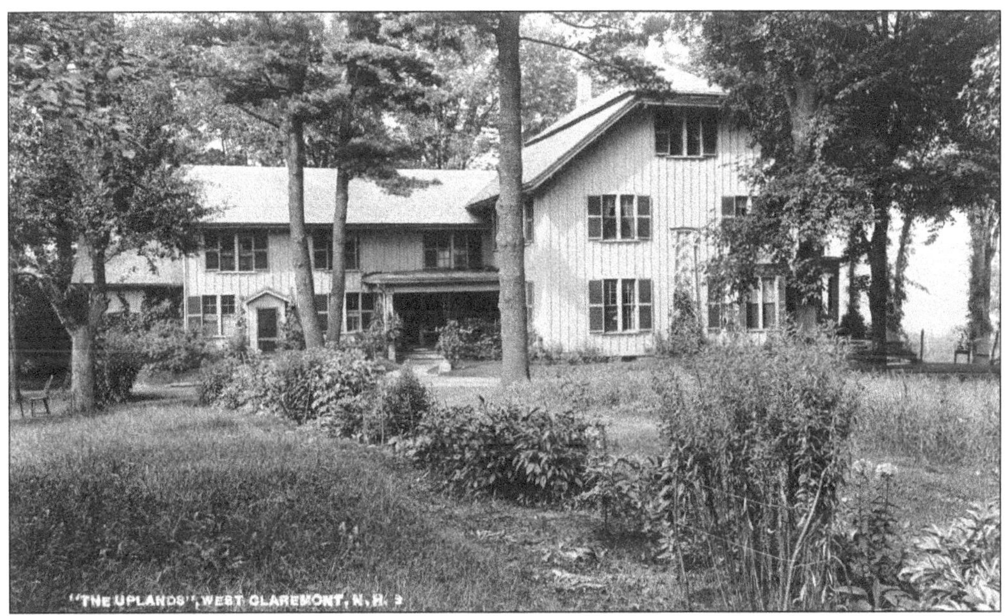

The Uplands was the name of the Upham estate in West Claremont c. 1910. (WLM.)

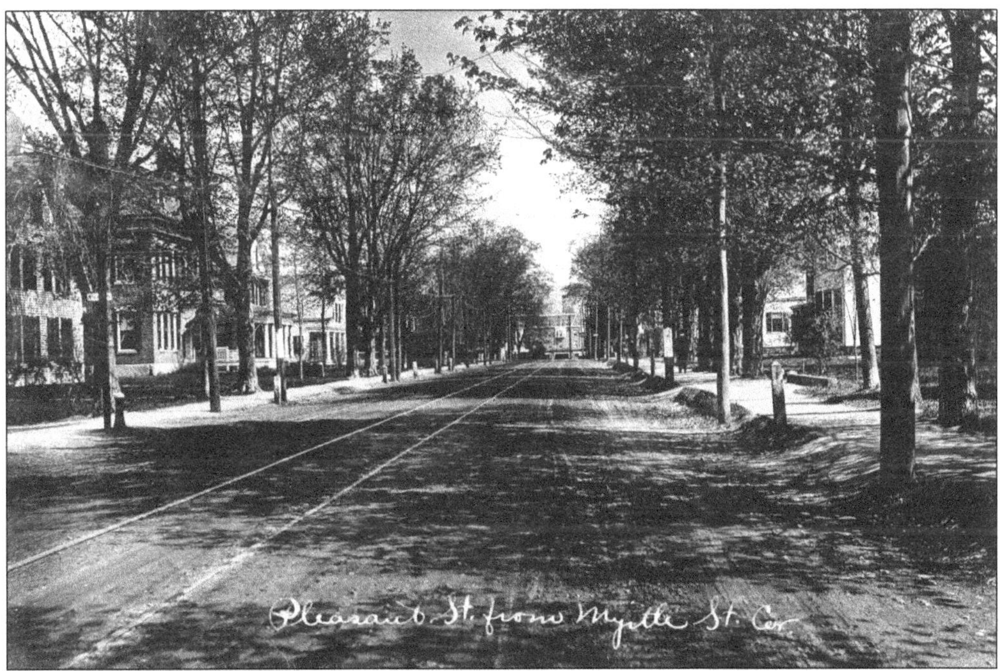

This 1912 photograph, facing north, shows the trolley tracks on Pleasant Street from the corner of Myrtle Street. (WLM.)

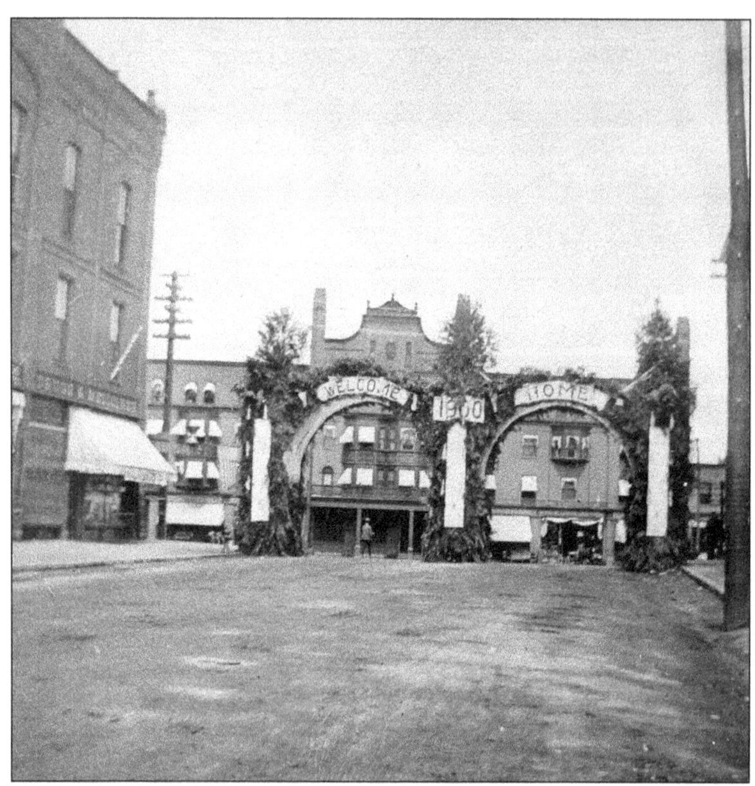

This sign at the end of Pleasant Street welcomes returning soldiers in 1900. (CHS.)

The old town hall, originally a Congregational meetinghouse, was constructed in 1785 on Maple Avenue about where the Goddard Bakery building now stands. It was dismantled in 1790 and reassembled at the site of the current city hall to serve as a hall for the church and the town. It was sold to the town in 1835. (CHS.)

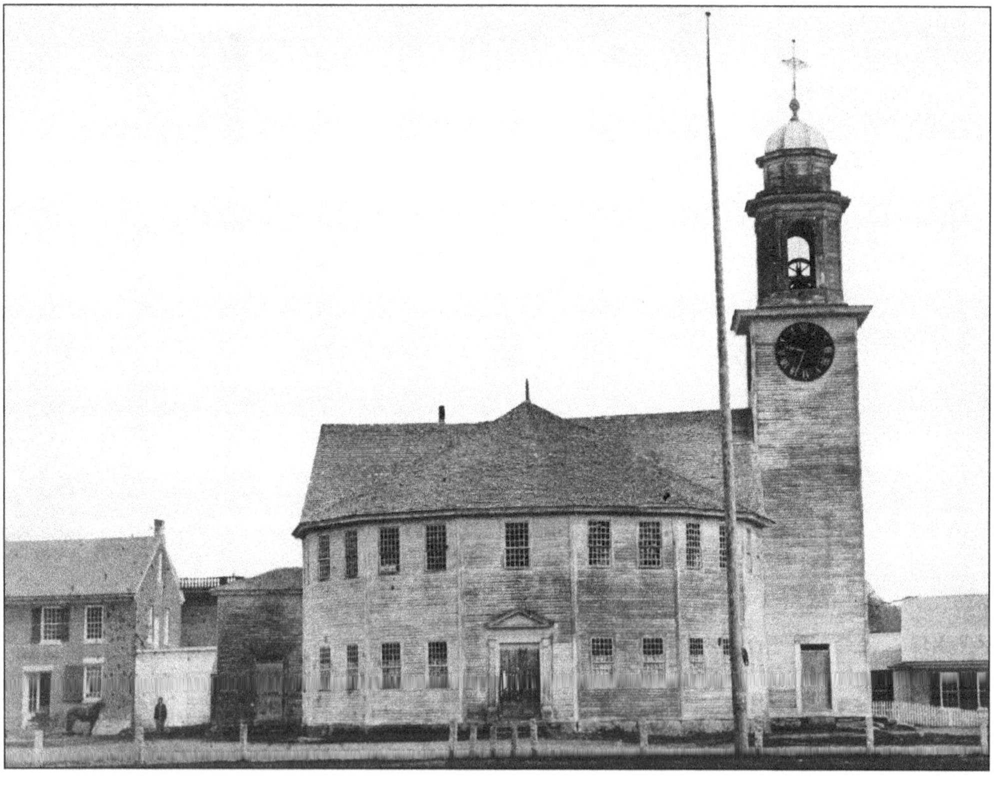

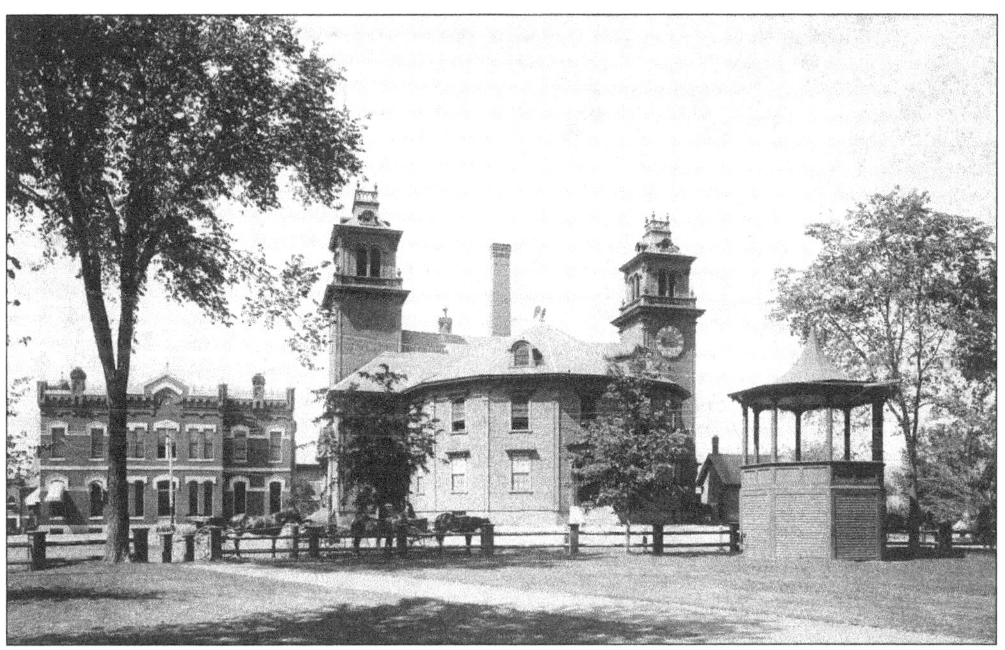

The old town hall is seen here after its second tower was added during the 1867–1868 modifications. (CHS.)

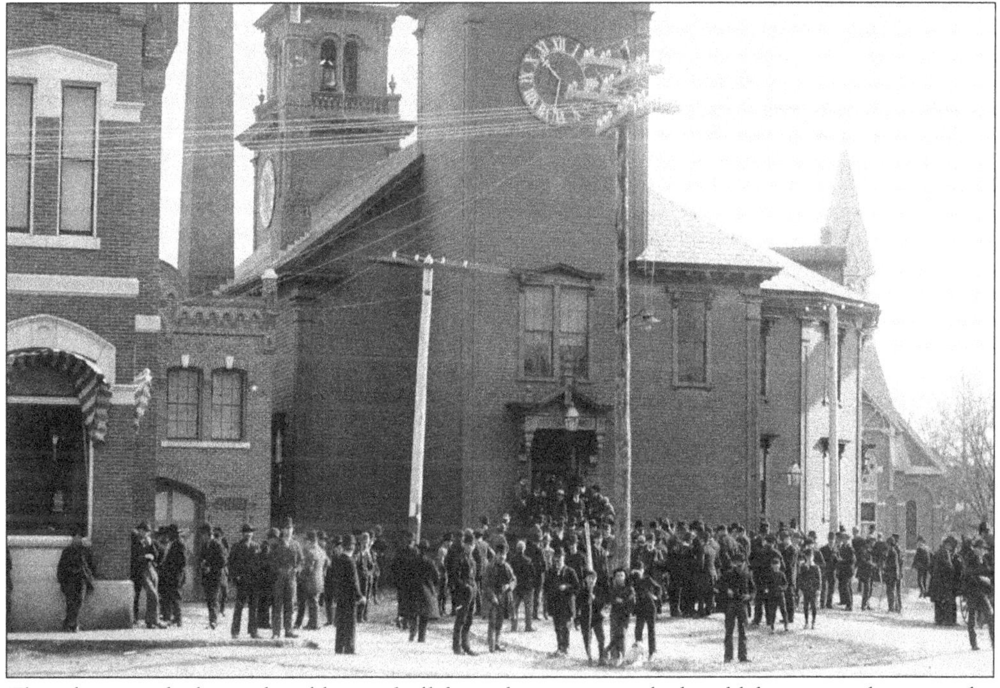

This photograph shows the old town hall from the square, with the old fire station between the hall and the Claremont National Bank. (CHS.)

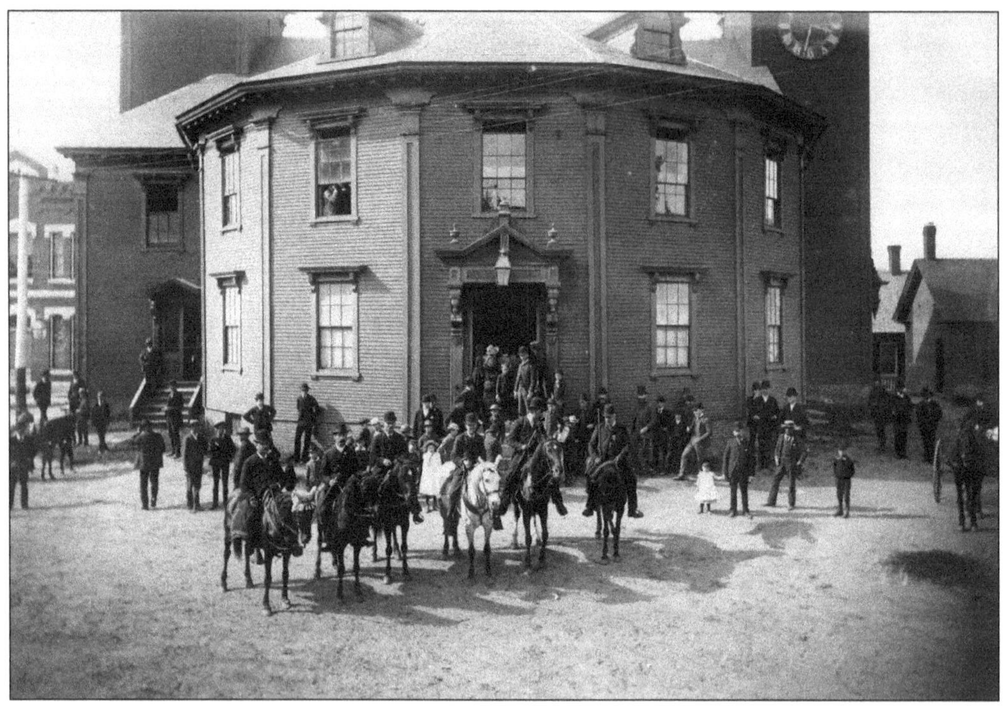

This photograph shows the town hall's octagonal south side. (CHS.)

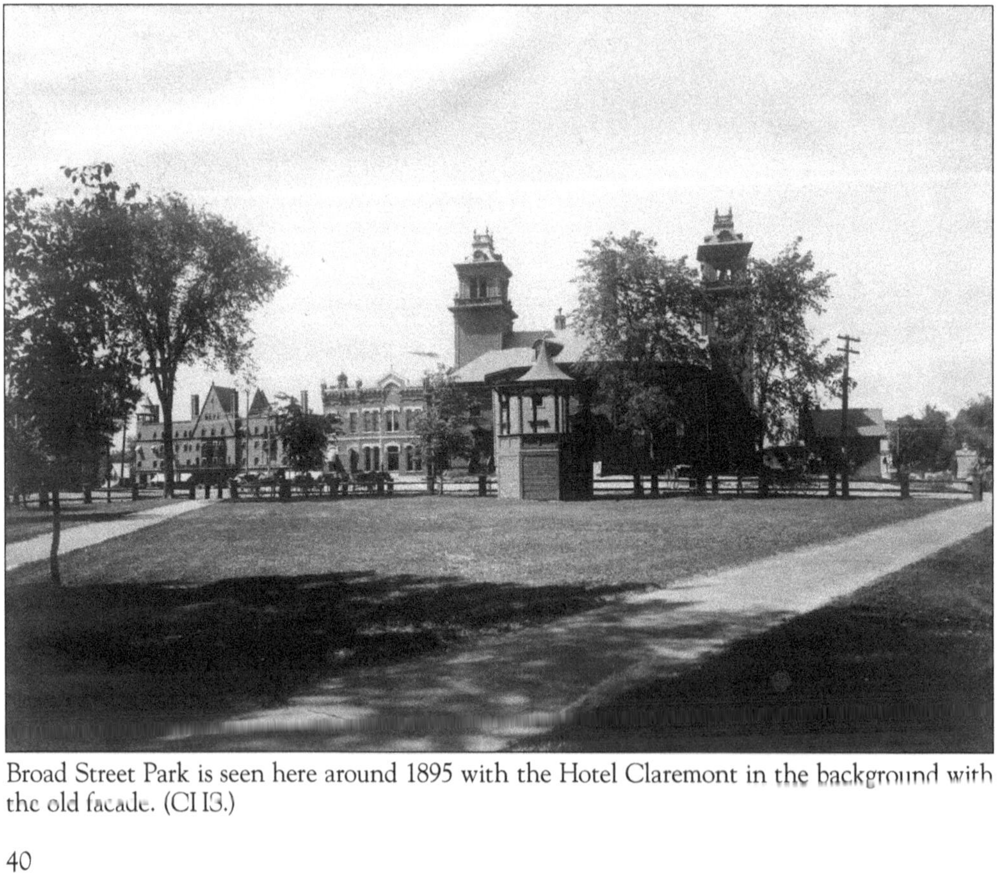

Broad Street Park is seen here around 1895 with the Hotel Claremont in the background with the old facade. (CHS.)

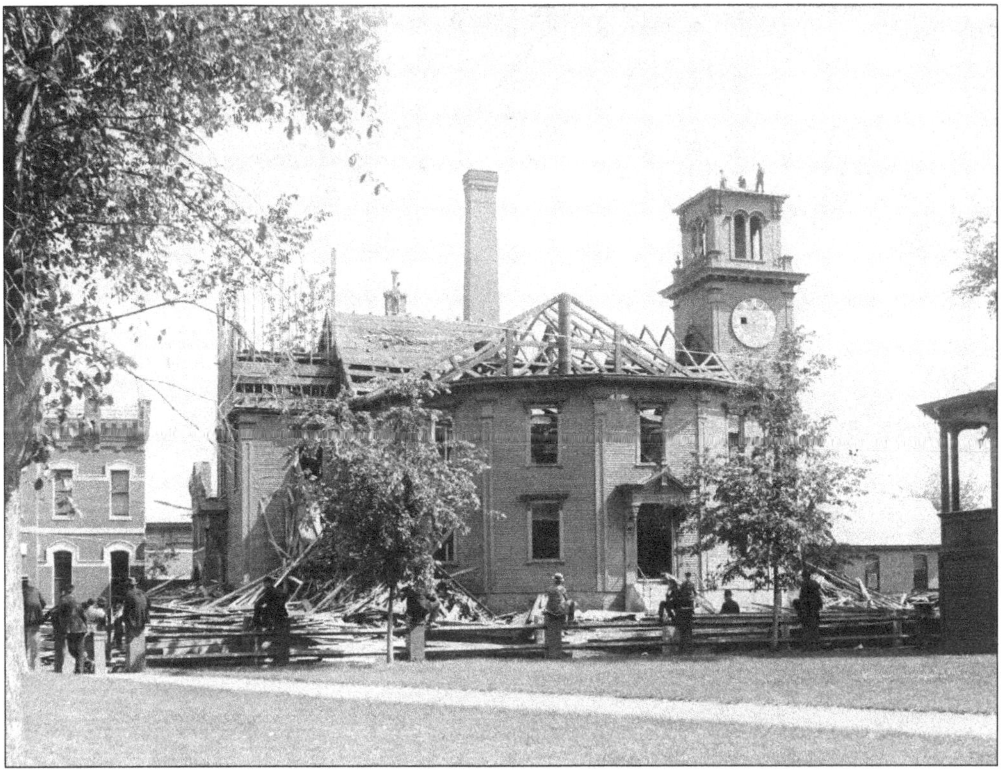

The old town hall is being dismantled to make way for the new one in 1896. (CHS.)

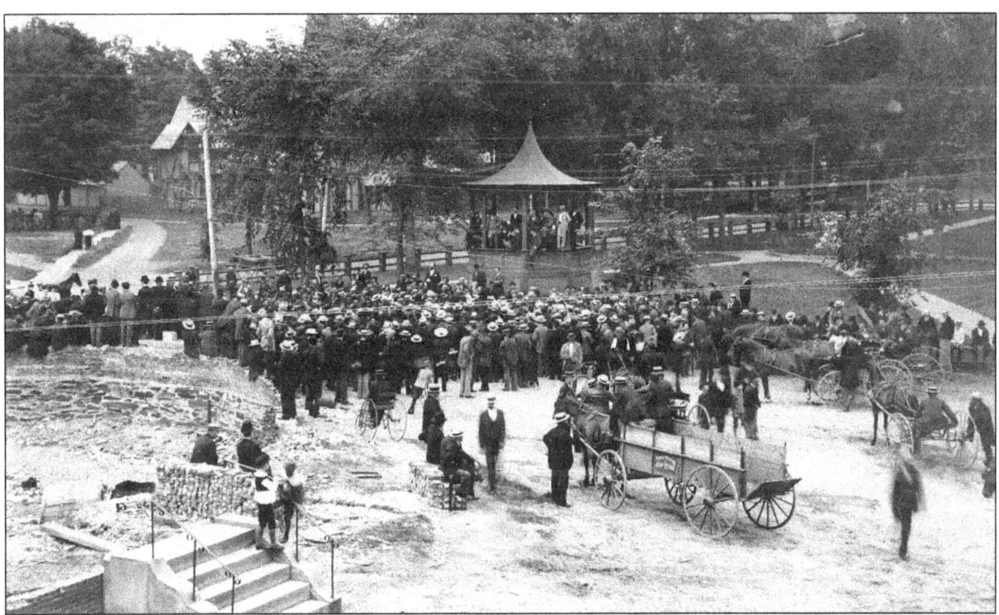

A crowd gathers in Broad Street Park in 1896. The foundation from the old town hall is in the lower left. (CHS.)

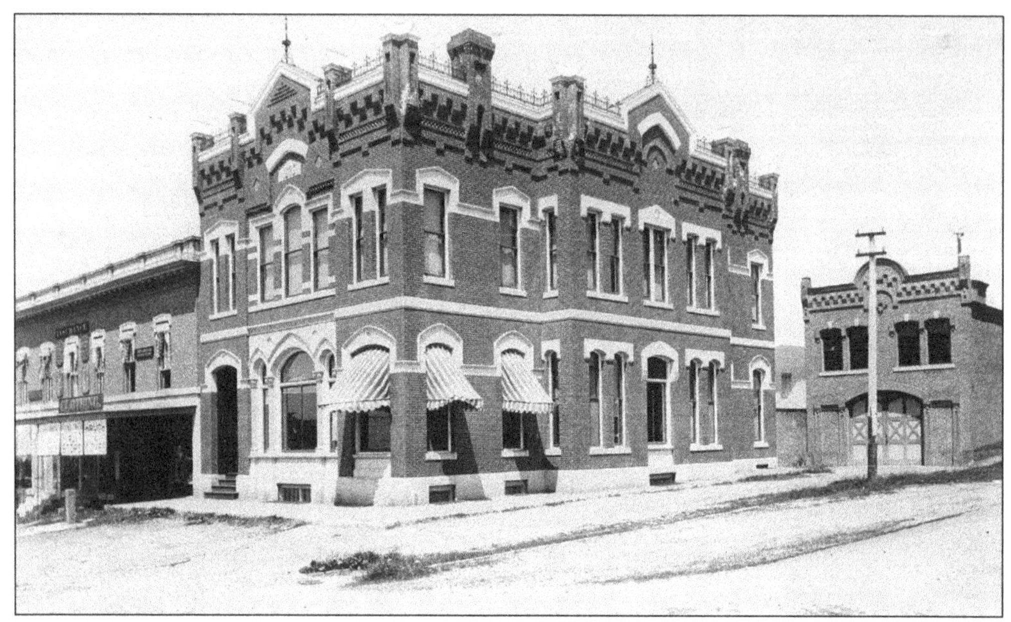

This 1896 photograph shows the Claremont National Bank with the old fire station to the right of it. (WLM.)

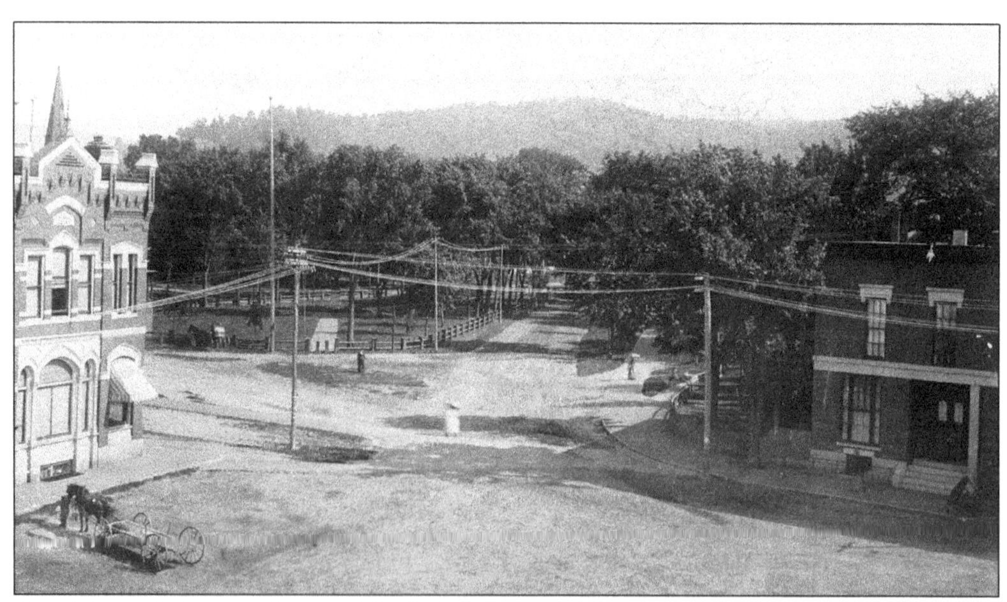

Broad Street Park is seen here in 1896 before construction of the new town hall. (CHS.)

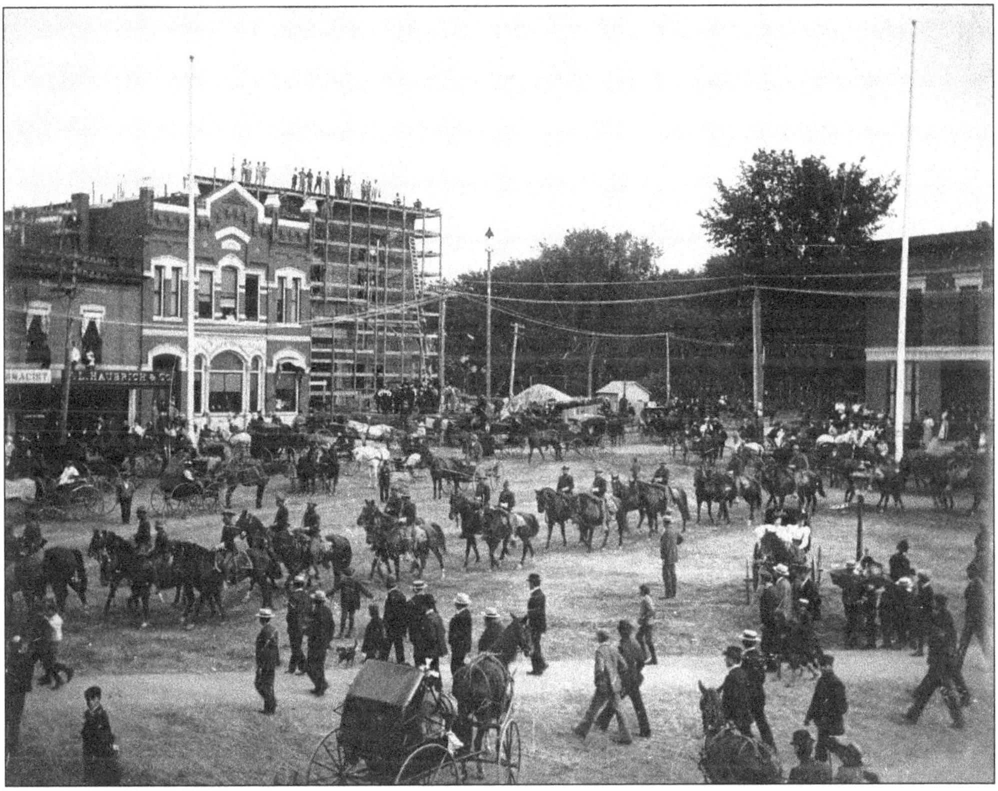

This view from the square shows the Claremont National Bank and the new town hall under construction. (CHS.)

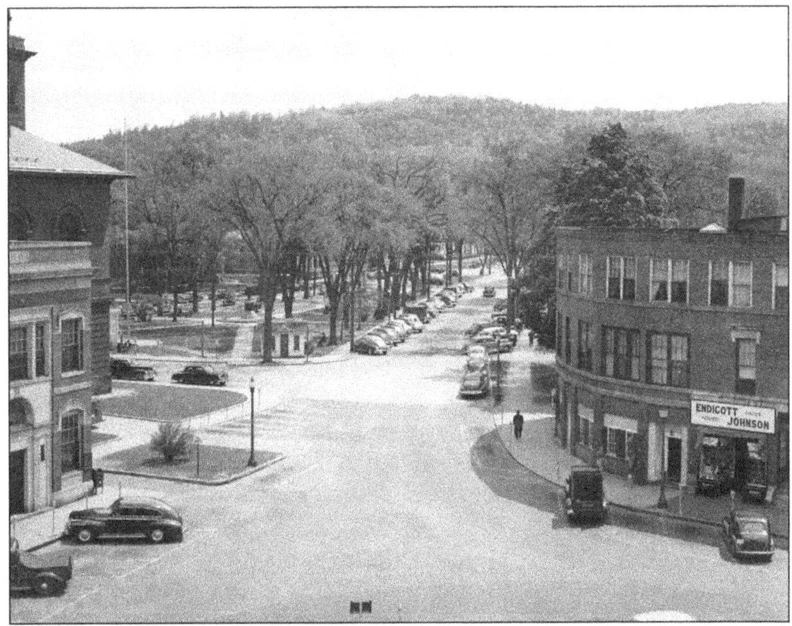

This view shows the southwestern side of the square in 1930. (CHS.)

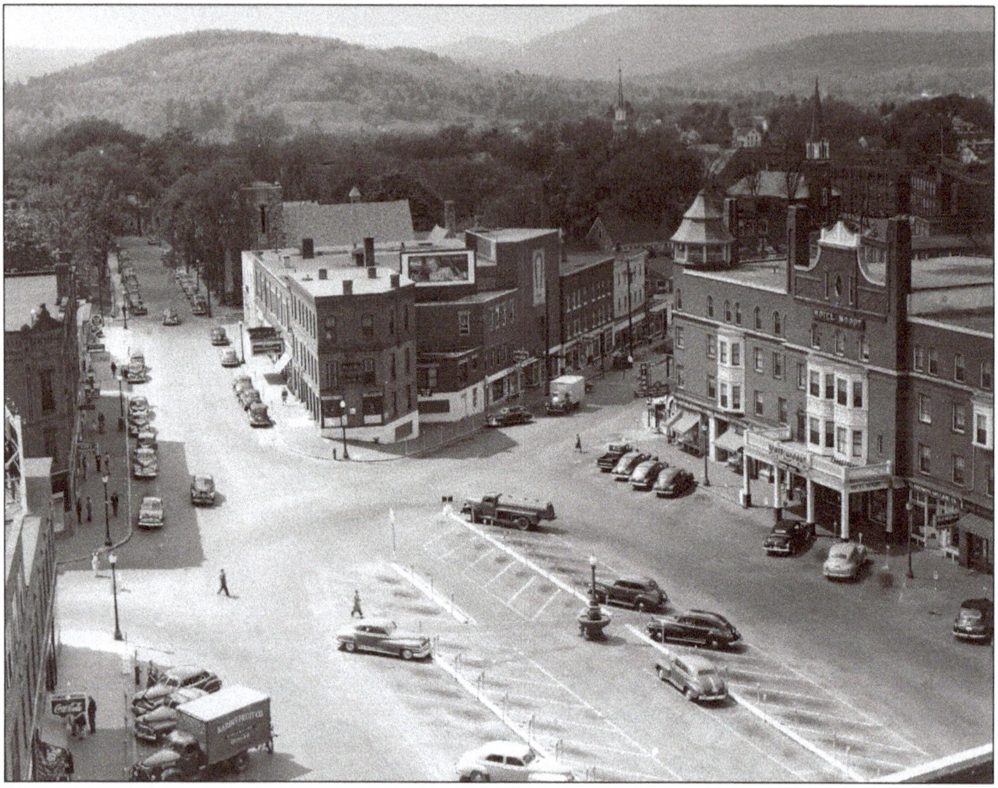

This view of the square faces west in 1930. (CHS.)

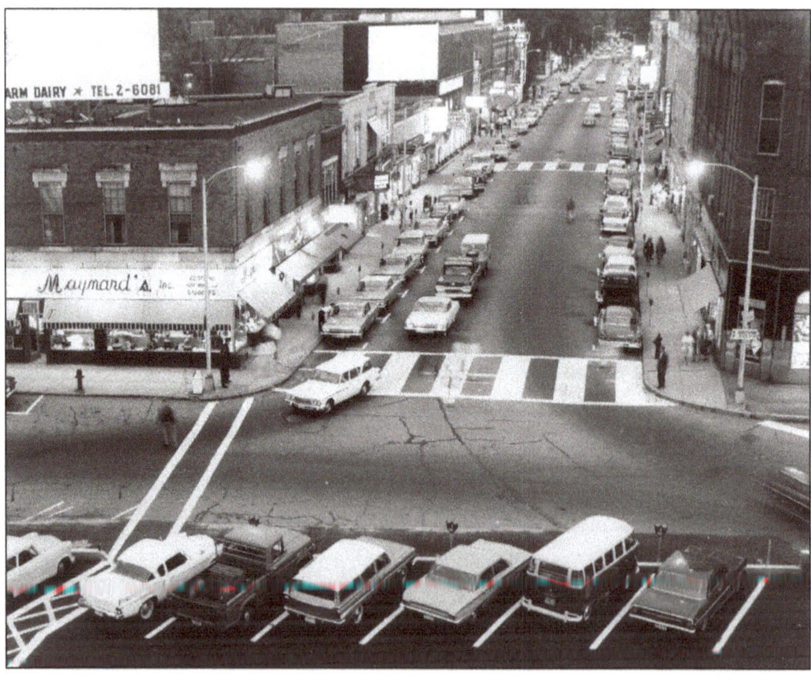

This night view of the square looks down Pleasant Street in 1930. (CHS.)

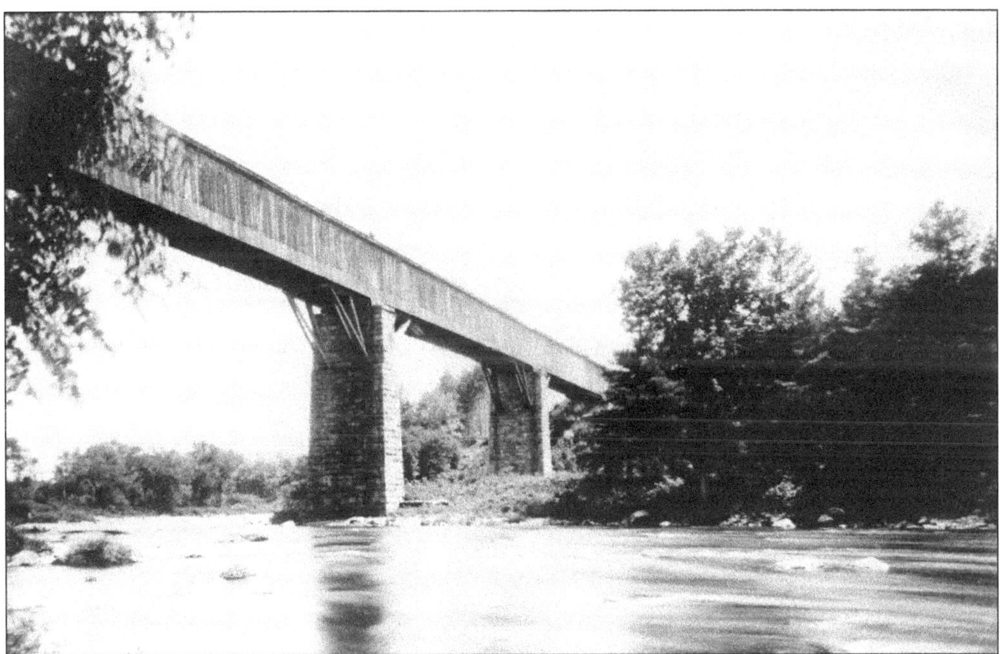

This is the original high bridge in West Claremont. Construction began in 1847 with the bridge opening on February 5, 1849. Construction is often misattributed to George Washington Whistler, who was in Russia from 1842 until his death in 1849, though the bridge may have been based on designs by him. (CHS.)

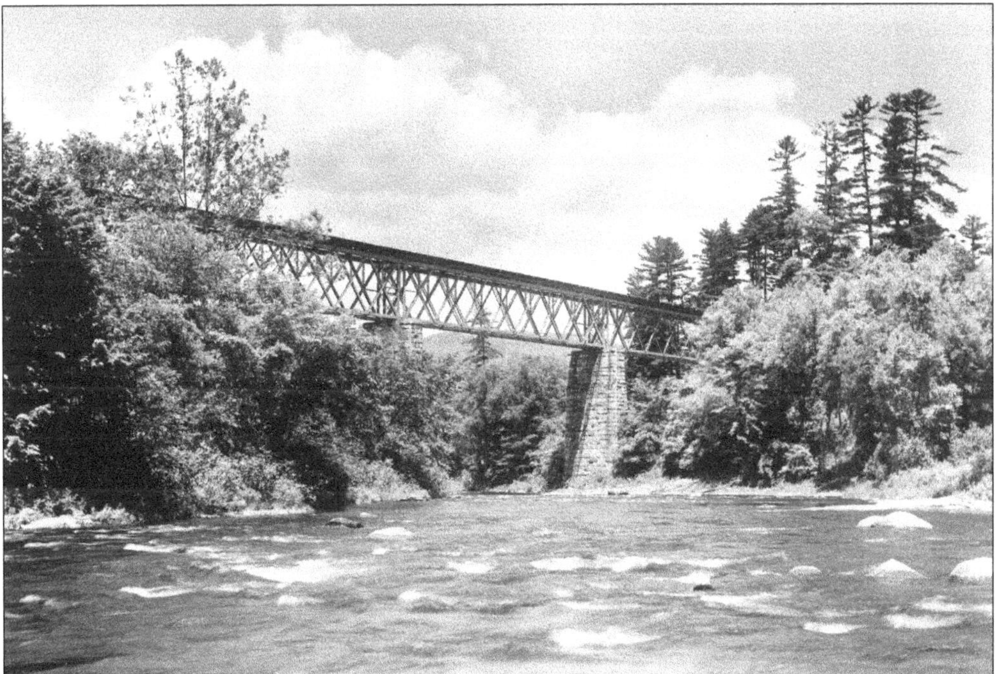

Pictured is the high bridge after the wooden covered deck truss was replaced by an iron lattice deck truss in 1889. This bridge was replaced by one 25 feet higher in 1929–1930, with the first train crossing the new structure on October 5, 1930. (CHS.)

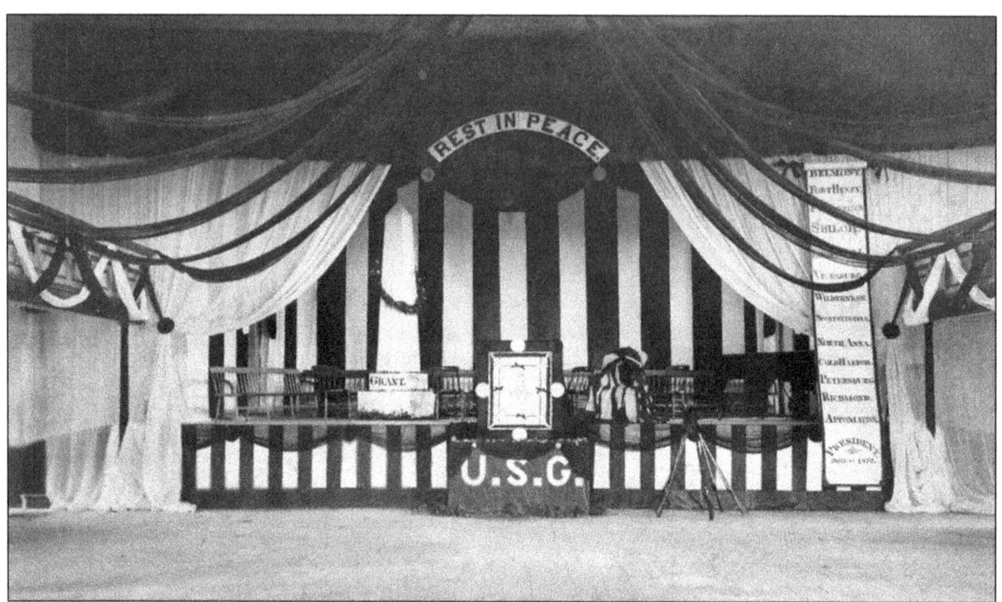

The interior of the old town hall was decorated for a memorial service for Pres. Ulysses S. Grant on August 8, 1885. Grant passed away on July 23, 1885. (CHS.)

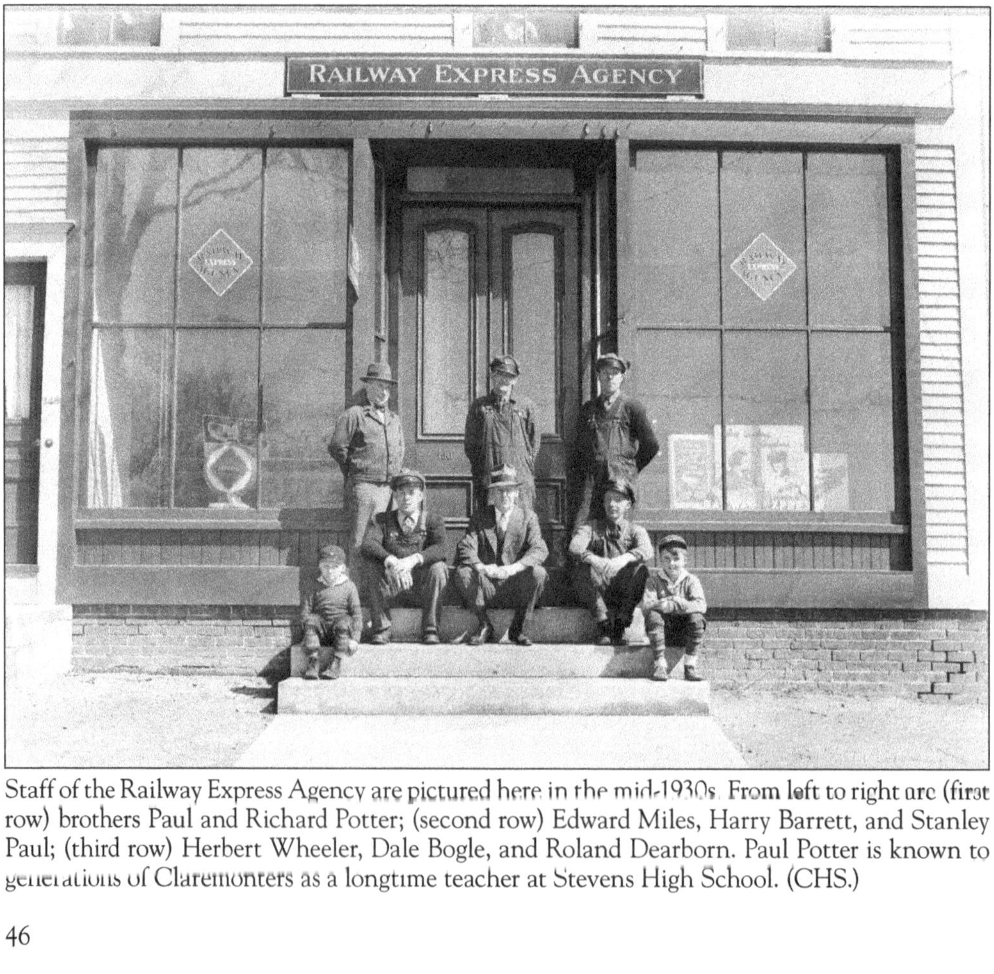

Staff of the Railway Express Agency are pictured here in the mid-1930s. From left to right are (first row) brothers Paul and Richard Potter; (second row) Edward Miles, Harry Barrett, and Stanley Paul; (third row) Herbert Wheeler, Dale Bogle, and Roland Dearborn. Paul Potter is known to generations of Claremonters as a longtime teacher at Stevens High School. (CHS.)

Two

THE MILLS

The mills propelled Claremont to prominence, starting when small mills began dotting the area between 1813 and 1820. The industry boom came in the 1830s with the creation of a number of mills, including the Sugar River Manufacturing Company (later Monadnock Mills). The addition of the Sullivan Machinery Company in the 1860s continued the town's rise.

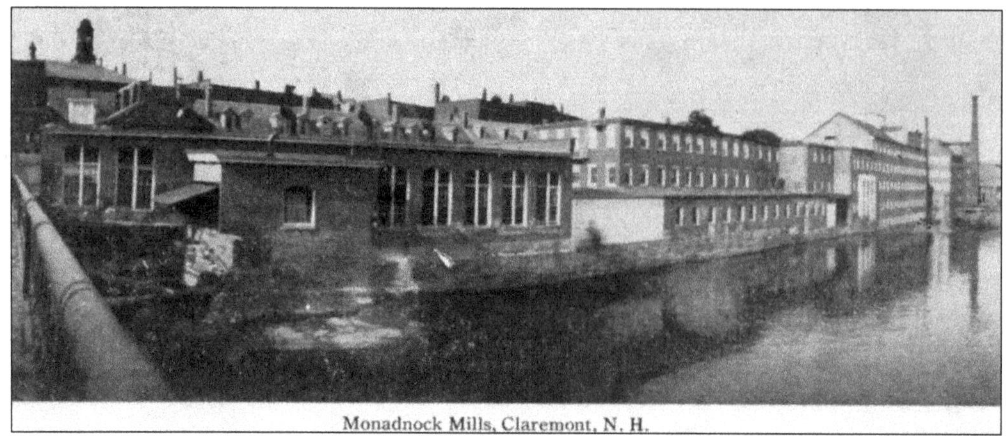
Monadnock Mills, Claremont, N. H.

This view of Monadnock Mills on the southern side of the Sugar River is from the north end of the Broad Street Bridge. (WLM.)

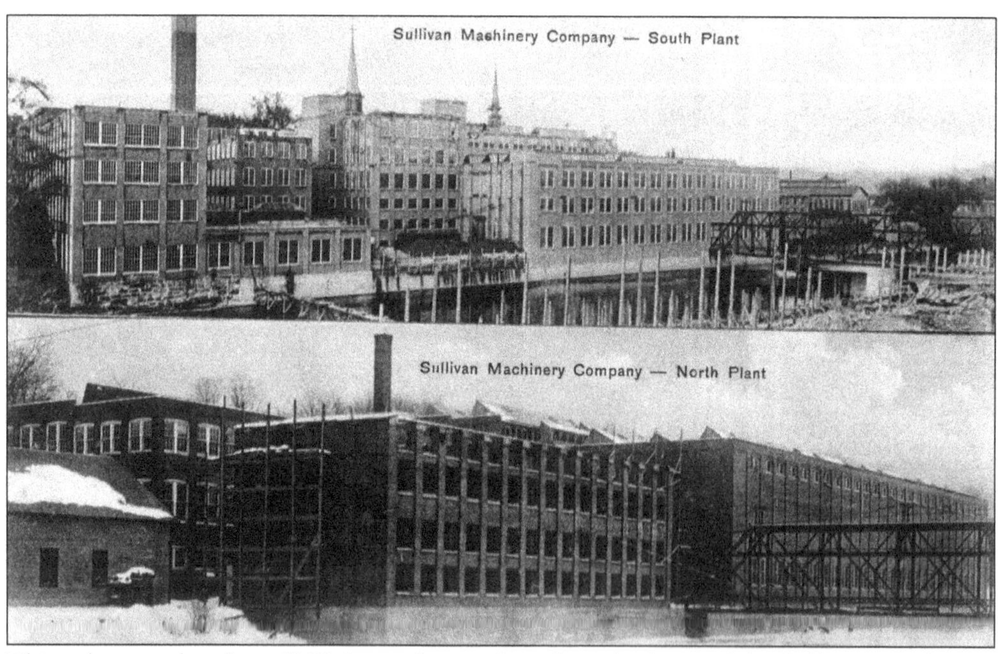
Sullivan Machinery Company — South Plant

Sullivan Machinery Company — North Plant

This split-view shot from 1908 shows the north and south plants of the Sullivan Machinery Company on both sides of the Sugar River. (WLM.)

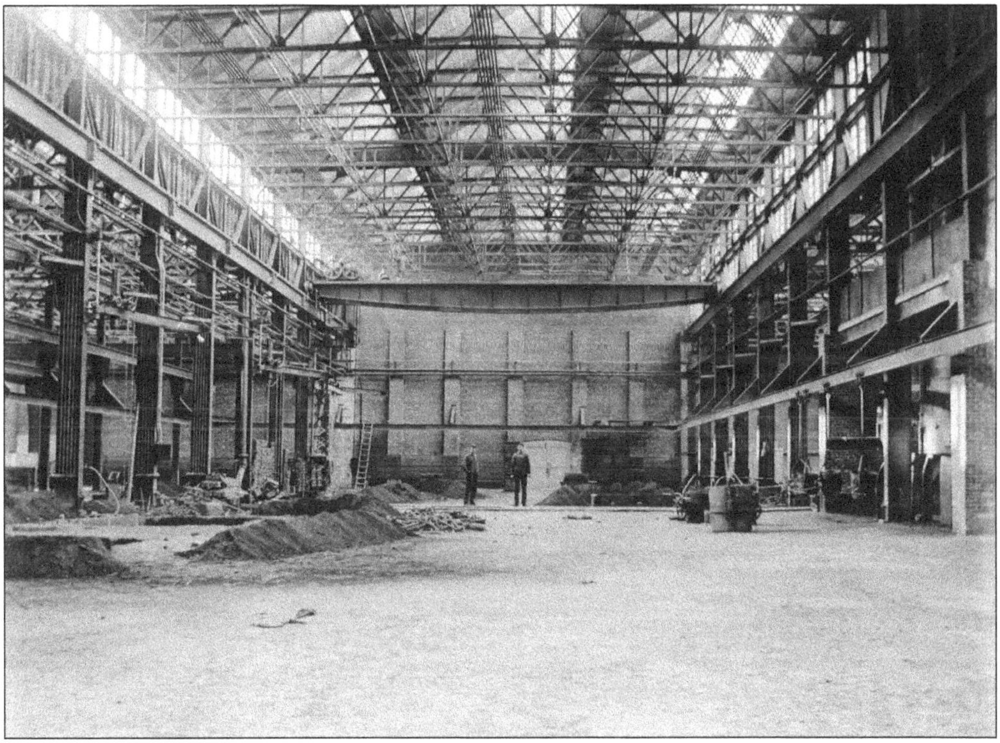

The interior of the Sullivan Machinery Company foundry is seen here in 1910. (WLM.)

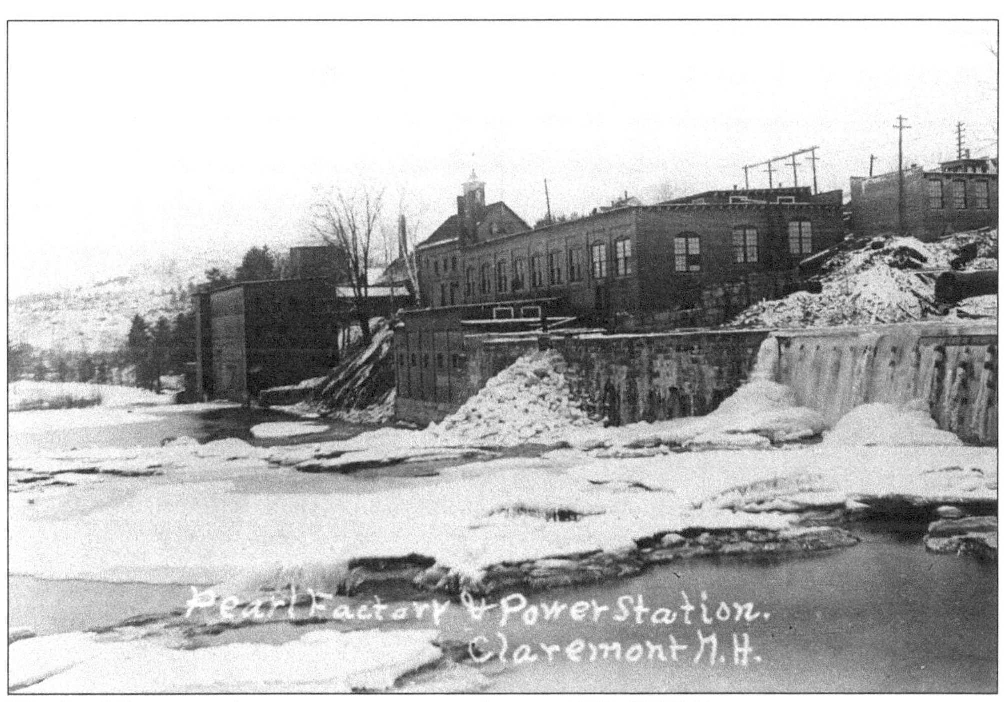

The Pearl Factory and power station are seen here in 1908. (WLM.)

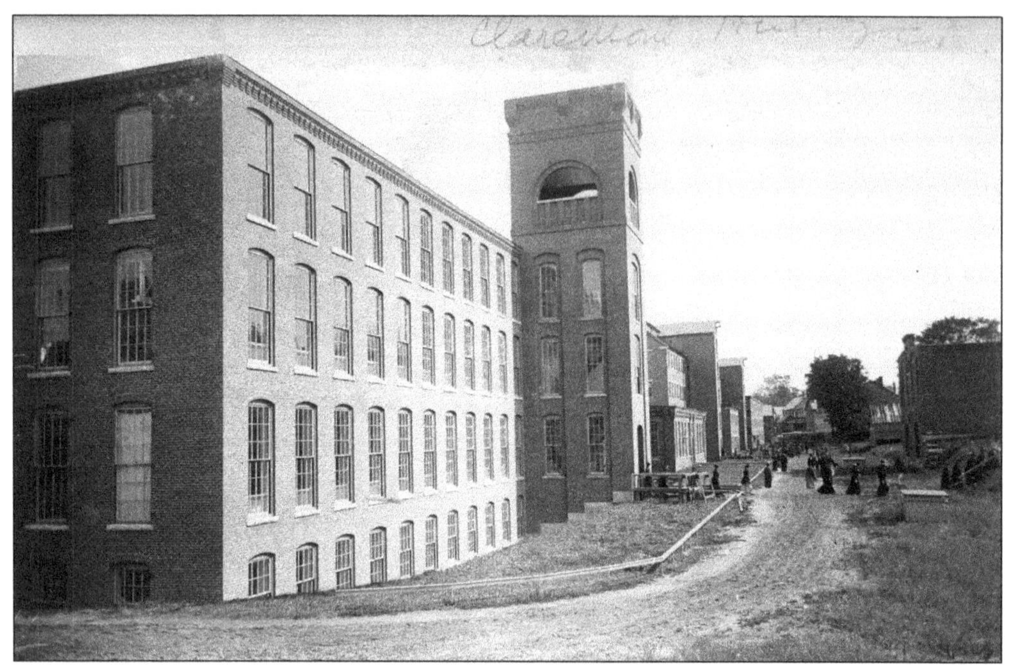

Monadnock Mill No. 3 on Water Street, seen here in 1895, is now commonly called the Peterson Building. A fourth floor was later added. (CHS.)

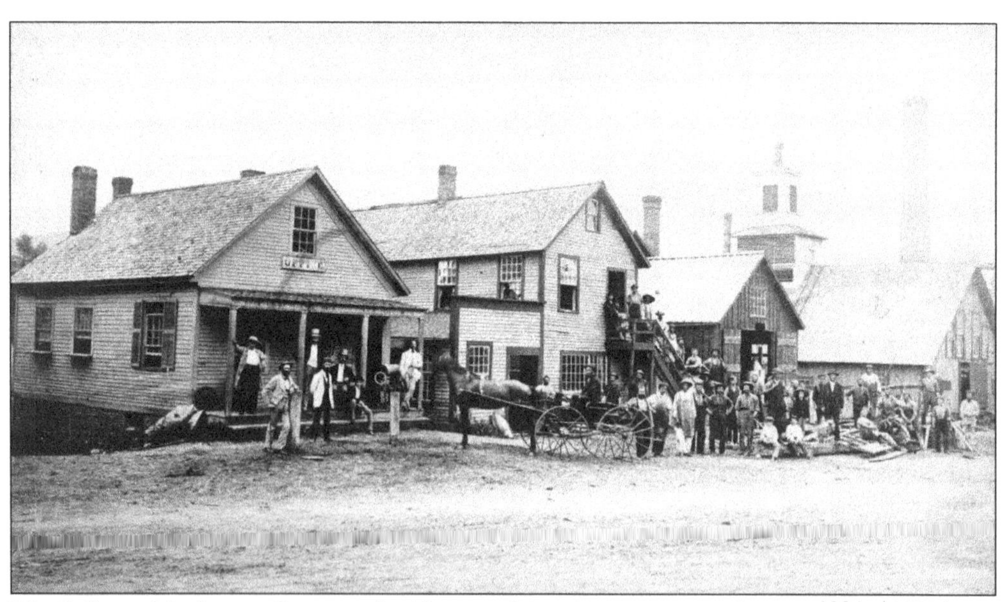

The Sullivan Machinery Company buildings on Main Street are seen here in 1890. (CHS.)

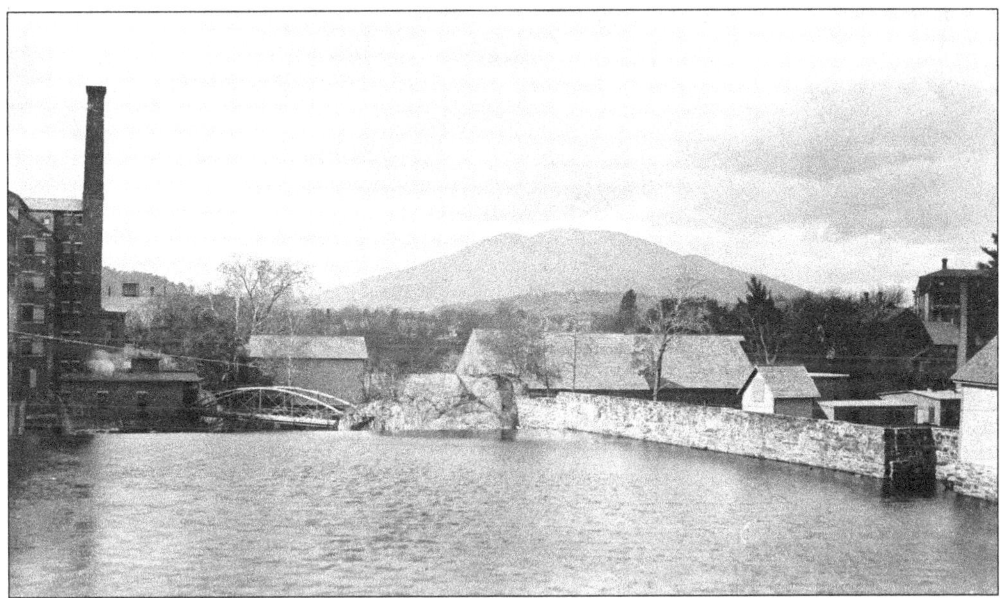

This is a view of Monadnock Mills from the Broad Street Bridge facing west. Mount Ascutney is in the background. (CHS.)

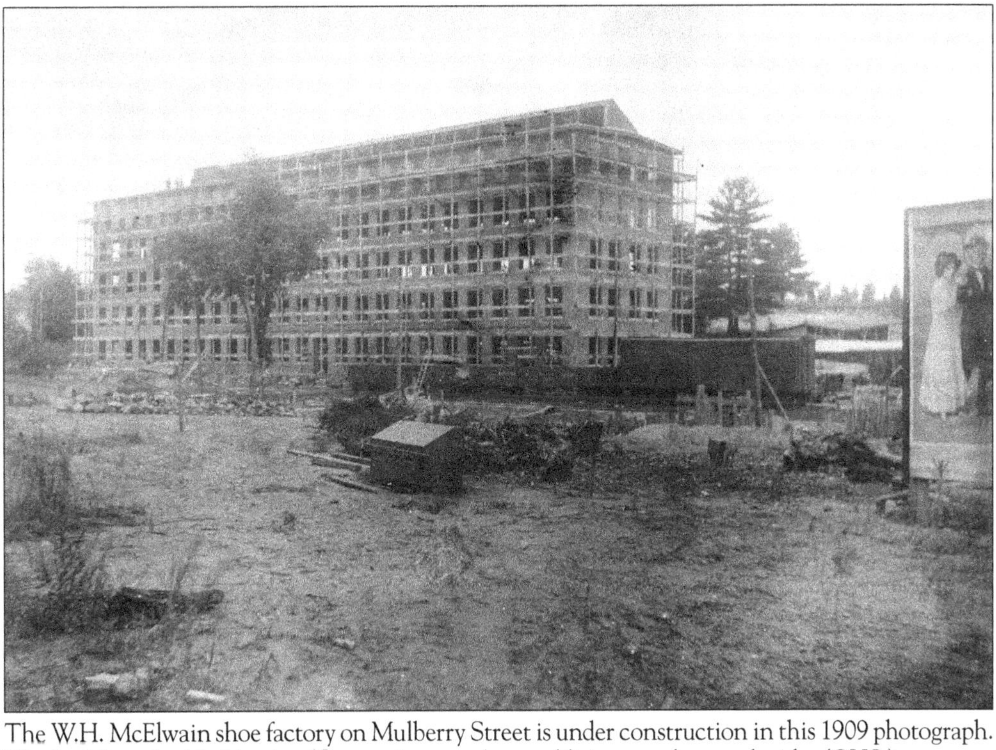

The W.H. McElwain shoe factory on Mulberry Street is under construction in this 1909 photograph. The building doubled in size 10 years later with an addition on the north side. (CHS.)

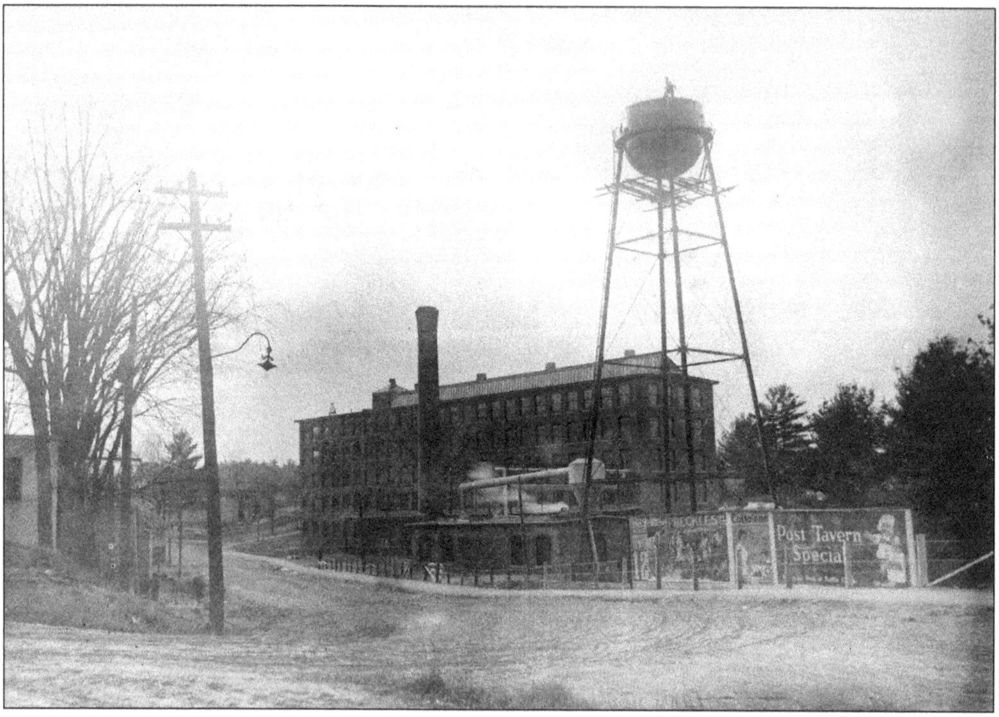

The McElwain shoe factory is seen here in 1915. Despite being home to a succession of shoe manufacturers until the late 1960s, the structure is now generally known as the Topstone Building after the furniture company that occupied it for most of the 1970s. (CHS.)

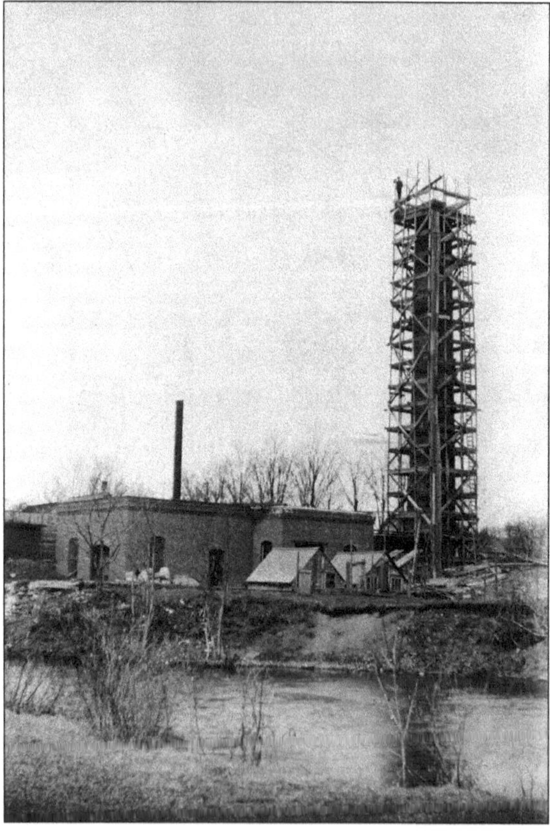

This is a photograph of the Claremont Water Works Company, constructed by Claremont builder Hira Beckwith and completed in the spring of 1907. The chimney is 90 feet high. (CHS.)

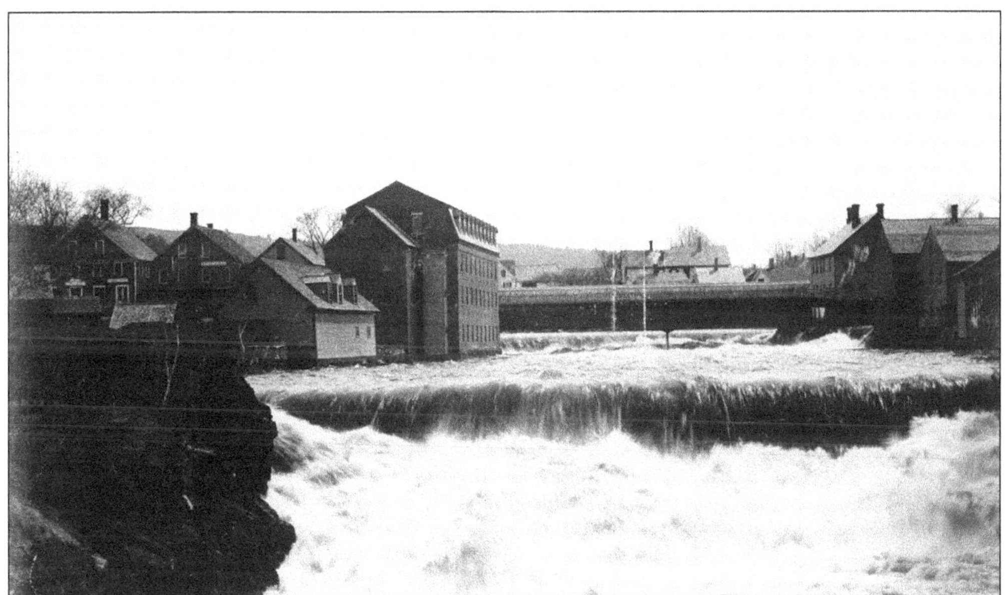

High water passes by the Sullivan Woolen Mill (left) and Monadnock Mills around 1900. This view faces east toward the Broad Street Bridge. (CHS.)

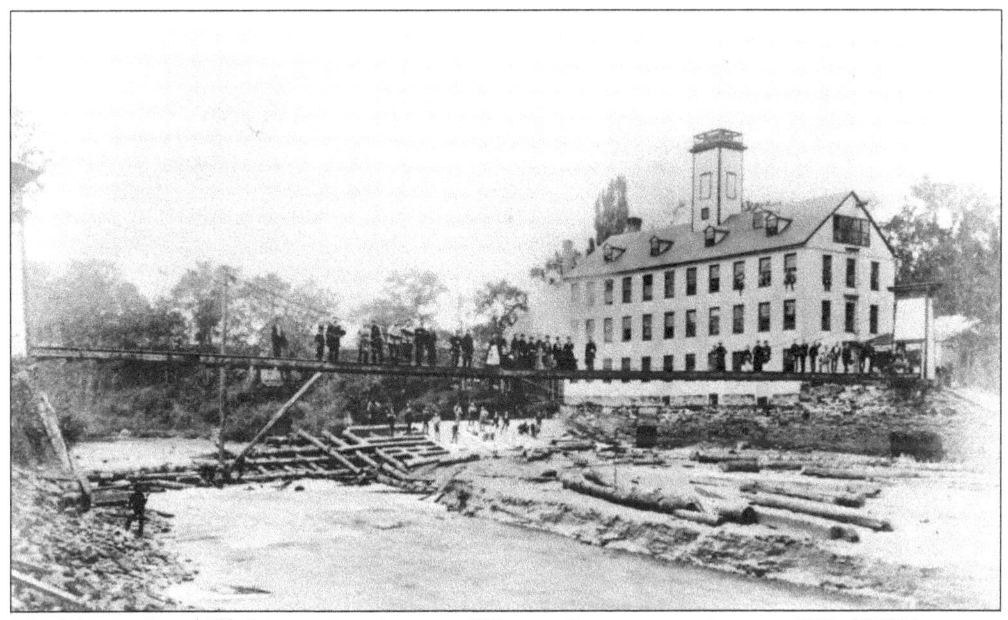

The Maynard and Washburn shoe factory off Spring Street is seen here in 1895. (CHS.)

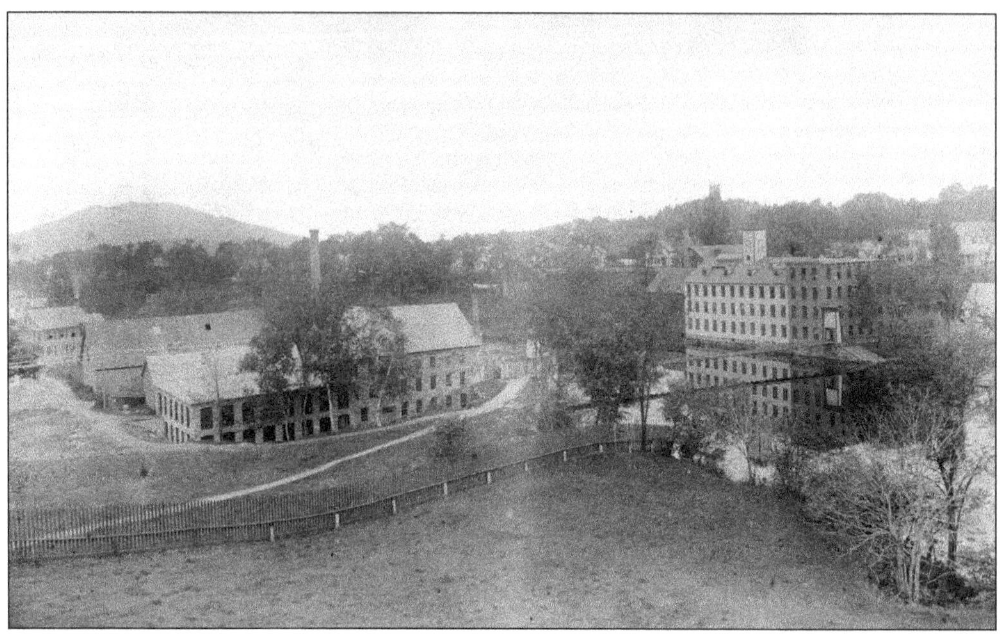

This photograph shows the Claremont Manufacturing Company on the south side of the river and the Maynard and Washburn shoe factory on the north side. Mount Ascutney is in the background. (CHS.)

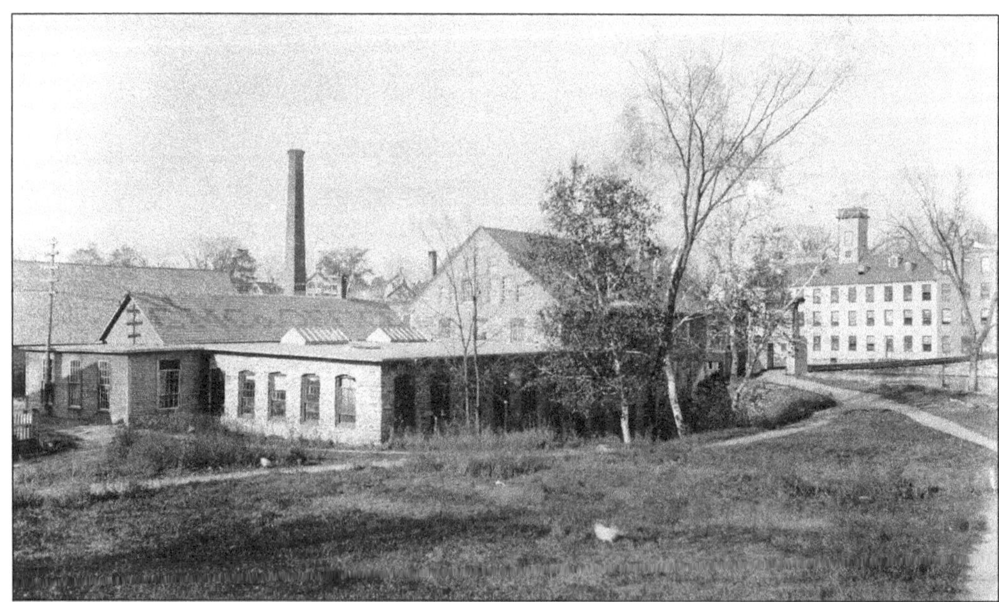

The Sullivan Machinery Company is seen here in 1900 with the Maynard and Washburn shoe factory to the right. (CHS.)

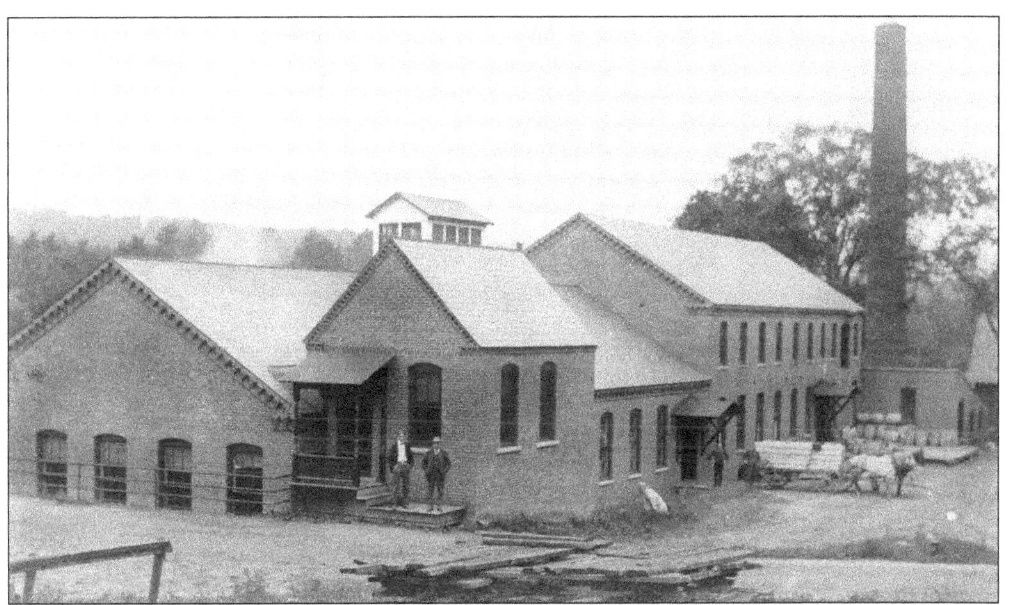

The Coy Paper Mill in West Claremont is seen here in 1885. (CHS.)

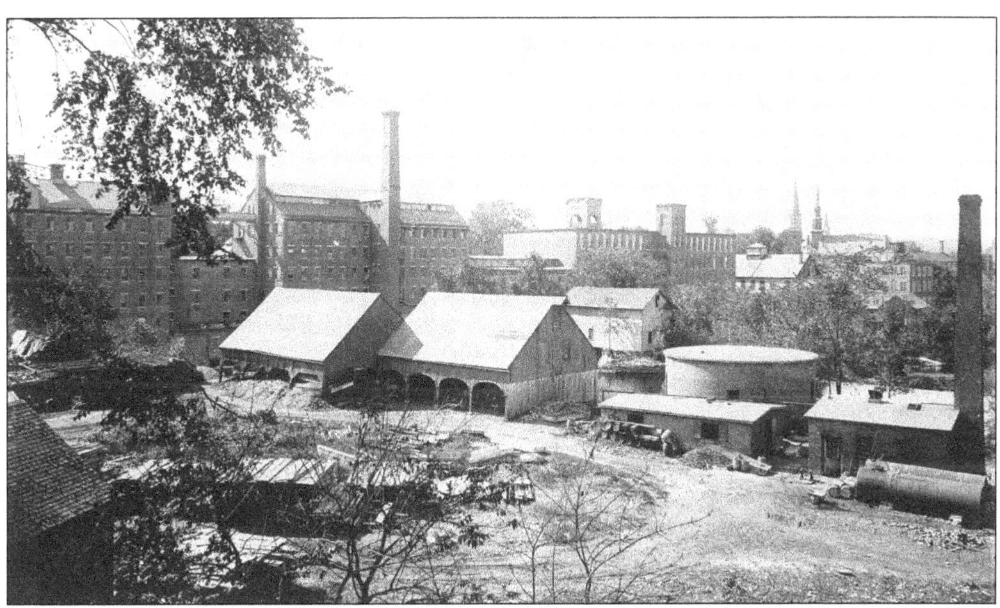

The Claremont Gas Company is seen here in 1895 with Monadnock Mills across the Sugar River. (CHS.)

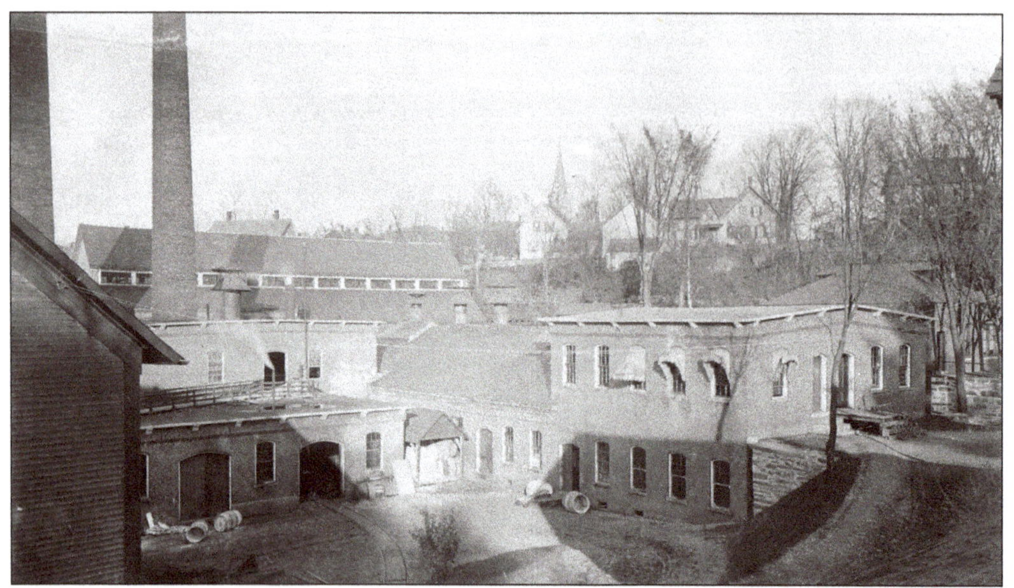

The Claremont Paper Mill on Sullivan Street is seen here in 1895. (CHS.)

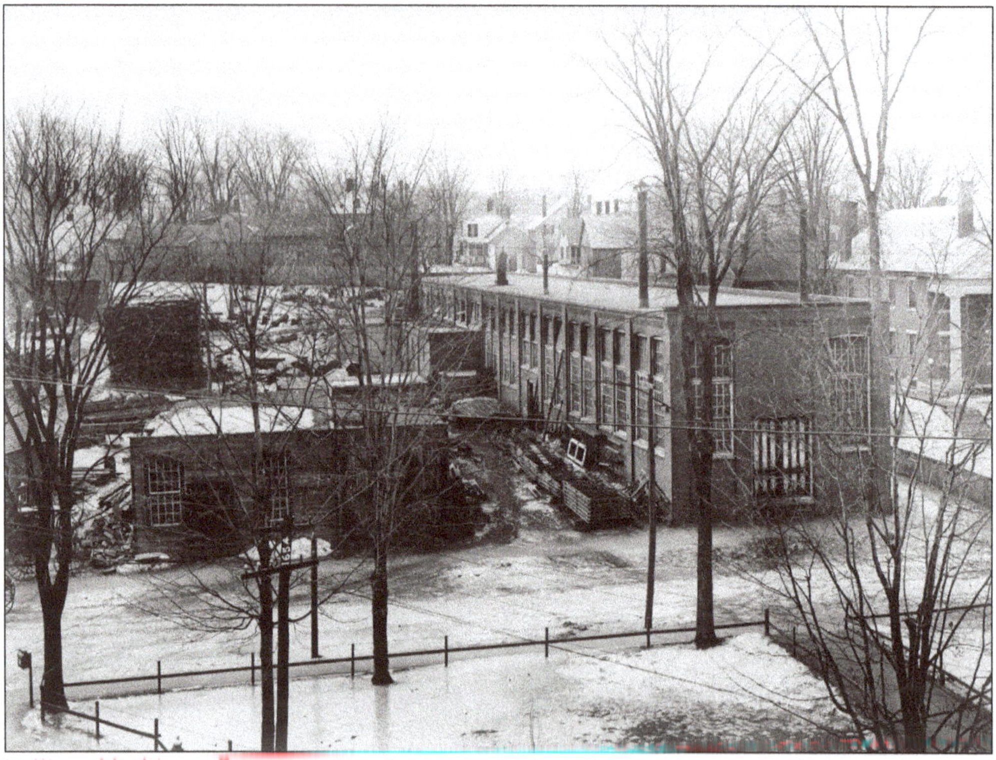

Sullivan Machinery Company's forge house was built in 1902 on the corner of Main and Central Streets. Additions in 1907 and 1911 tripled its size and gave it its distinctive sawtooth roof design. (CHS.)

Buildings at Monadnock Mills are seen here in 1910. Much of this area was lost in the fires of 1979 and 1981. (CHS.)

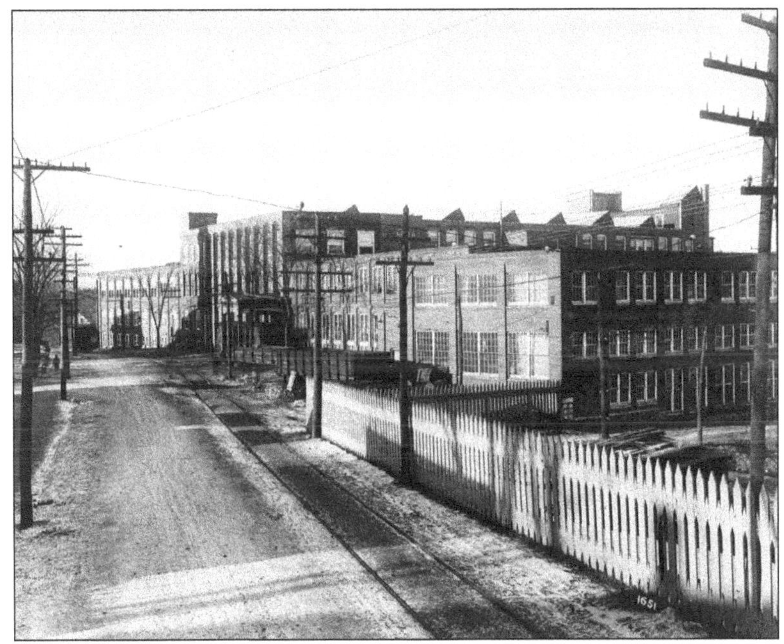

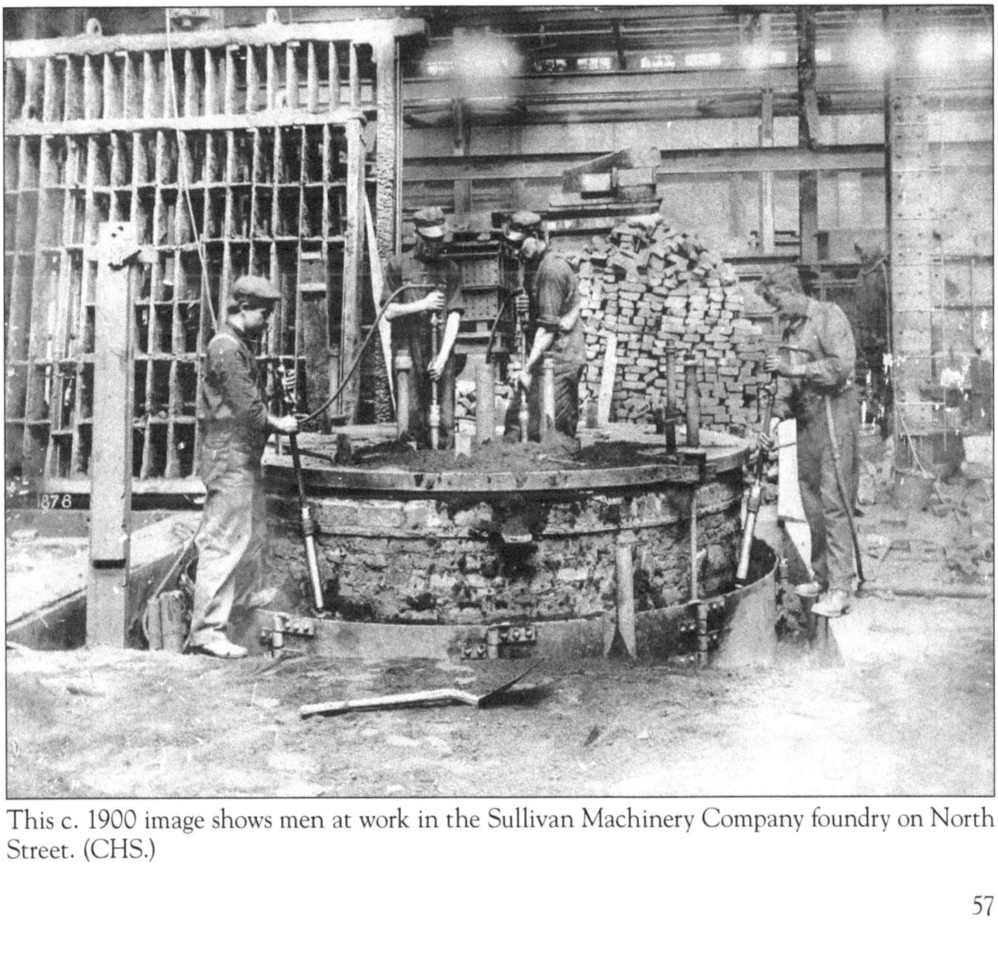

This c. 1900 image shows men at work in the Sullivan Machinery Company foundry on North Street. (CHS.)

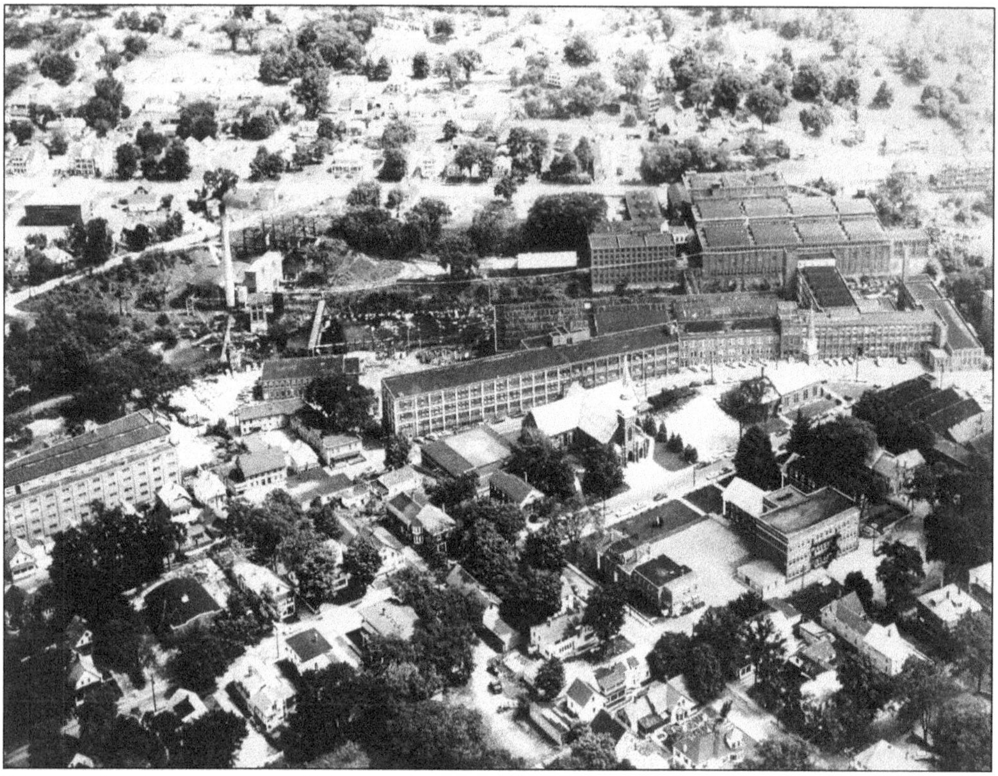

This overhead view of the mill district faces north around 1950. (CHS.)

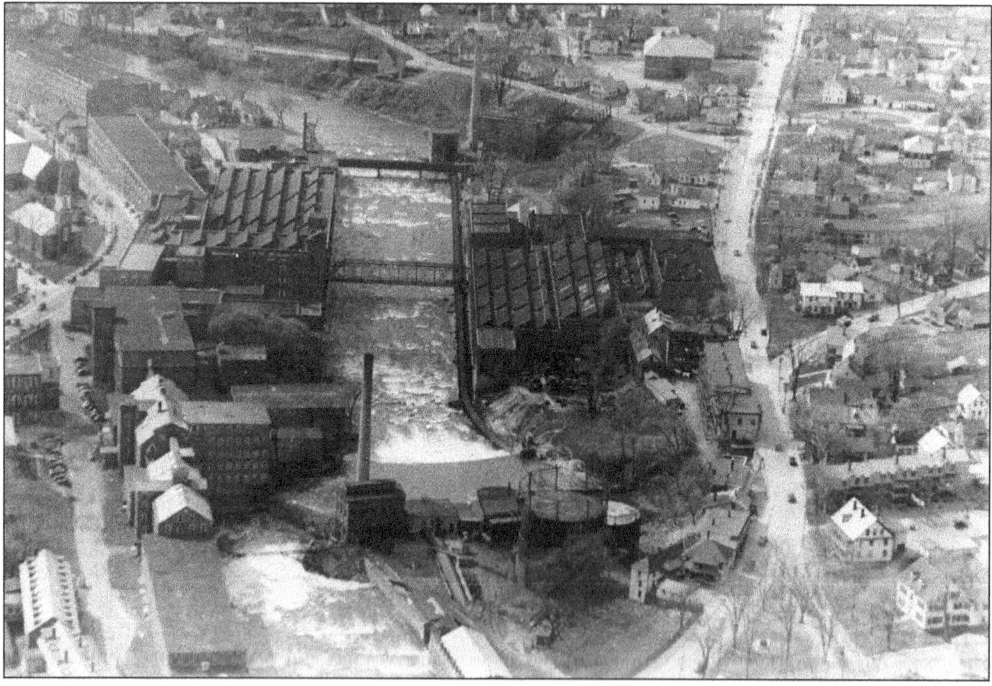

This is an overhead view of the mill district facing west, taken around 1940. Main Street is on the left, and North Street is on the right. Lacasse Park is in the lower right. (CHS.)

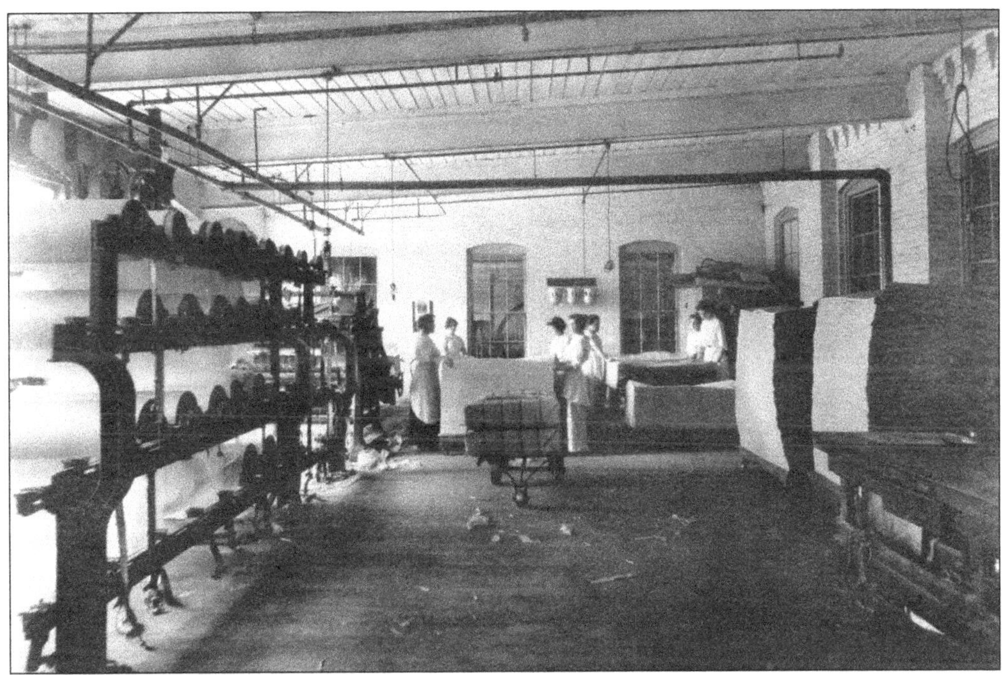

Women are at work inside the Coy Paper Mill around 1900. (CHS.)

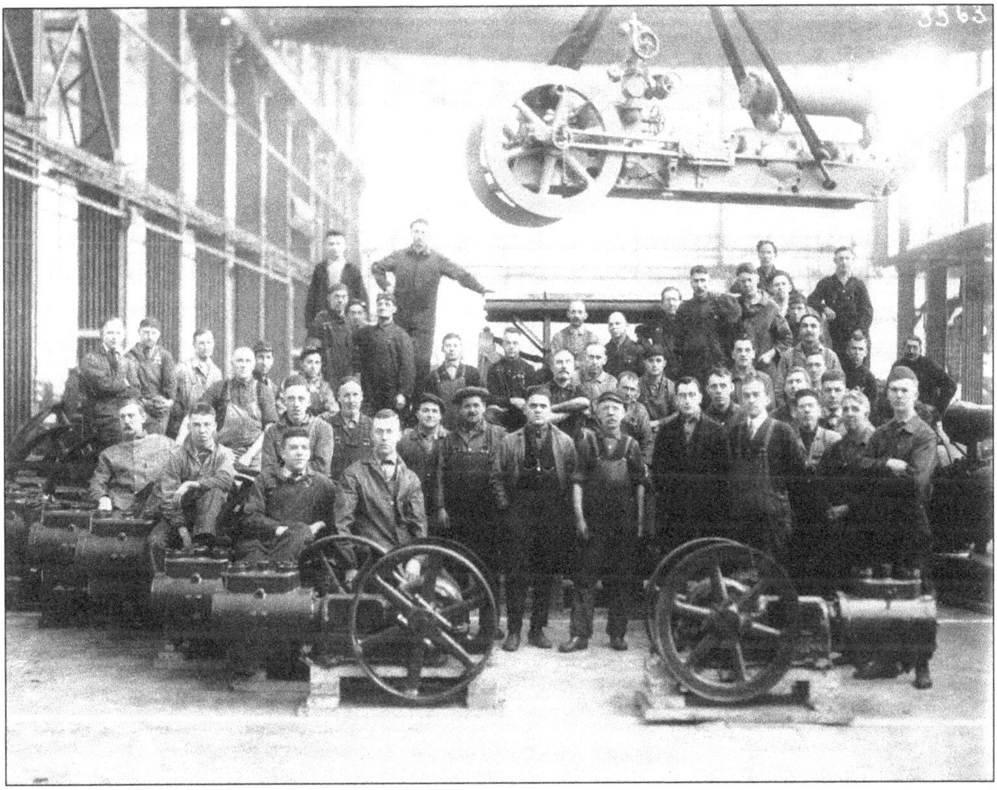

A work crew for the Sullivan Machinery Company is seen inside the business around 1910. (CHS.)

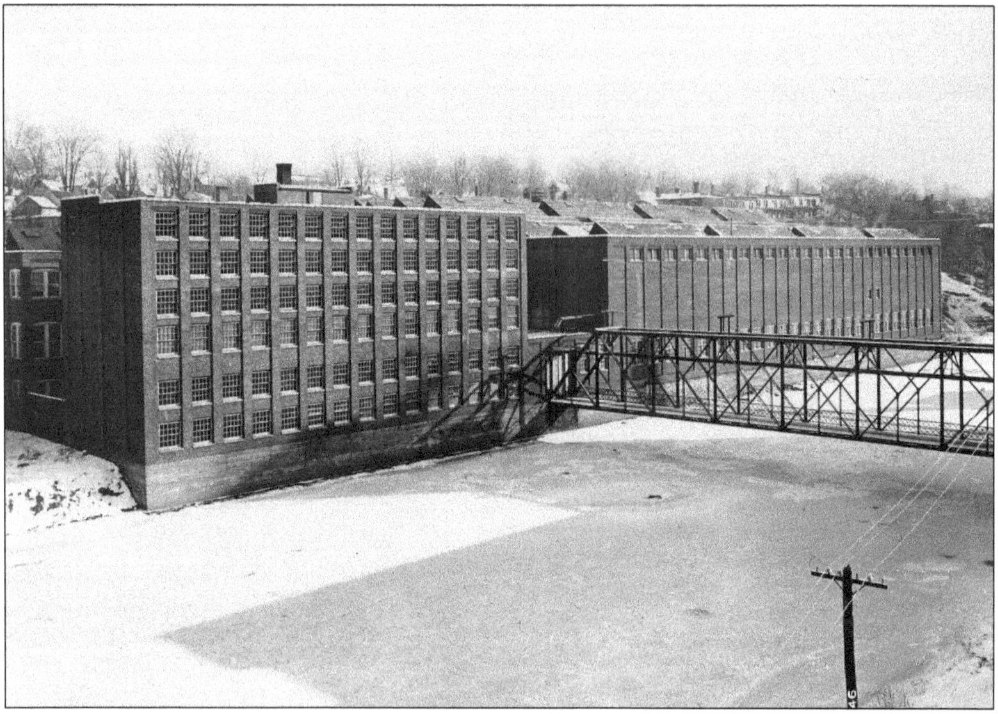

This view, taken from across the Sugar River, shows the Sullivan Machinery Company foundry on North Street in 1909. (CHS.)

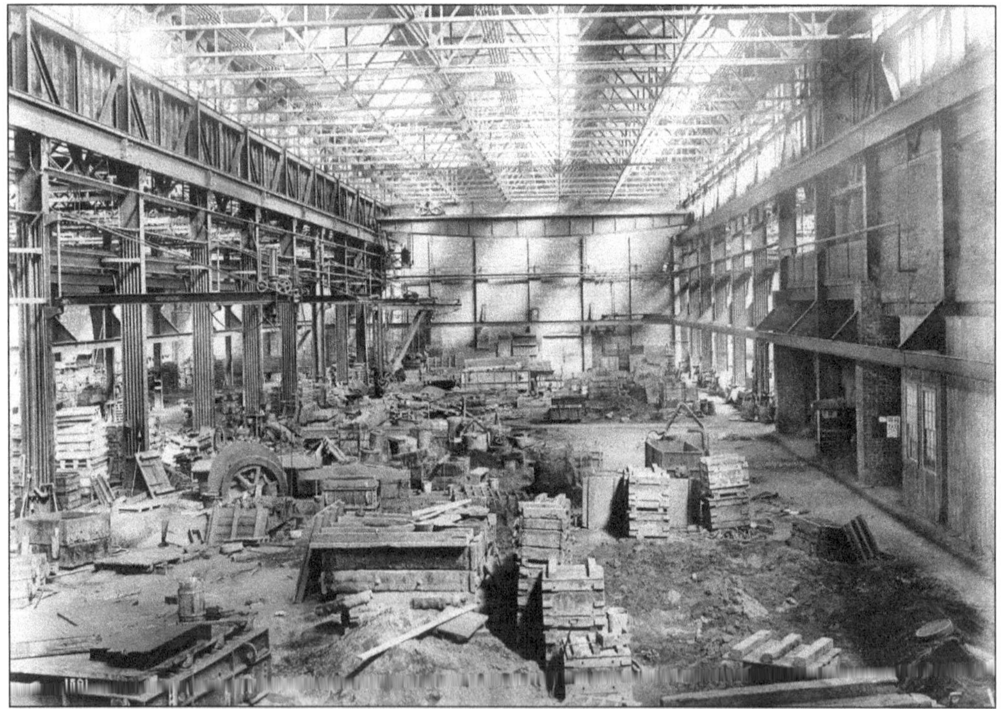

The work floor of the Sullivan Machinery Company foundry on North Street is pictured here around 1910. (CHS.)

Three

BUSINESSES

A number of businesses helped make Claremont the retail hub of the area. Long before Washington Street changed from a residential street to a commercial street, residents did their shopping in the Pleasant Street/Tremont Square area and on down to the lower village on Main Street.

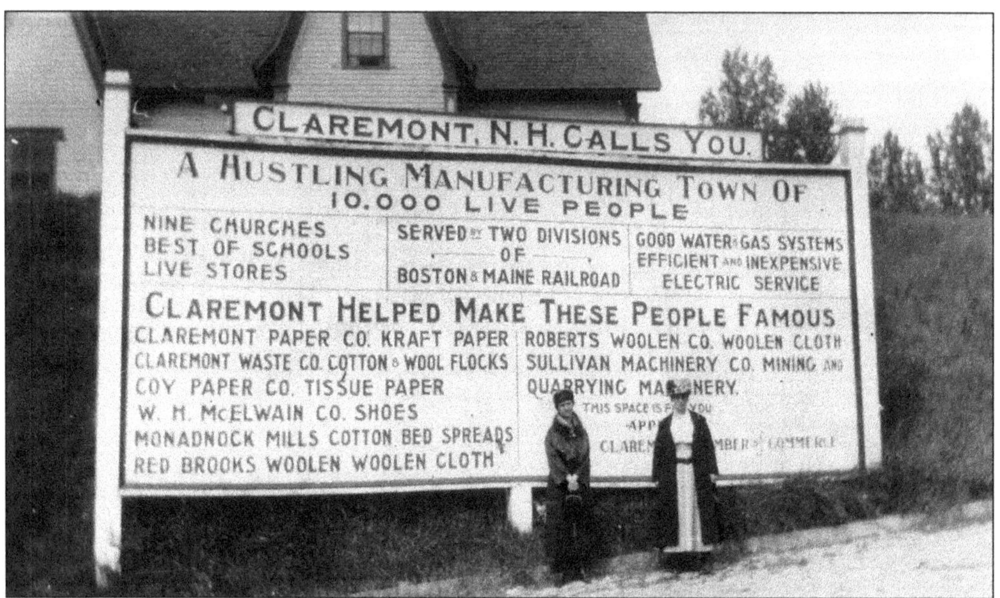

This sign, seen here around 1920, stood at the corner of Pleasant and Green Streets noting some of the prominent businesses in town. (CHS.)

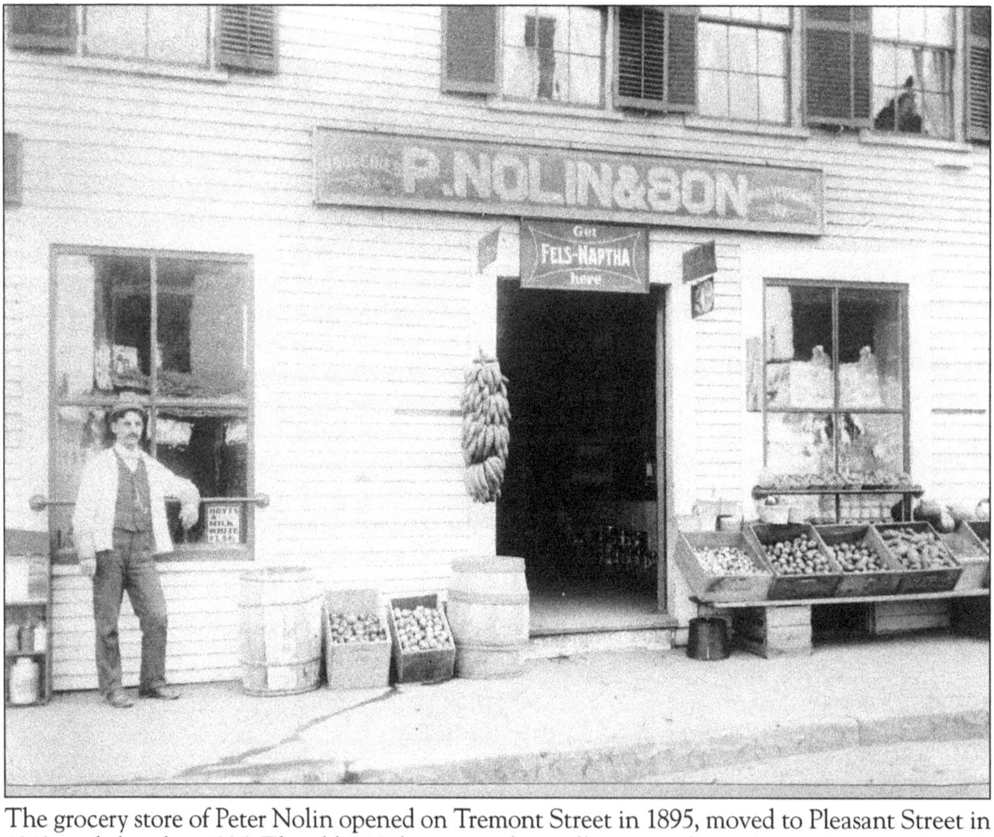

The grocery store of Peter Nolin opened on Tremont Street in 1895, moved to Pleasant Street in 1919, and closed in 1935. The elder Nolin was such a well-respected member of the town that all businesses were closed in observance of his funeral in 1909. (CHS.)

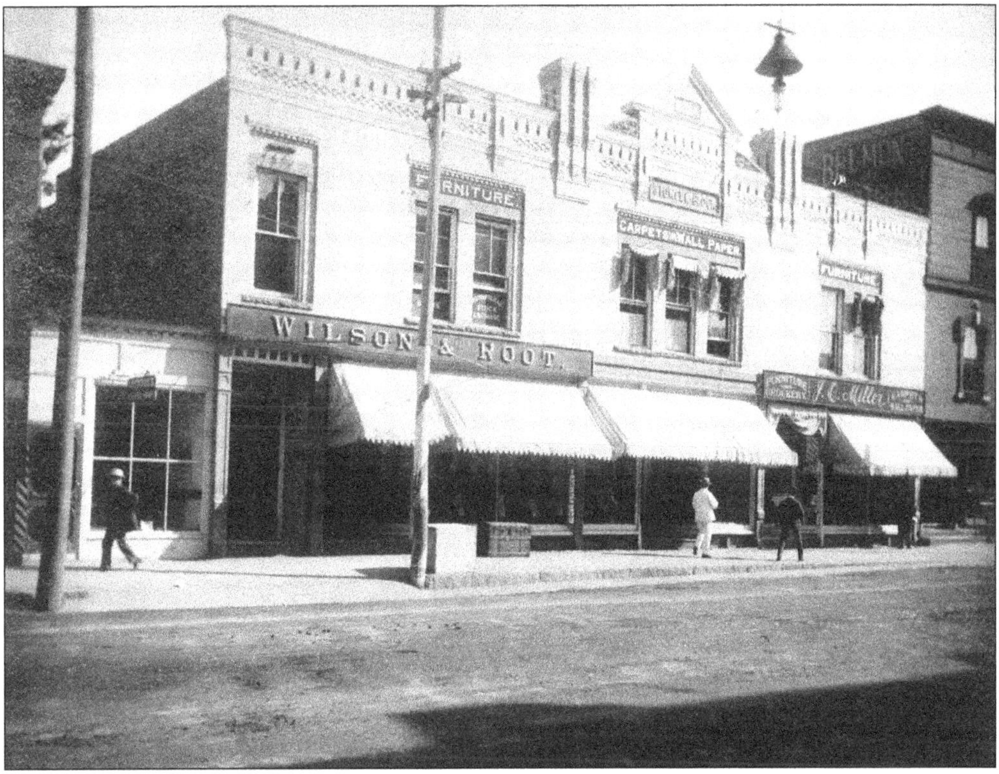

The men's furnishings store Wilson & Root opened in the Stowell Block in May 1896. (CHS.)

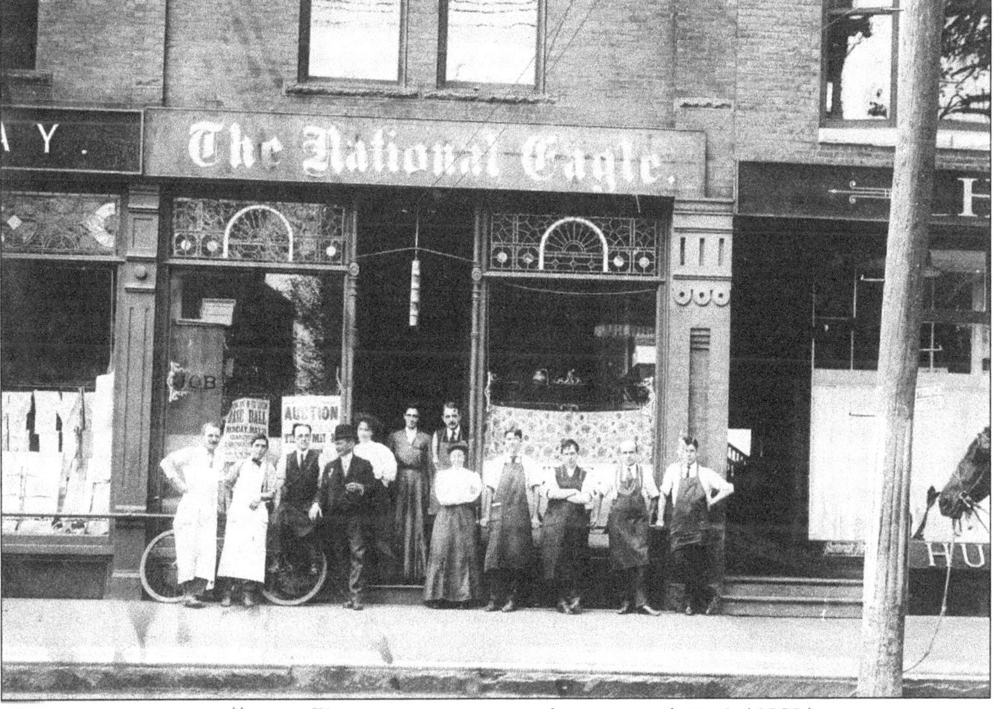

The National Eagle office on Pleasant Street is seen here around 1885. (CHS.)

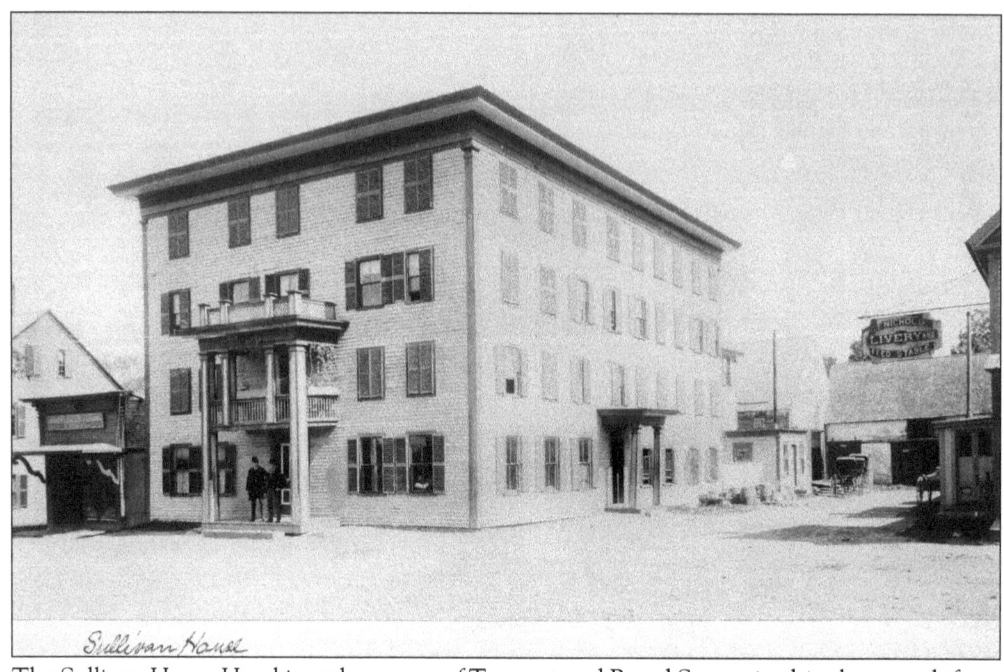

The Sullivan House Hotel is at the corner of Tremont and Broad Streets in this photograph from around 1890, with Nichols Livery and Feed Stable next door. (CHS.)

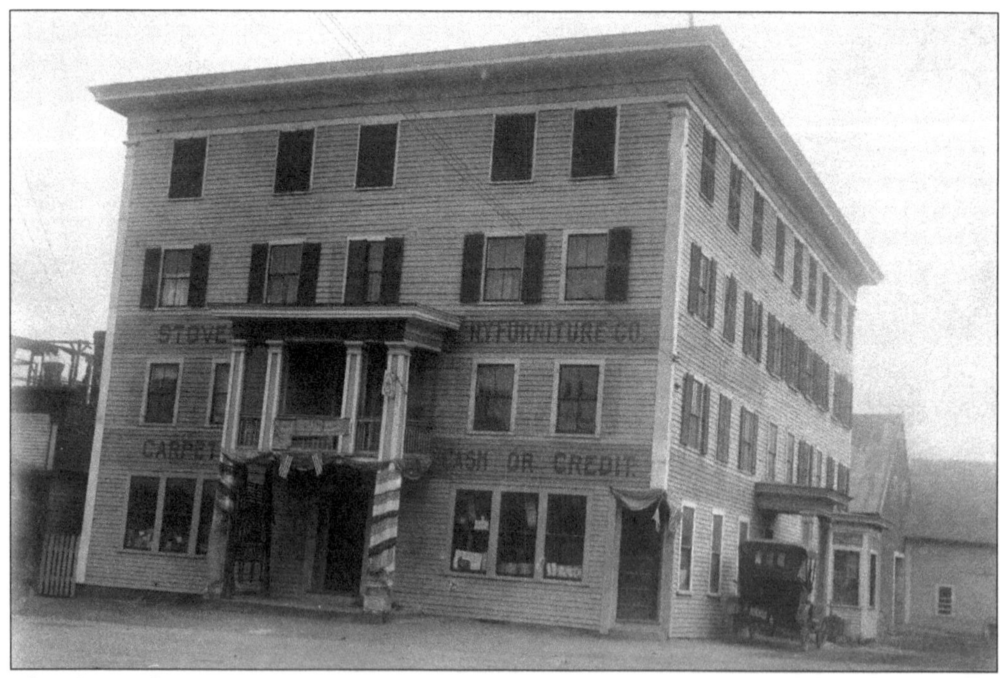

The New York Furniture Company occupied the old Sullivan House Hotel by the time this photograph was taken around 1895, and Welch & Riley operated the neighboring livery stable. (CHS.)

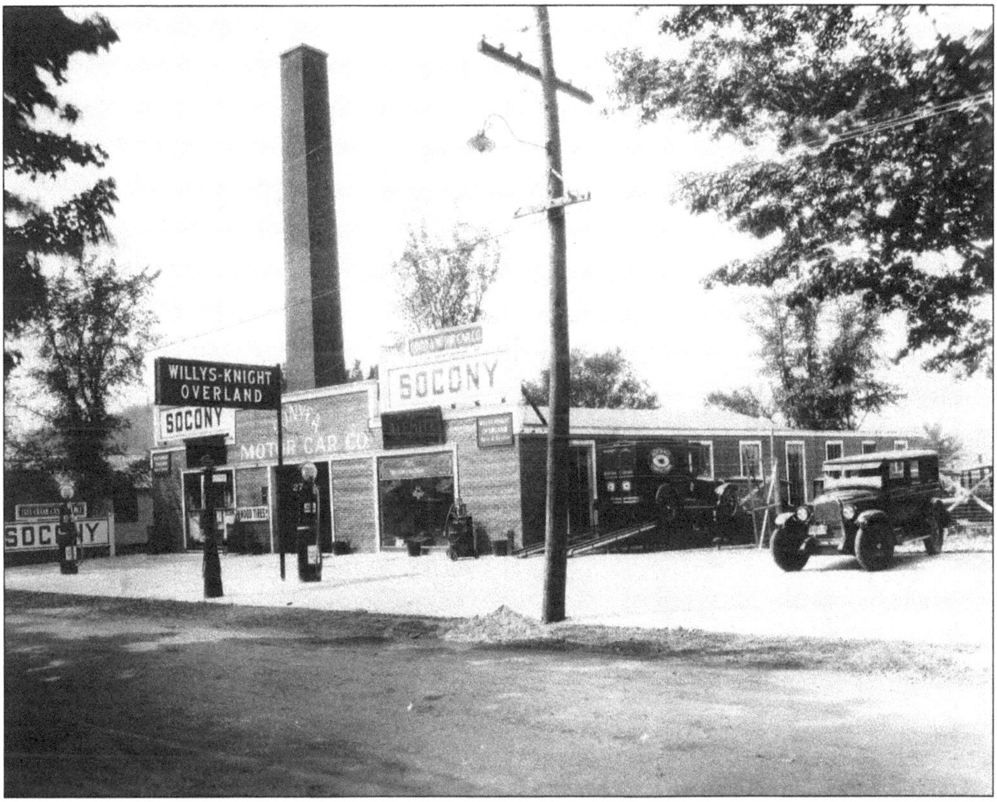

Gonyea Motor Car Company on Washington Street is seen here around 1915. (CHS.)

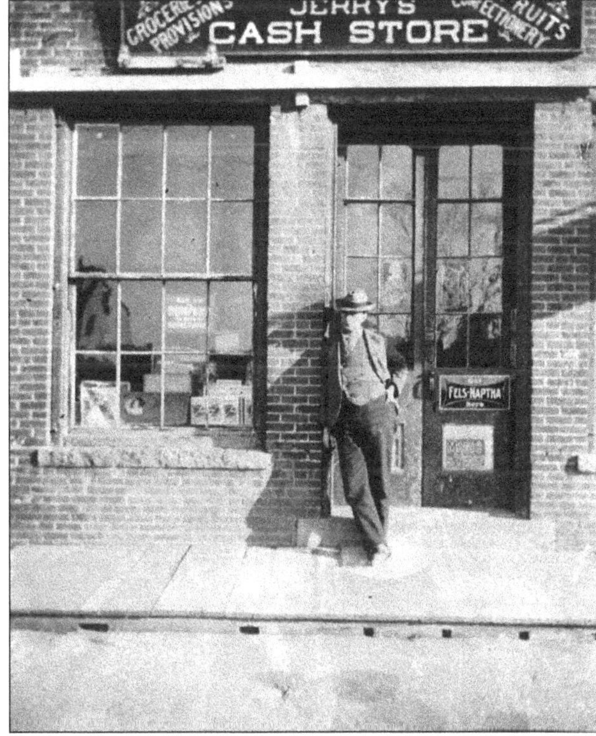

Albert Jerry stands in front of his grocery store at 25 Tremont Street around 1895. (CHS.)

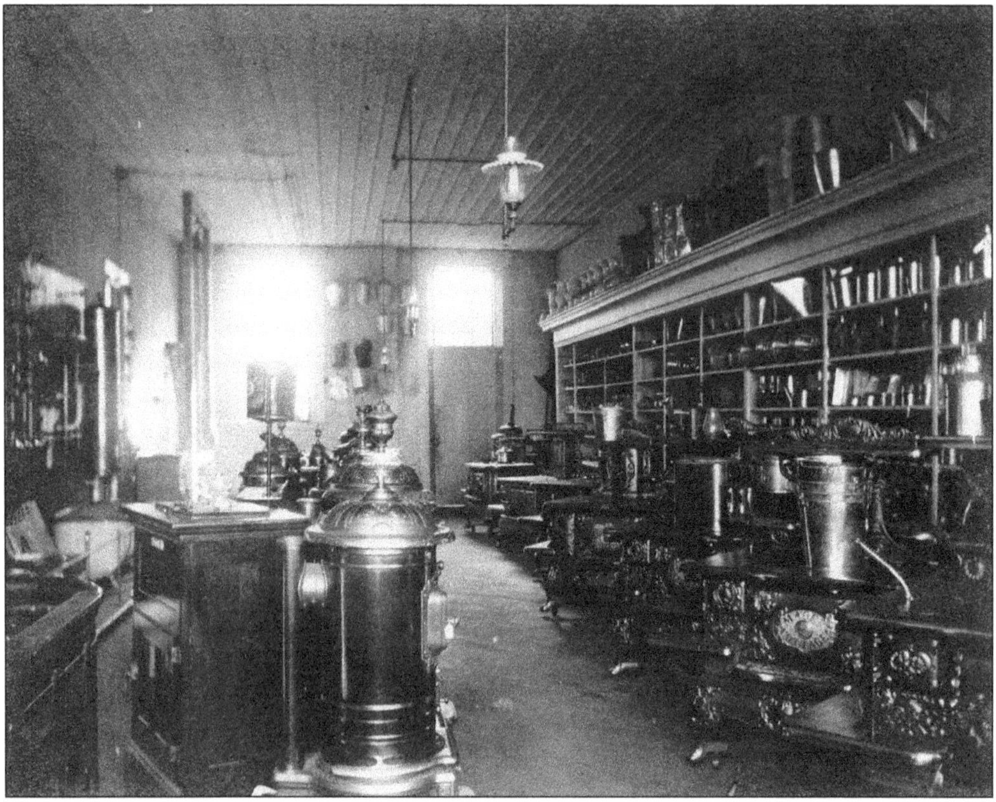

The interior of the Crossman & Polmatier plumbing store is seen here around 1900 on Tremont Square. (CHS.)

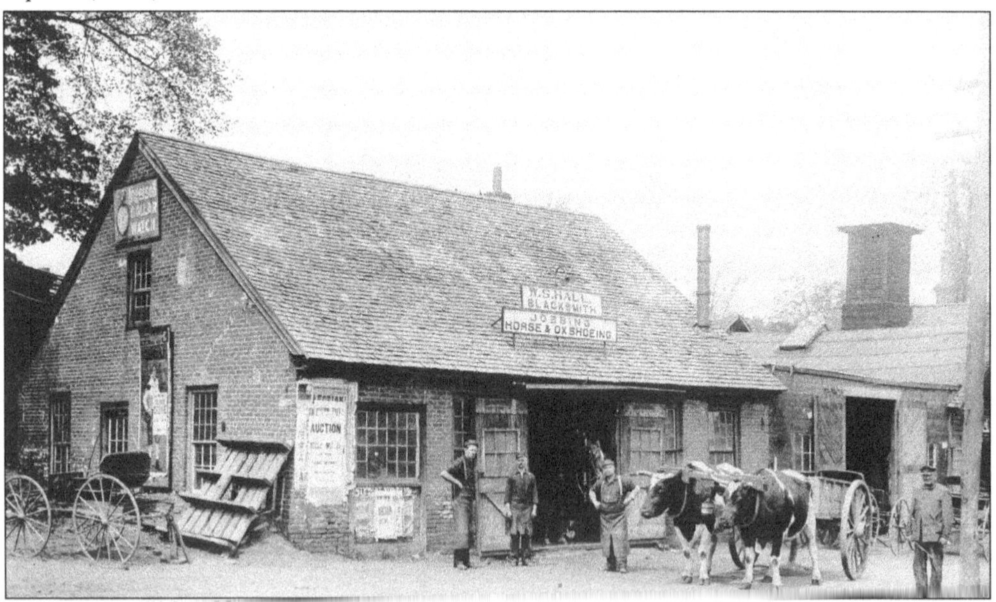

Walter Hall, Walter Howe, George Cook, and Frank Johnson stand in front of Hall's blacksmith shop on Main Street around 1900. Hall worked for carriage-smith Edmund Wheeler before branching out on his own. (CHS.)

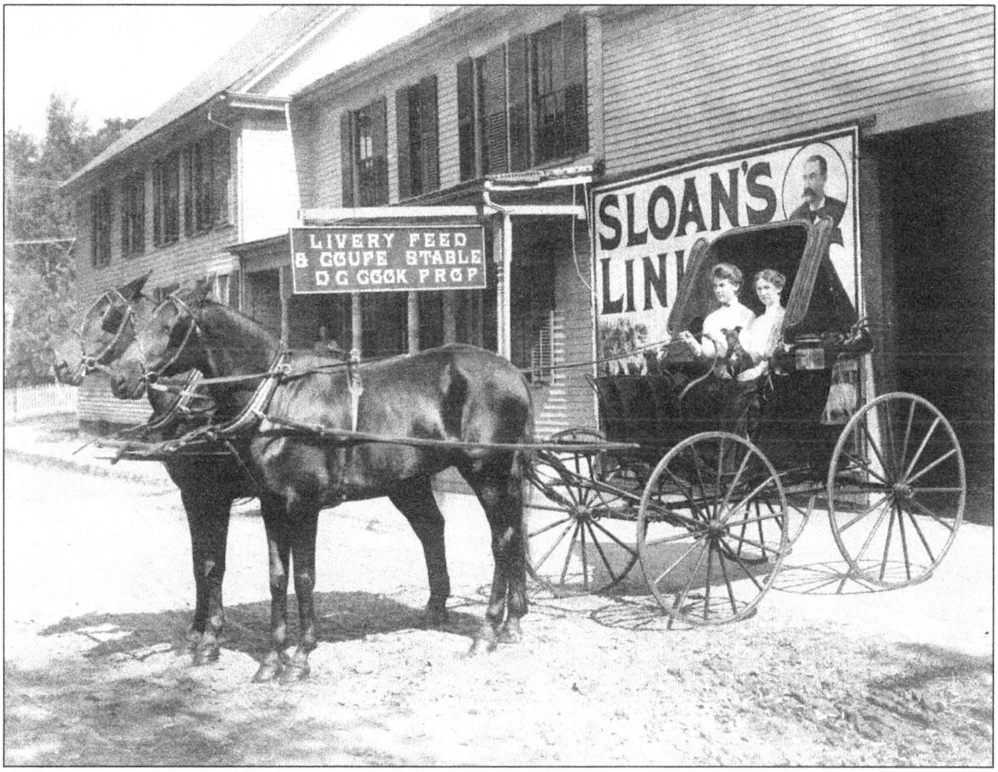

This c. 1900 image shows D.G. Cook's livery stable at the corner of Spring and Elm Streets. (CHS.)

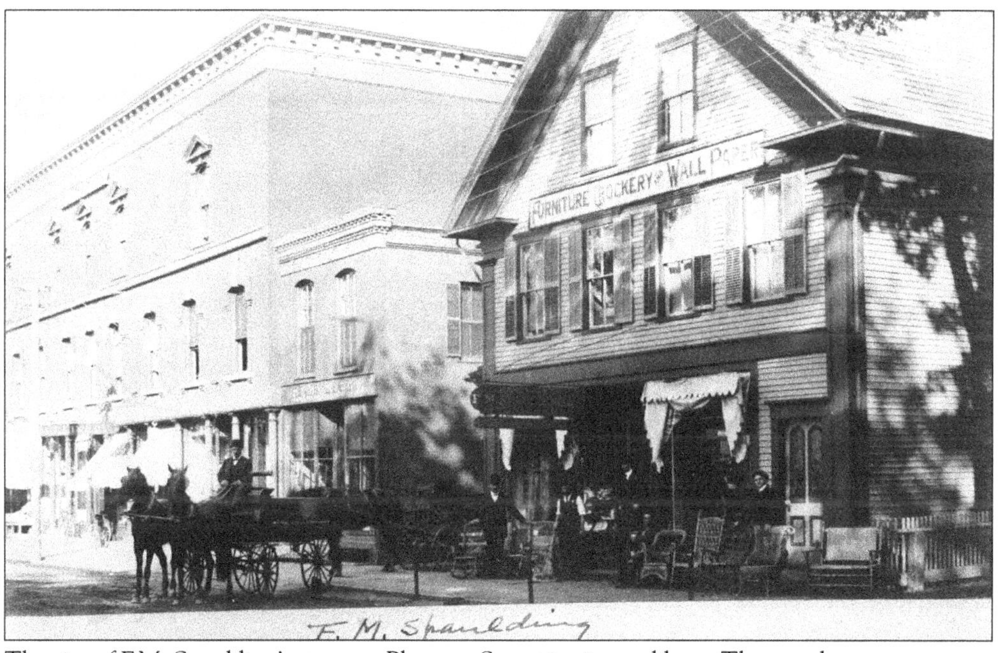

The site of F.M. Spaulding's store on Pleasant Street is pictured here. The wooden structure was replaced by a brick building best known as Marson's. (CHS.)

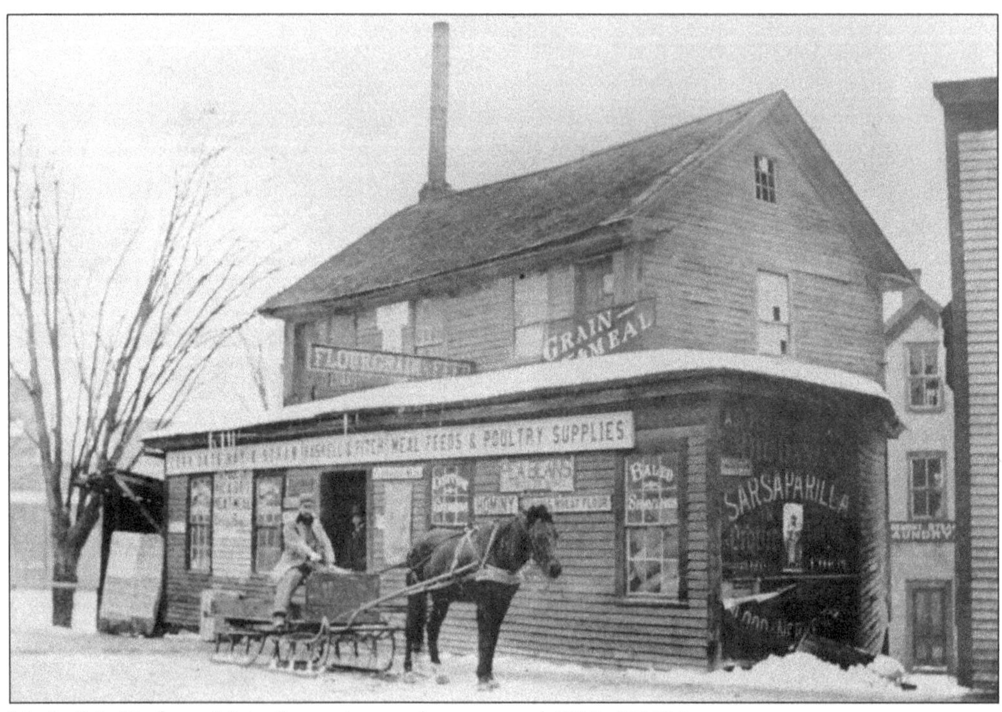

Haskell & Fitch on Main Street is seen here around 1910. (CHS.)

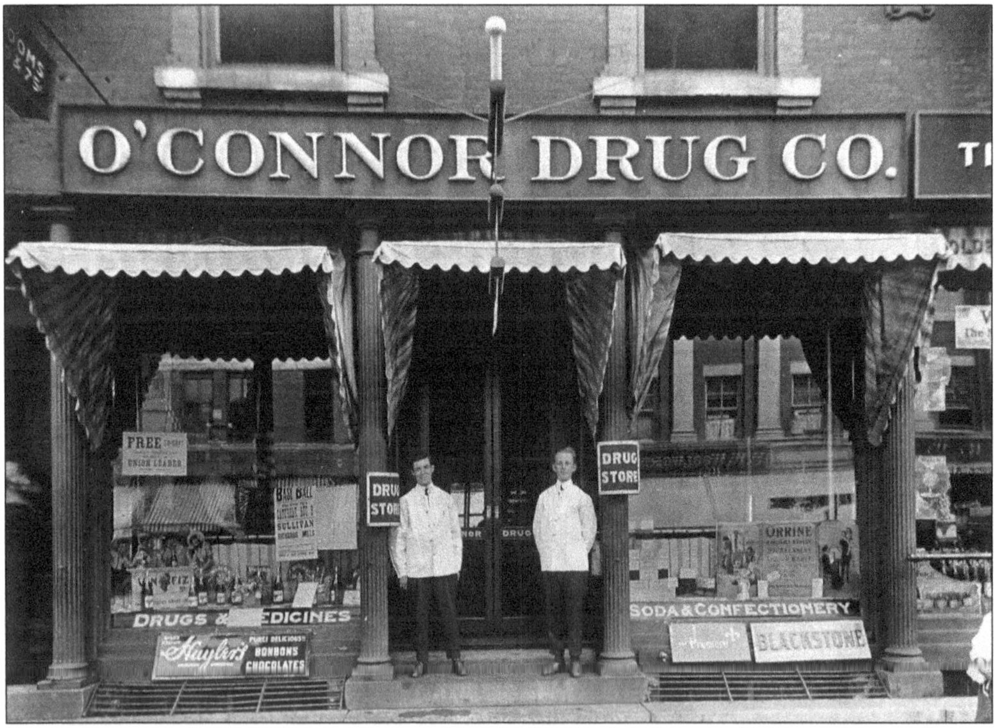

The O'Connor Drug Company, located at 30 Pleasant Street, is seen here around 1910. (CHS.)

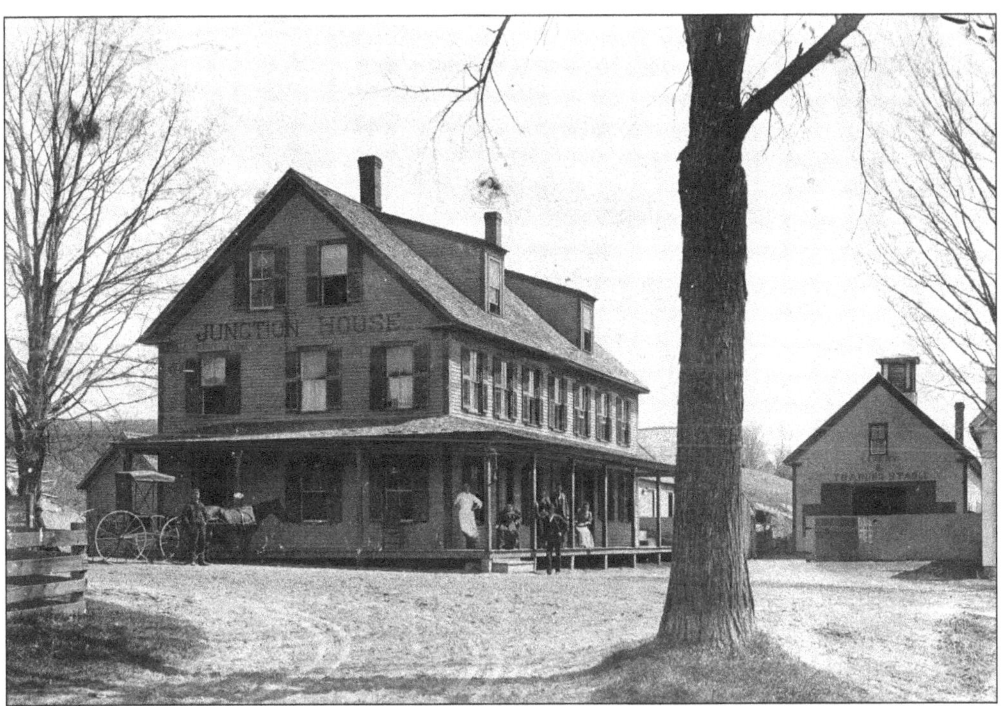

The Junction House hotel is seen here around 1895. (CHS.)

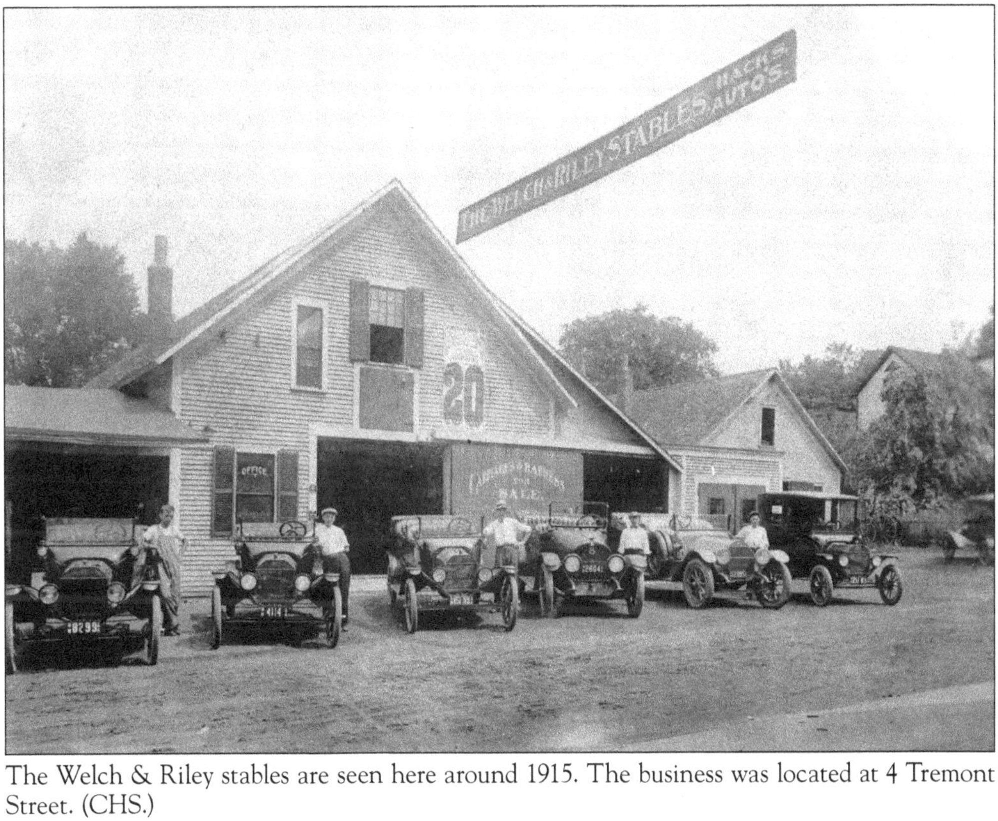

The Welch & Riley stables are seen here around 1915. The business was located at 4 Tremont Street. (CHS.)

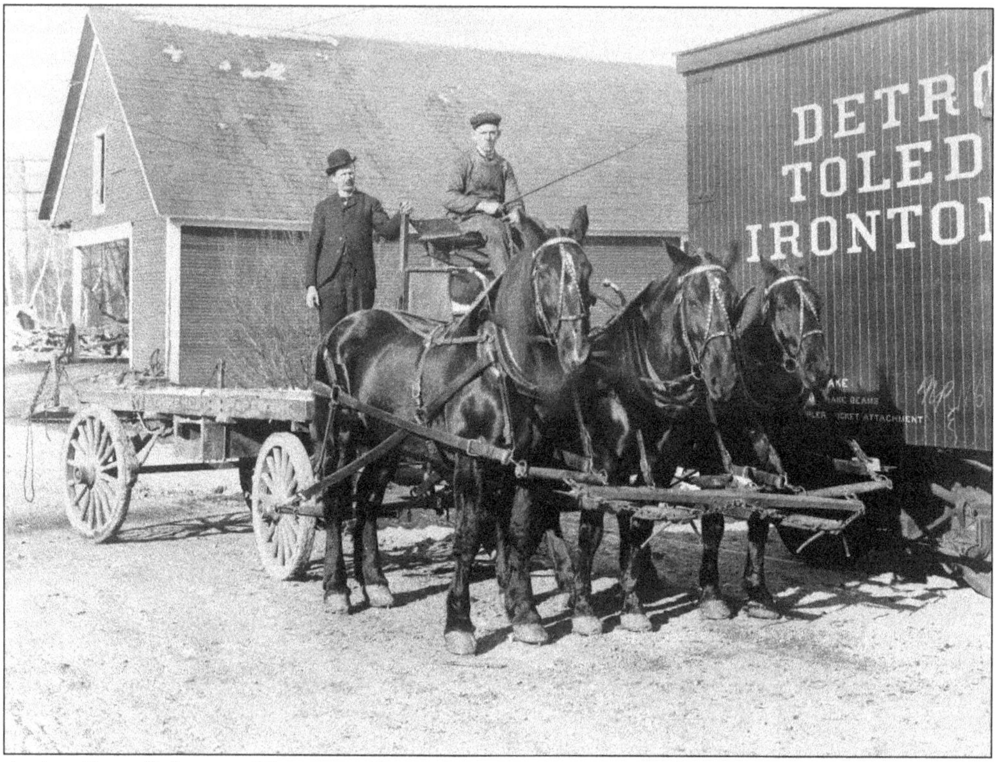

Arthur Stowell drives a Claremont Paper Company buggy around 1895. (CHS.)

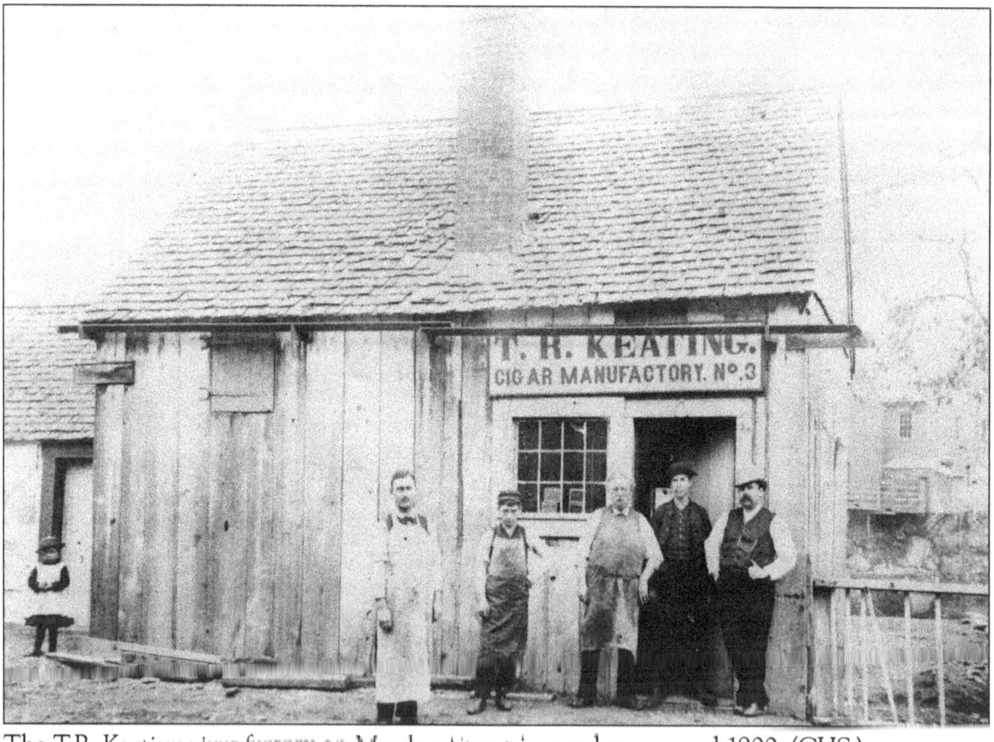

The T.R. Keating cigar factory on Meadow Street is seen here around 1900. (CHS.)

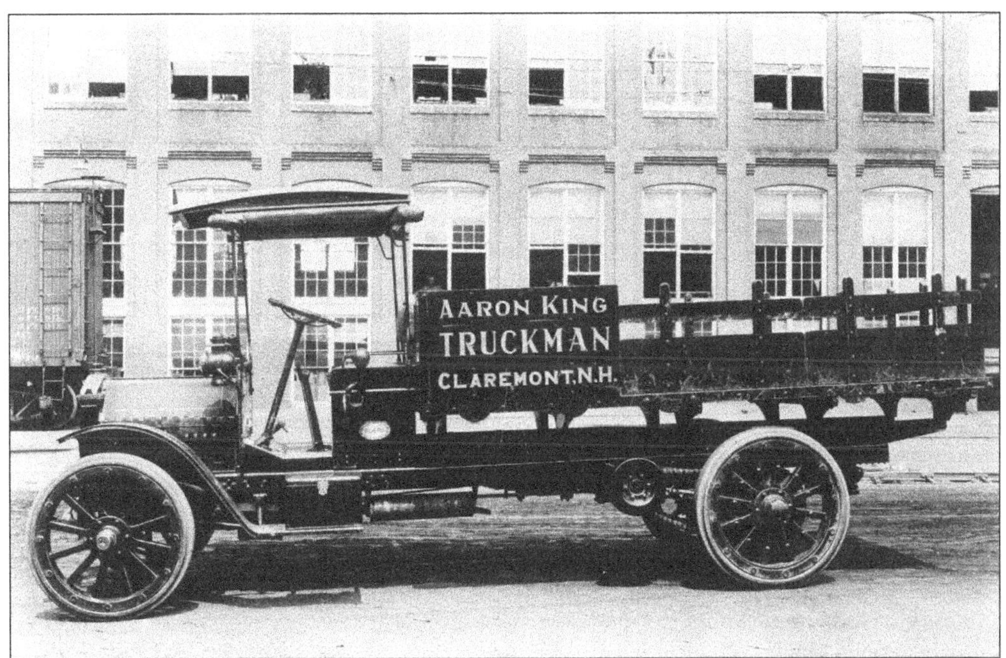

This vehicle belonged to Aaron King, truck man, around 1915. King provided short- and long-haul runs for several decades. (CHS.)

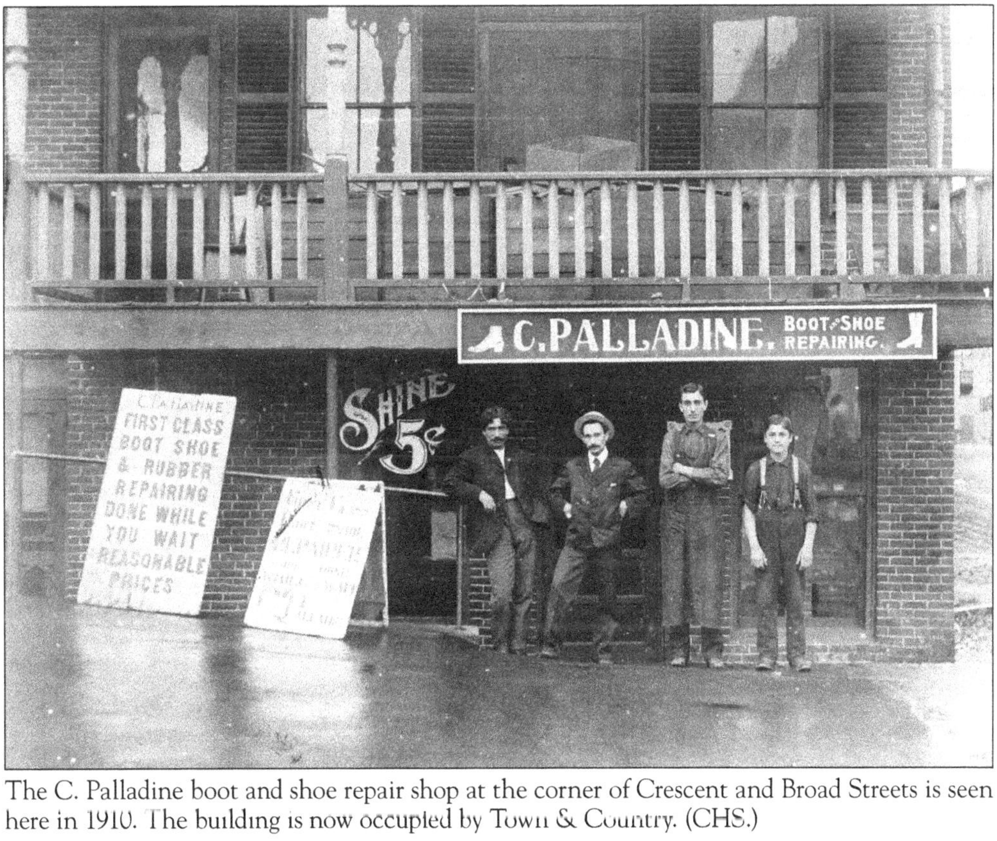

The C. Palladine boot and shoe repair shop at the corner of Crescent and Broad Streets is seen here in 1910. The building is now occupied by Town & Country. (CHS.)

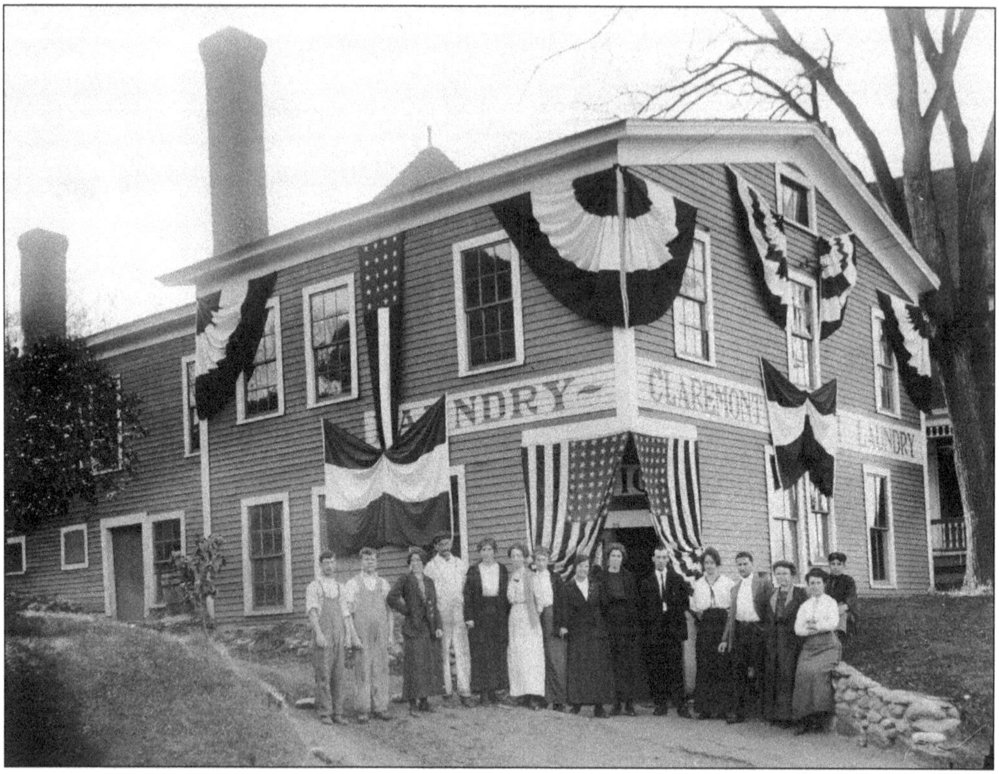

The Claremont Steam Laundry, seen here around 1910, operated at 30 Main Street from the early 1900s through the late 1950s. (CHS.)

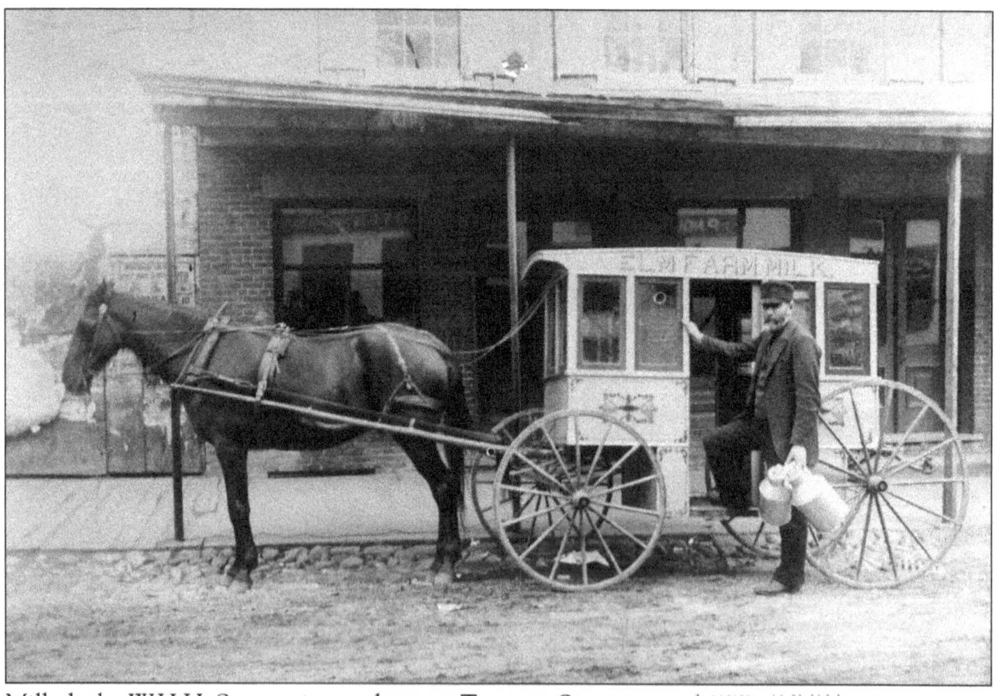

Milk dealer W.H.H. Stewart is seen here on Tremont Street around 1905. (CHS.)

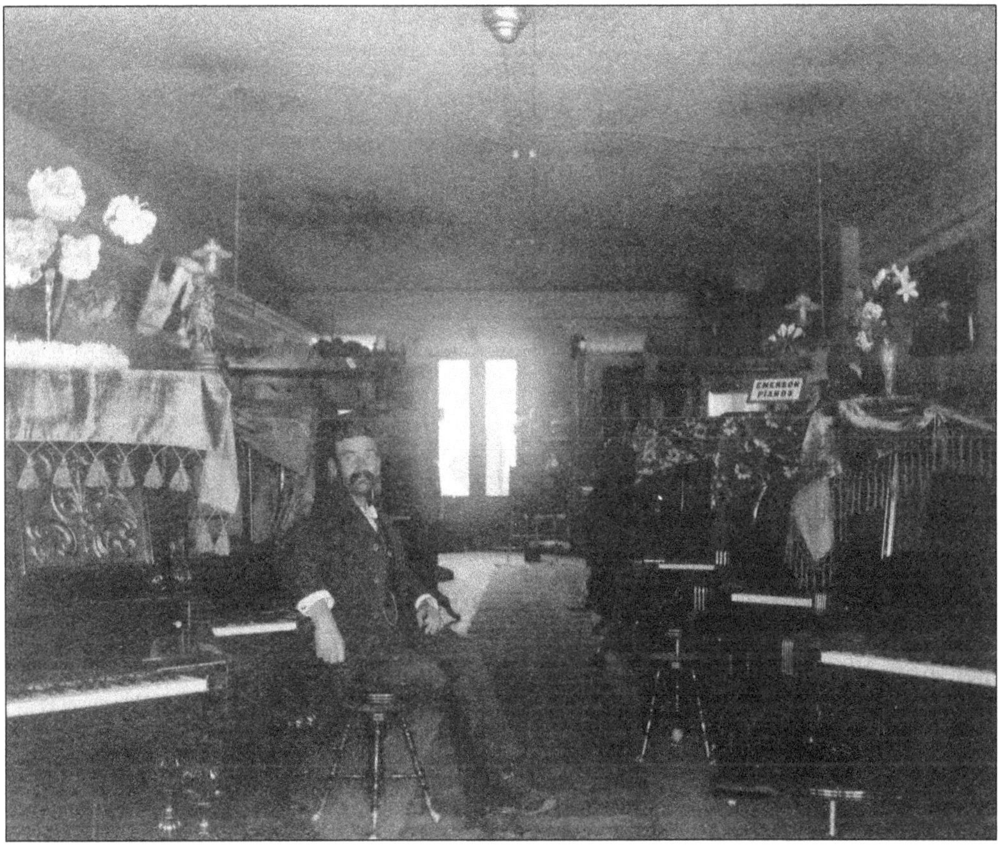

H.F. Olmstead sold musical instruments in the Brown Block in 1899 before moving to the Farwell Block in 1900. (CHS.)

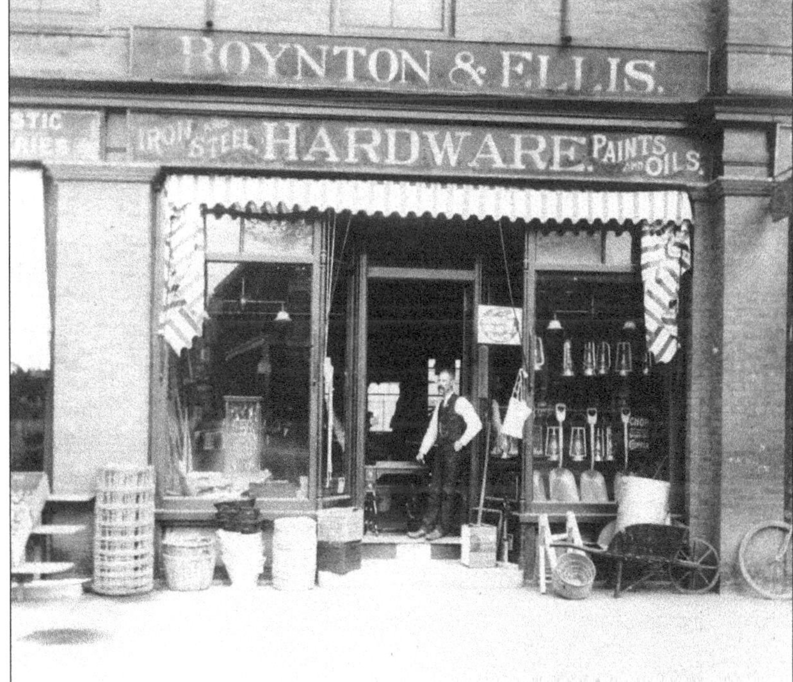

Boynton & Ellis Hardware is seen here around 1910. The store was located at 28 Tremont Square. (CHS.)

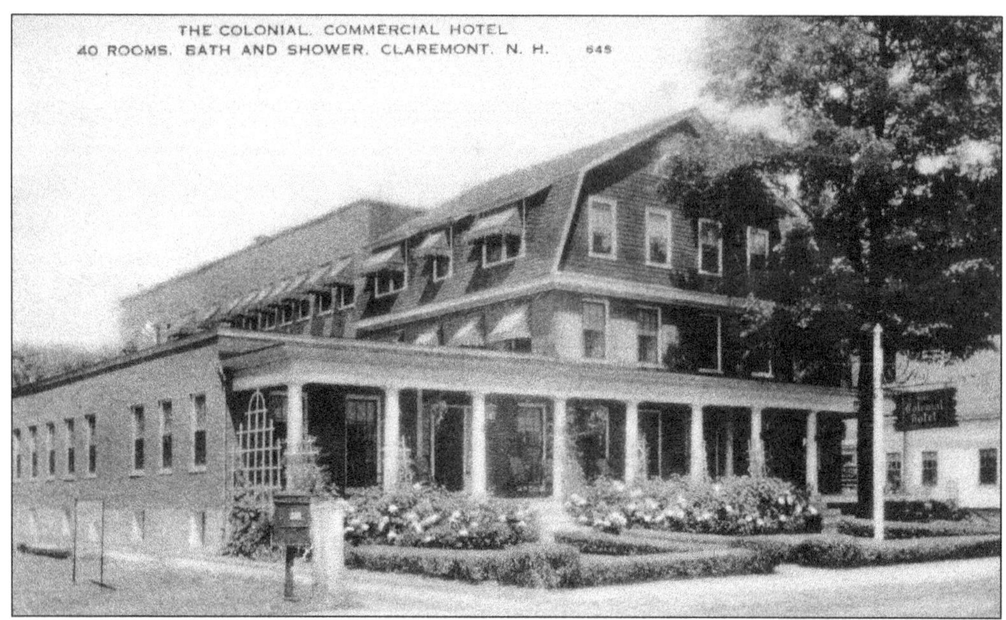

The Colonial Hotel, at 85 Pleasant Street, is seen here around 1925. It was later named the King's Arrow Inn and was a prominent feature of Pleasant Street until the mid-1960s. (WLM.)

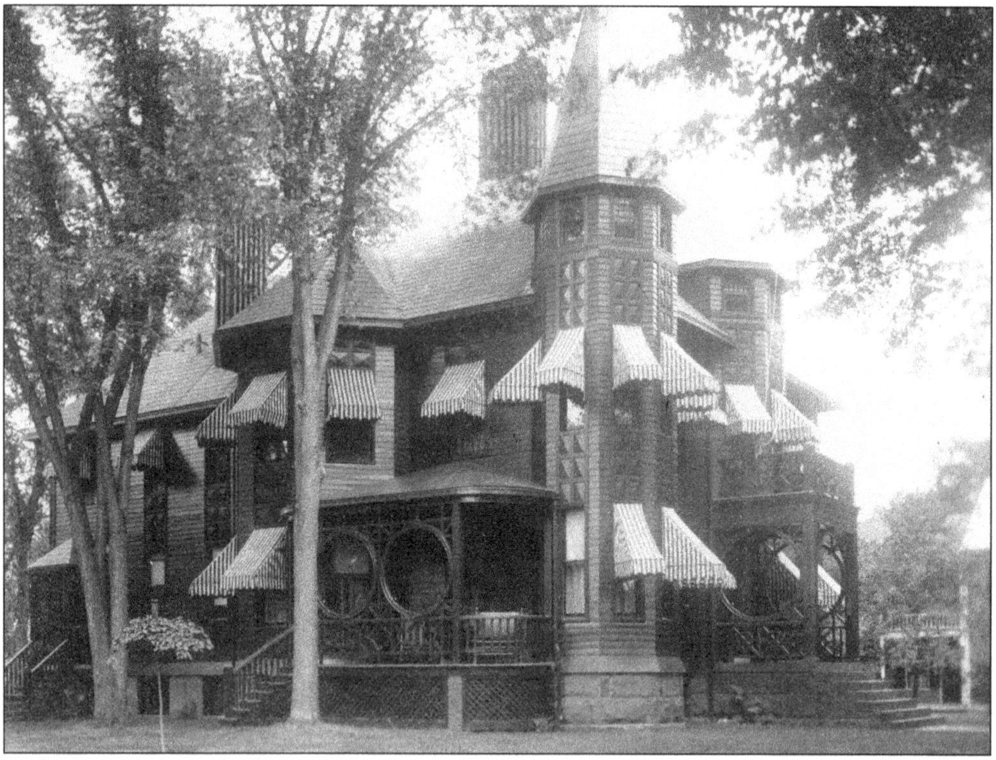

Built on Broad Street by George Farwell in 1887, this house was later converted into Huntley's Inn, seen here around 1910. It became the Blondin Funeral Home in 1948 and later had several uses, including that of Sullivan County offices, before being razed in the 1970s. The new Claremont Savings Bank is on this site today. (WLM.)

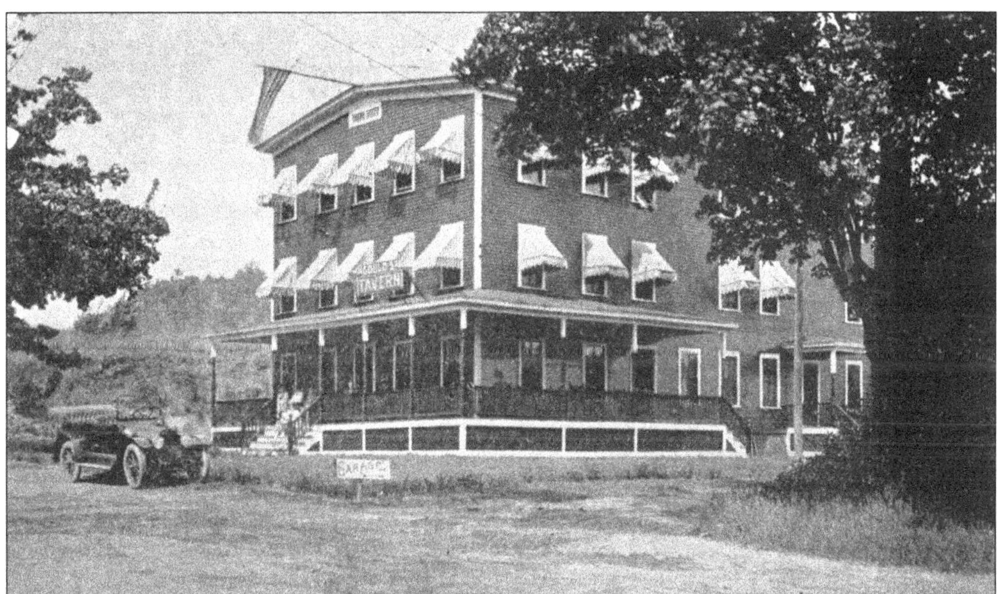

Gould's Tavern, seen here around 1915, was at the junction across the road from the railroad station. It closed when business declined due to the stigma of having been used as a makeshift hospital during the 1918 swine flu epidemic. (WLM.)

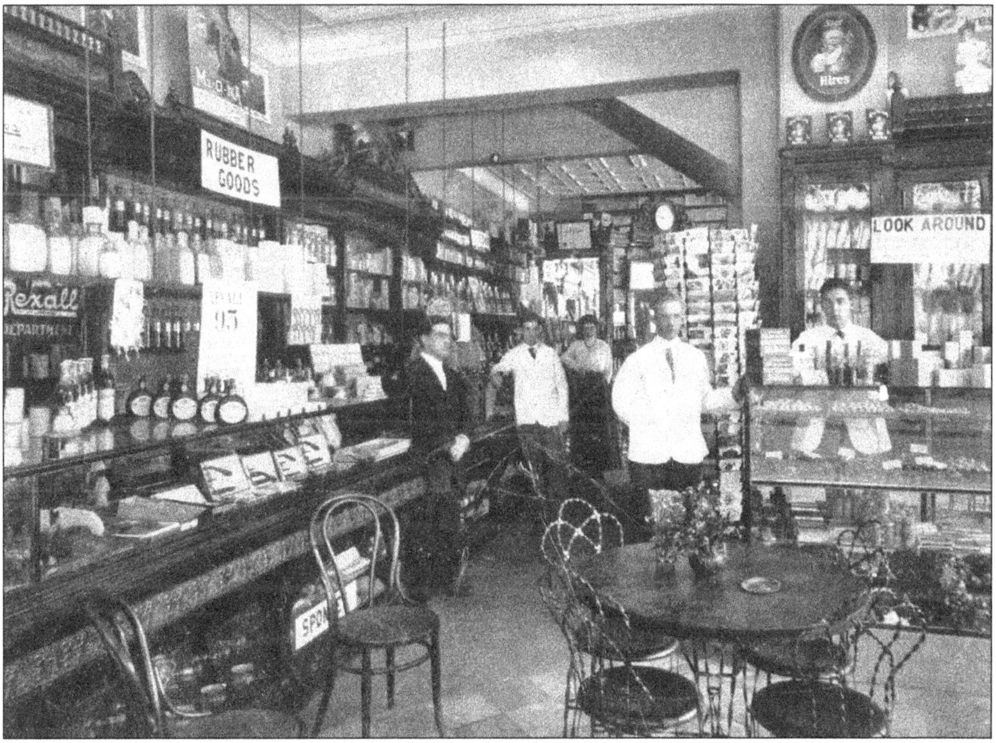

The staff is seen inside Dodge's Pharmacy in 1909. The pharmacy was located on Tremont Square. (CHS.)

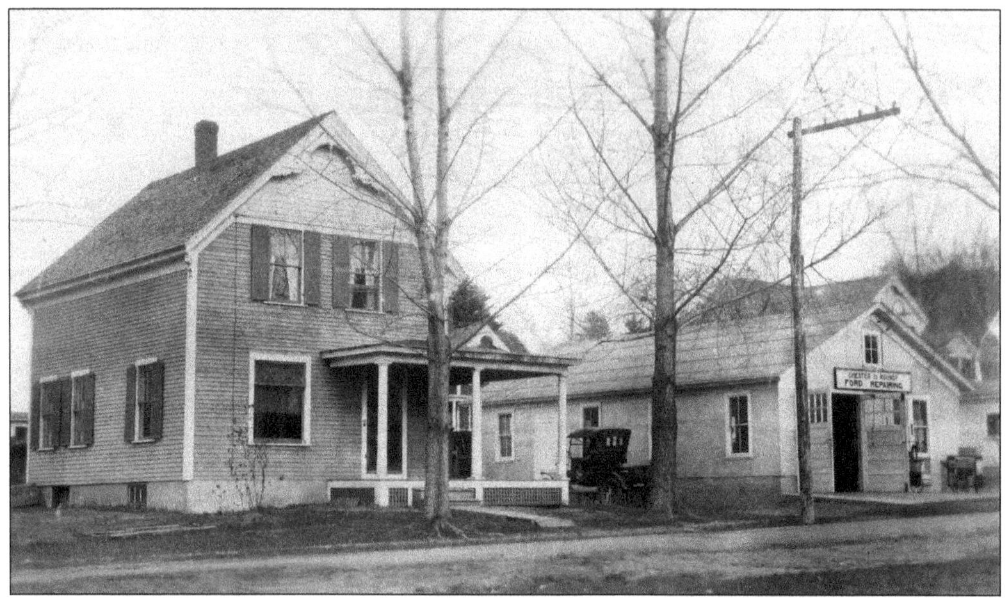

Chester H. Roundy operated this Ford repair shop, seen here around 1925, at 12 Benton Avenue. (WLM.)

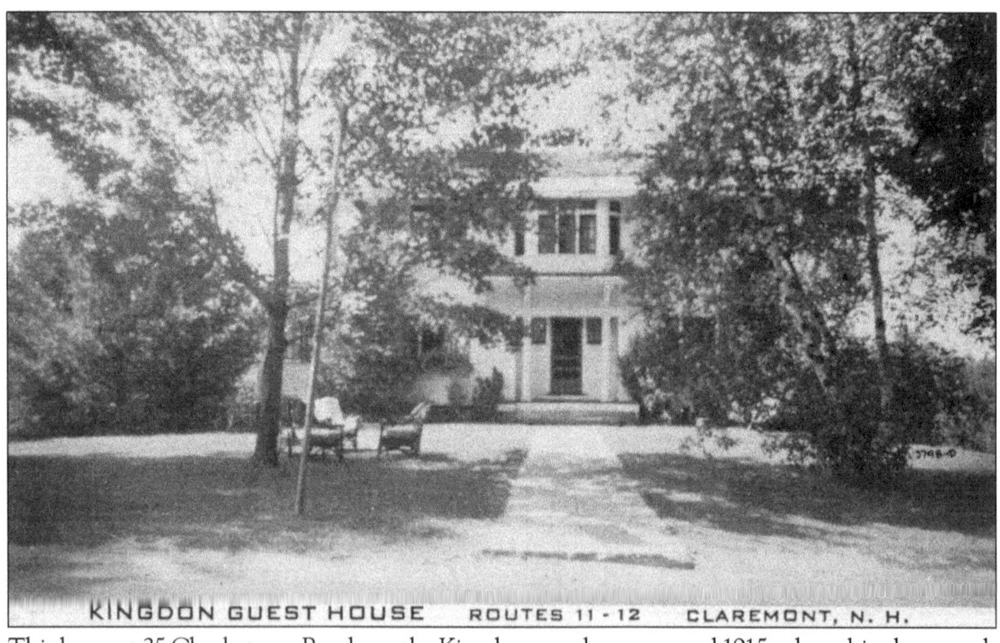

This home at 25 Charlestown Road was the Kingdon guesthouse around 1915, when this photograph was taken. It was later the longtime home of Charlestown Road Realty. (WLM.)

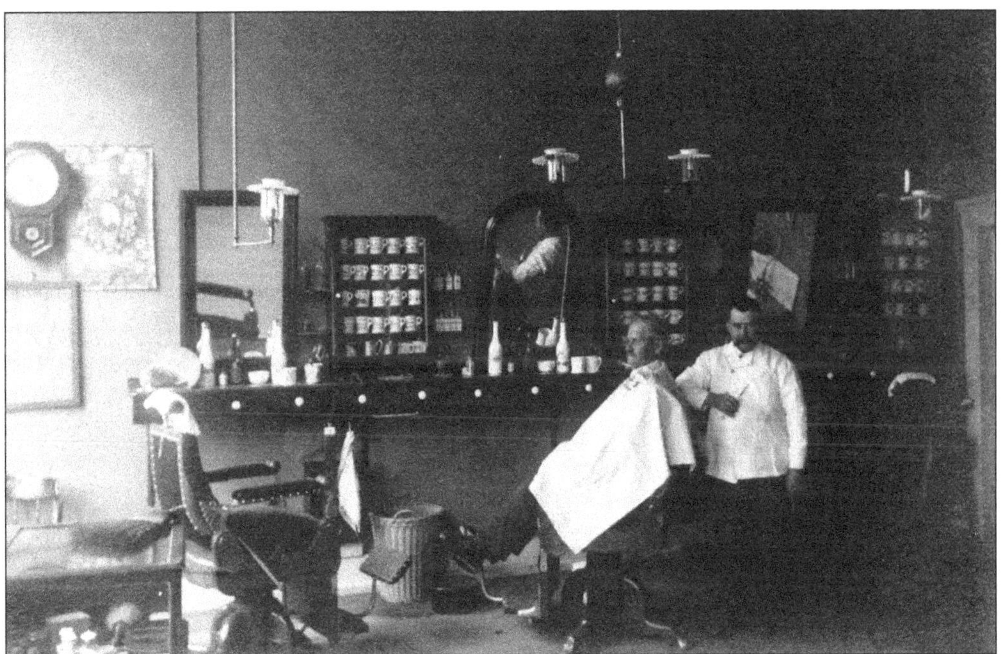

The barbershop of David H. Cushion was in the Stone Block on Tremont Square around 1900. (CHS.)

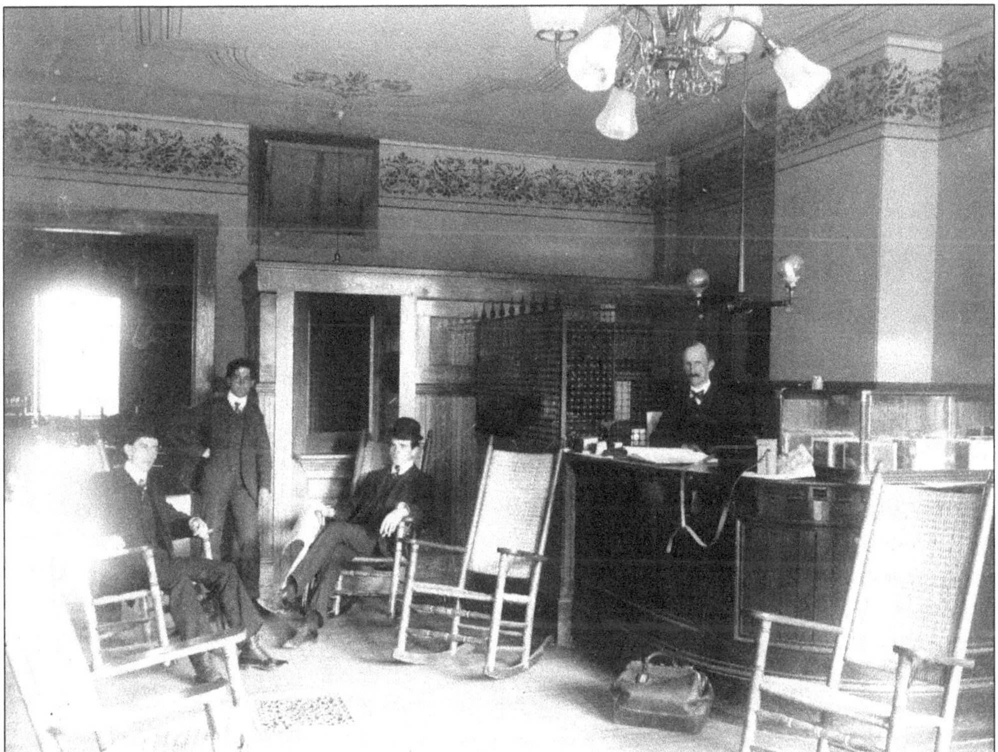

The lobby of the Hotel Belmont on Pleasant Street is seen here around 1895. (CHS.)

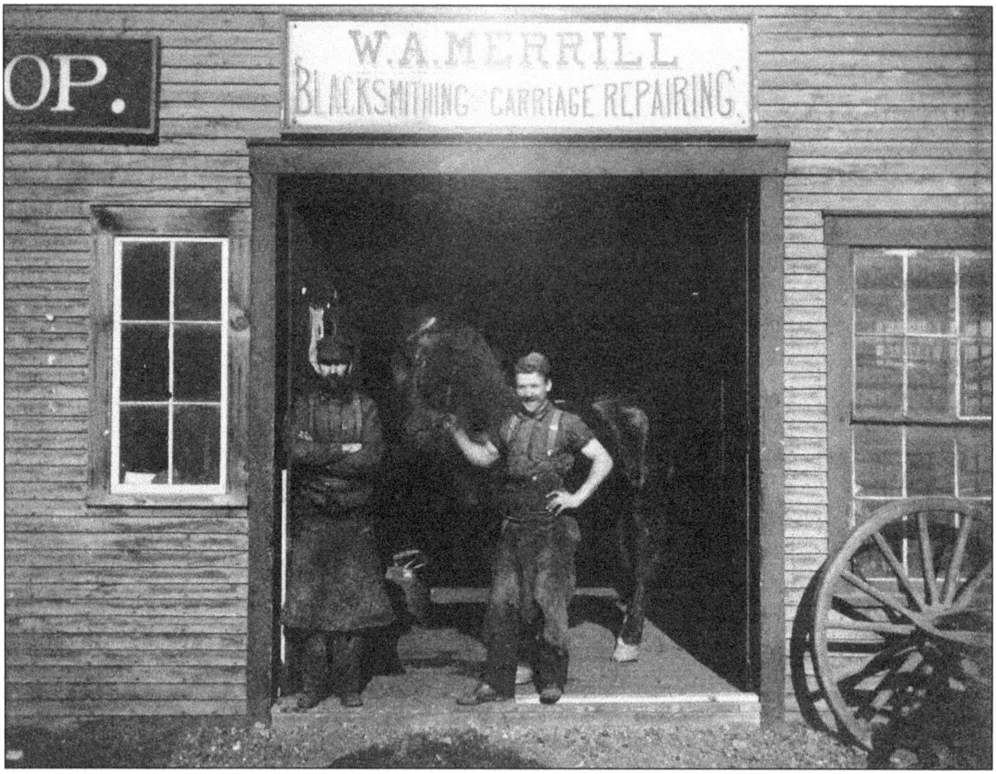

The William A. Merrill's blacksmith shop, seen here around 1900, was located at 127 Main Street. (CHS.)

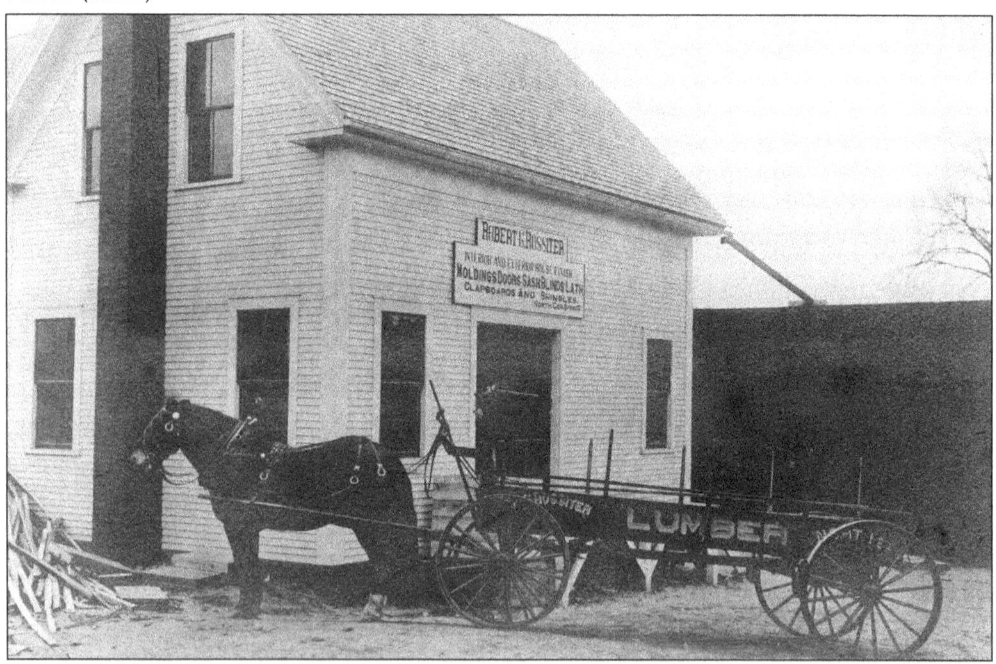

Robert Rossiter operated out of this shop, seen here around 1905, at the corner of North and Spring Streets. (CHS.)

Four

SCHOOLS AND CHURCHES

Claremont has had dozens of schools through the years, but photographs do not exist for many of them. A few of the Claremont churches seen in this chapter also served as schools at one time.

In the mid-1800s, there were as many as 25 schools in use at the same time, which became consolidated over time. The first building solely for high school children was the Claremont Academy. Built in 1840 on the corner of Sullivan and Walnut Streets, it was sold in 1869 when Stevens High School opened.

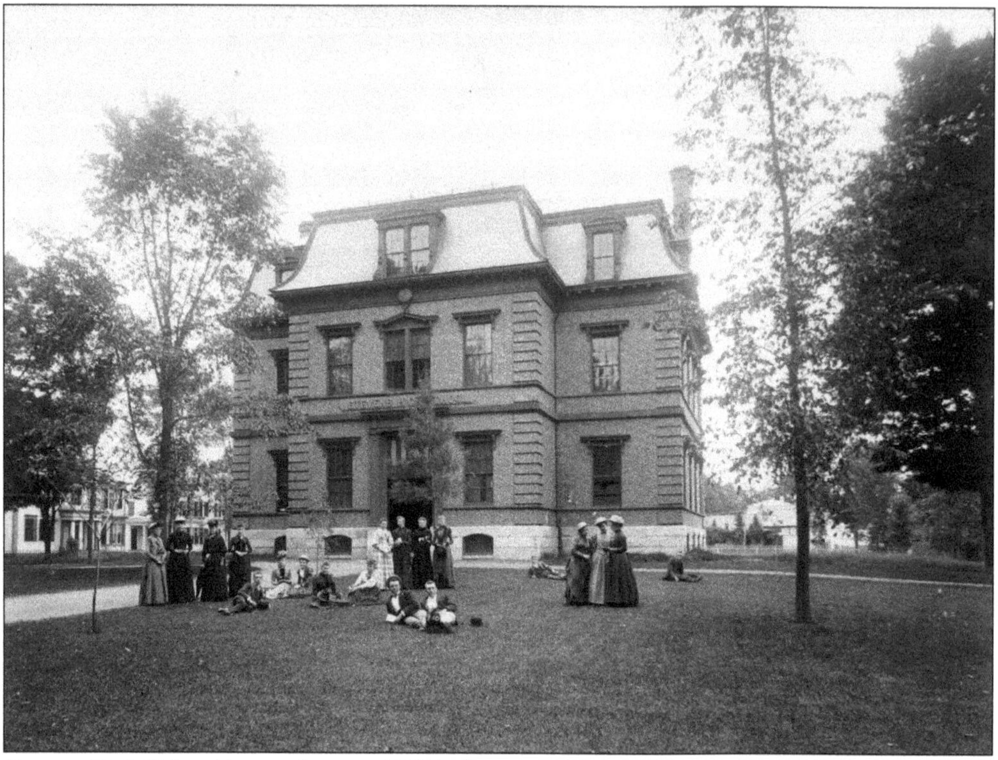

Stevens High School is seen here in 1870 before any additions were made. (CHS.)

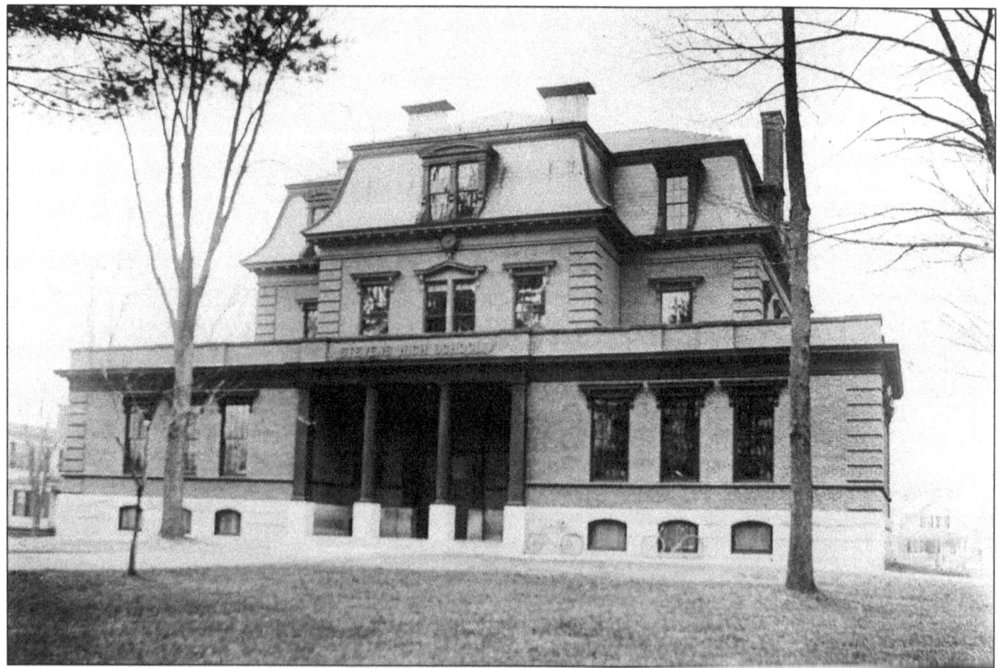

Stevens High School is seen here with the 1909 addition across the front of the building. The construction of a laboratory, a classroom, a manual training room, and a headmaster's office increased the school from five to nine rooms. (WLM.)

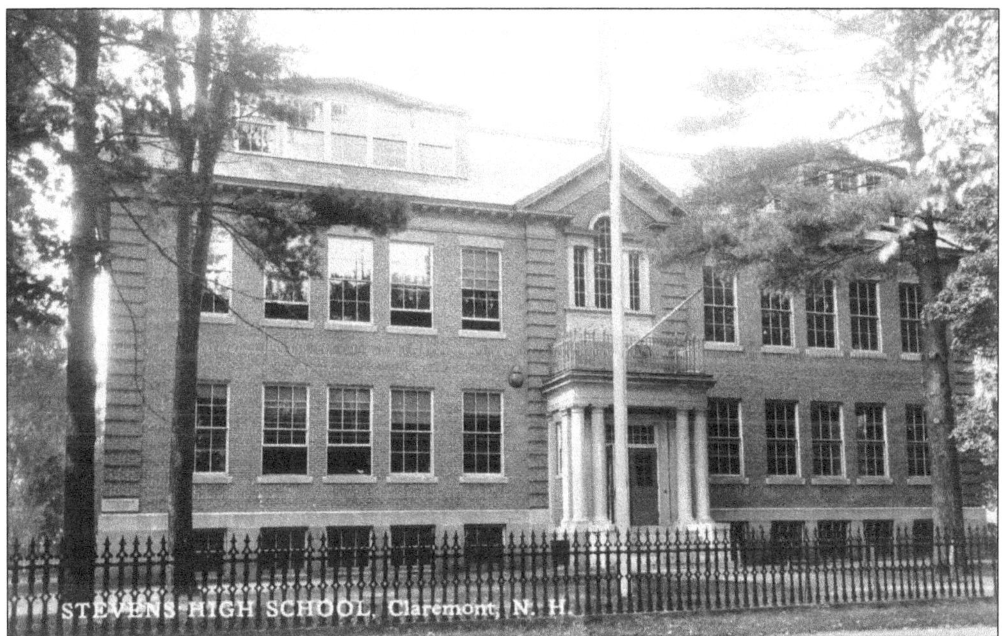

Stevens High School is seen here following the 1915 modifications that increased the school to 21 rooms and added the auditorium still in use today. The iron fence around the property was donated as scrap metal for the war effort during World War II. (WLM.)

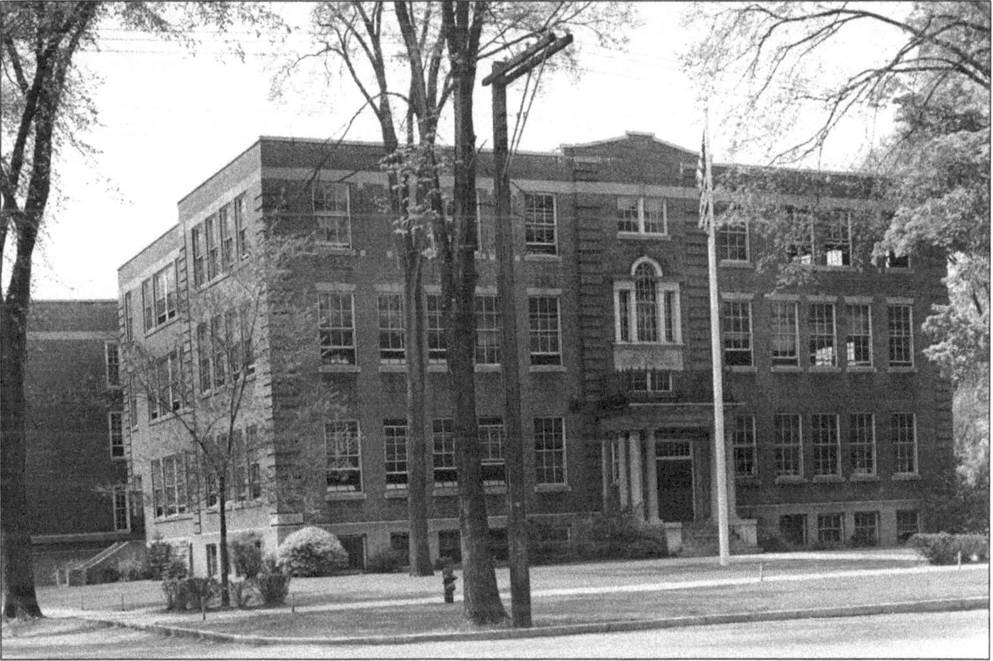

The junior high school classes, added in 1929, are visible on the Summer Street side. The high school made use of these rooms after the junior high school was built on South Street in 1958. Changes to the footprint to the building since 1958 have included new classrooms, a new cafeteria, and an extension to the gymnasium, taking the school to the Middle Street sidewalk. New locker rooms were added in 1990. (WLM.)

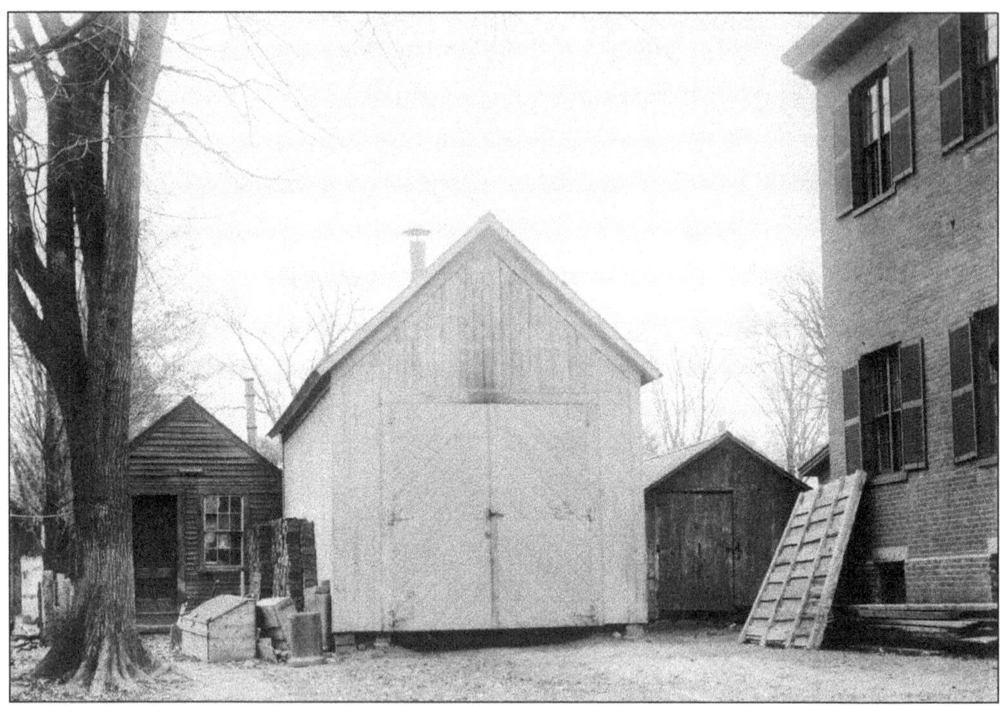

This shack is the remnants of a school that once stood on Broad Street about where the fire department is now located. (CHS.)

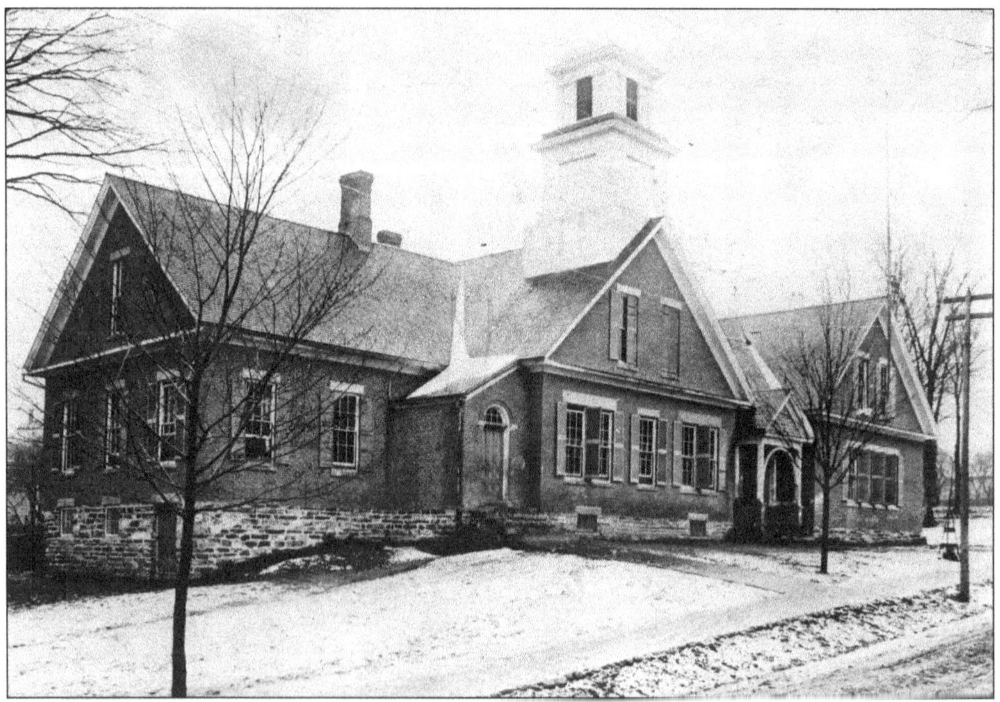

The Pearl Street School is seen here from the School Street side. An armory was later built on this spot. When the armory moved into a new building, this structure housed the Junior Sports League. (CHS.)

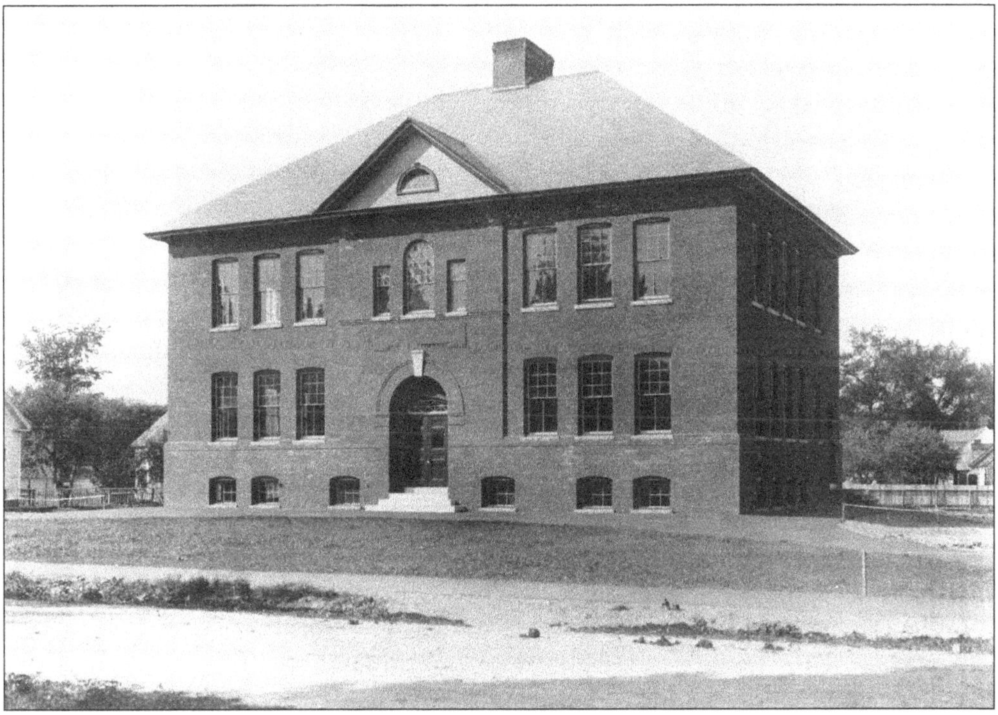

North Street School is seen here in 1906 before the 1909 additions were made. It replaced an earlier school that had been located near the end of Hanover Street and was moved to make room for construction of the Sullivan Machinery Company foundry. The old school was moved to the corner of North and Jones Streets (now Bernard Way) and was last used as a convenience store before it was razed in the 1990s. (WLM.)

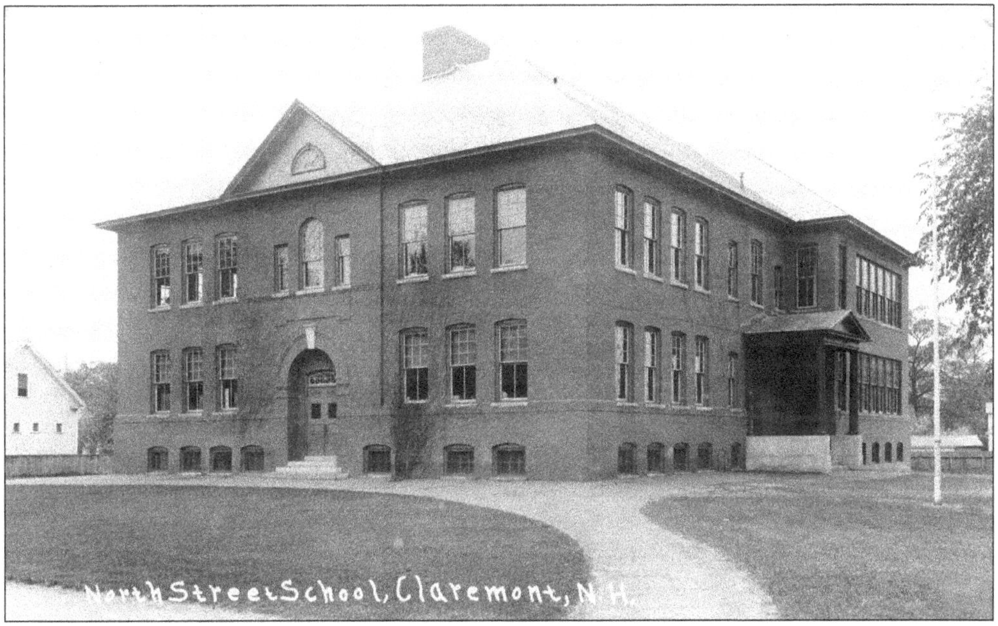

The North Street School is seen here following the 1909 addition. This school was closed in the 1990s along with Way School and West Terrace School. (WLM.)

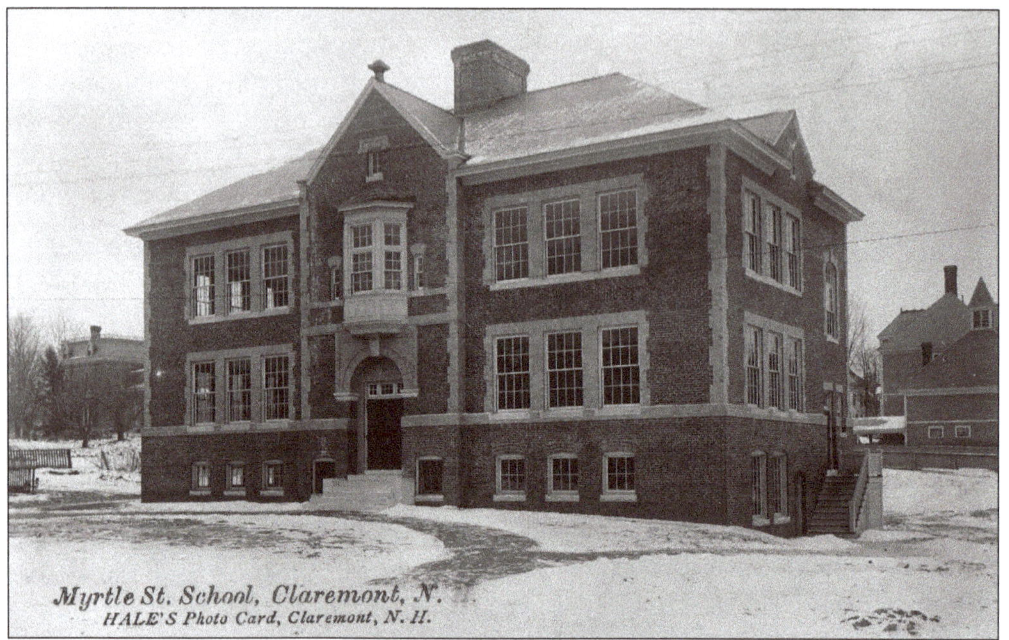

This school on Myrtle Street, seen here around 1910, was named after Dr. Osmon B. Way, who, prior to practicing medicine, had been a teacher and superintendent for 15 years. (WLM.)

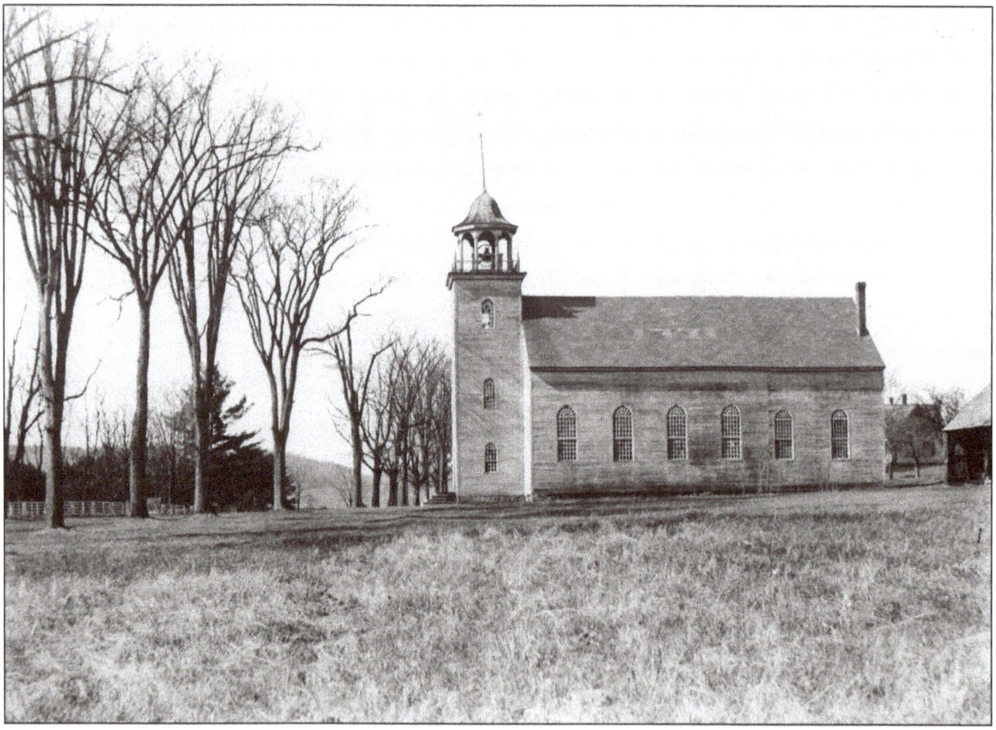

The Union Church in West Claremont was constructed in 1773 and is the oldest surviving Episcopal church in the state as well as the state's oldest building used exclusively for religious purposes. The tower and belfry were added in 1801, and the building was extended by 25 feet in 1820. (CHS.)

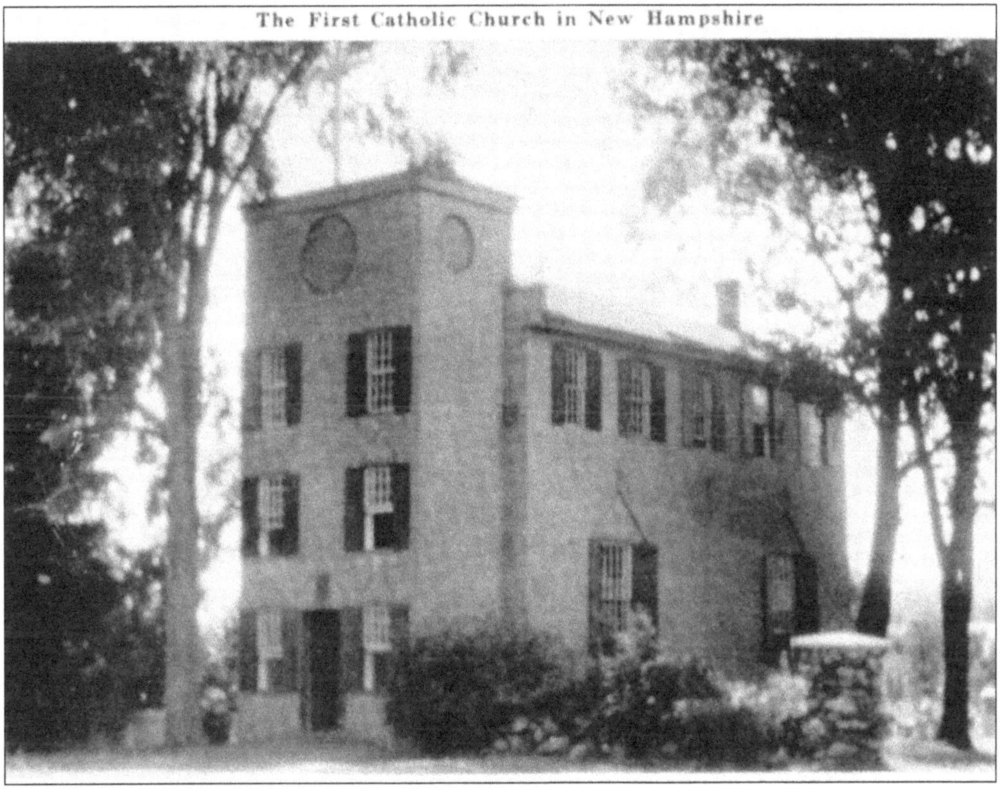

The First Catholic Church in New Hampshire

The old St. Mary Church in West Claremont was the first Roman Catholic church in the state. Construction began in 1823 and was completed a few years later. The top floor served as a school for many years. (WLM.)

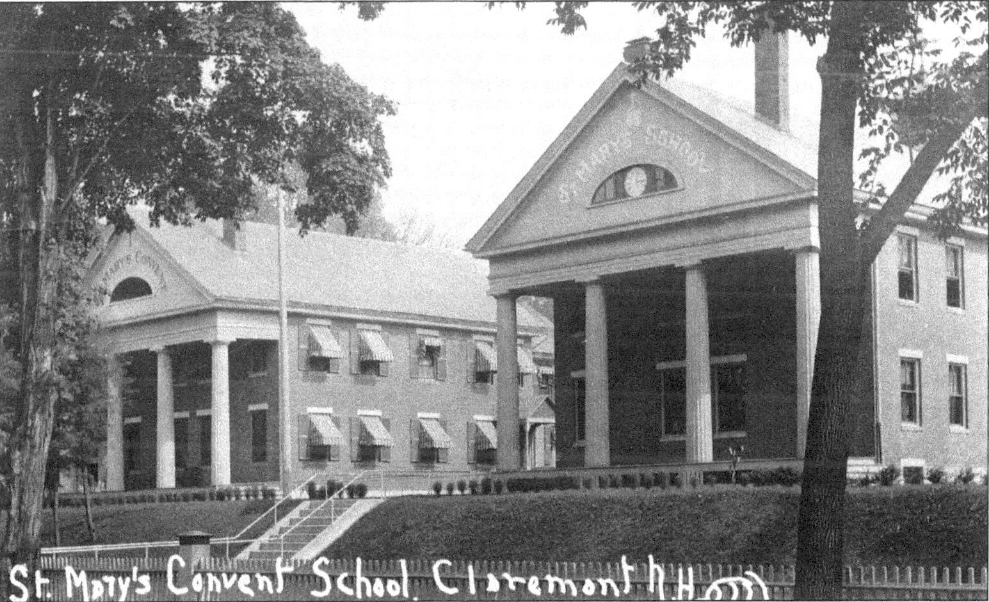

St. Mary's Convent and St. Mary's School are both seen here around 1930 on Central Street. (WLM.)

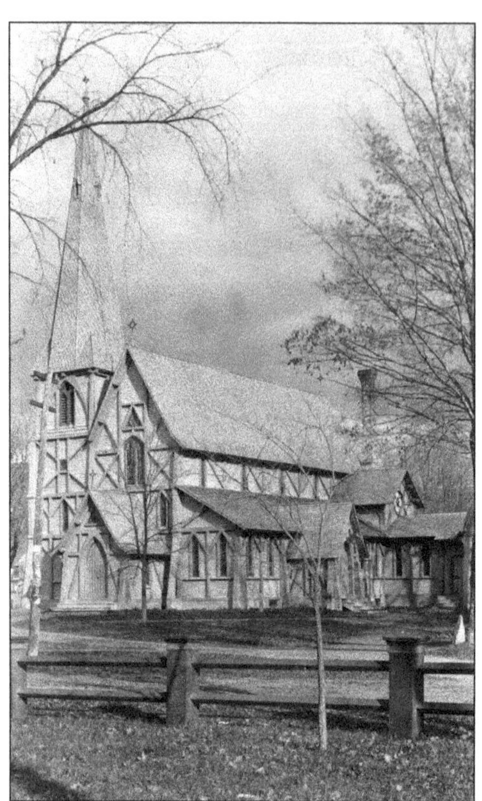

In 1852, construction began on the Trinity Episcopal Church on Broad Street. The building replaced a chapel that had occupied that spot for 34 years. The spire toppled during the 1938 hurricane and speared through the roof onto the floor below. (CHS.)

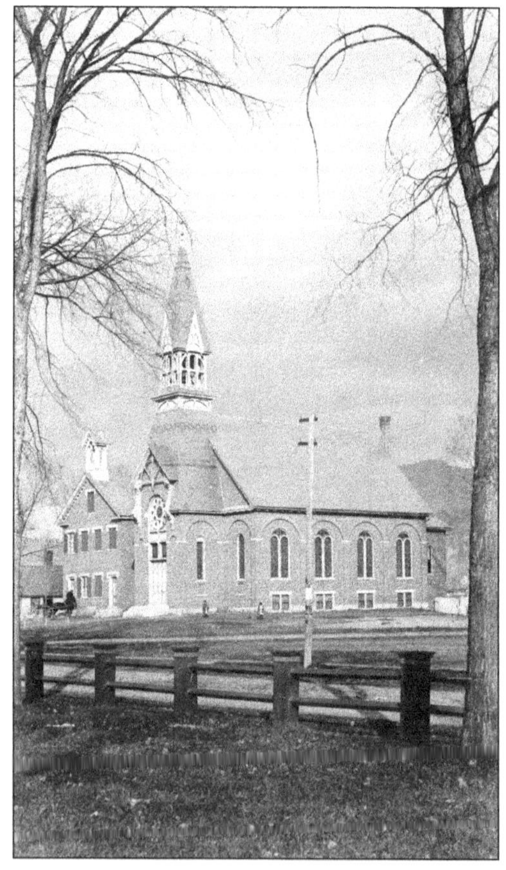

The Universalist church on Broad Street is seen at right. (WLM.)

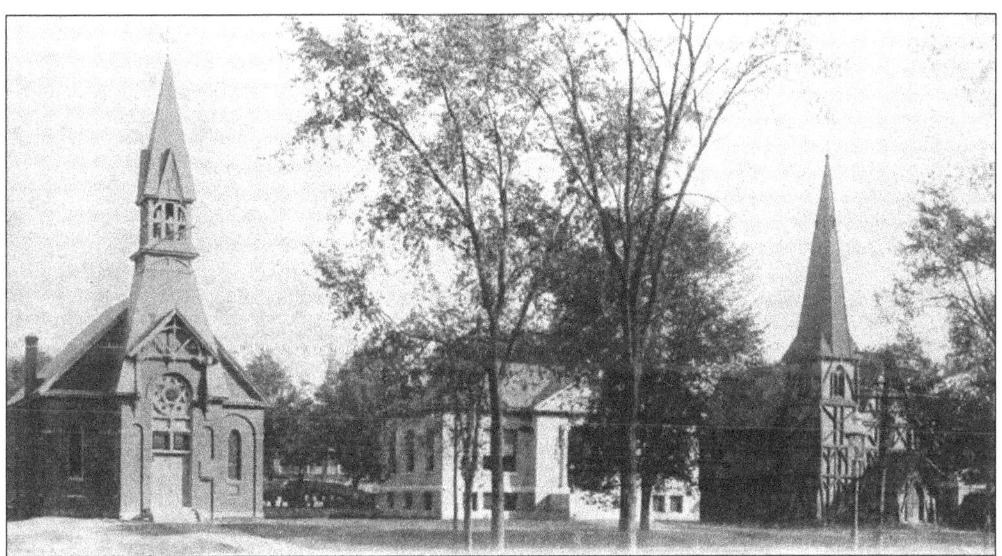

This photograph from around 1910 shows the Universalist church, the library, and the Trinity Episcopal Church on Broad Street. (WLM.)

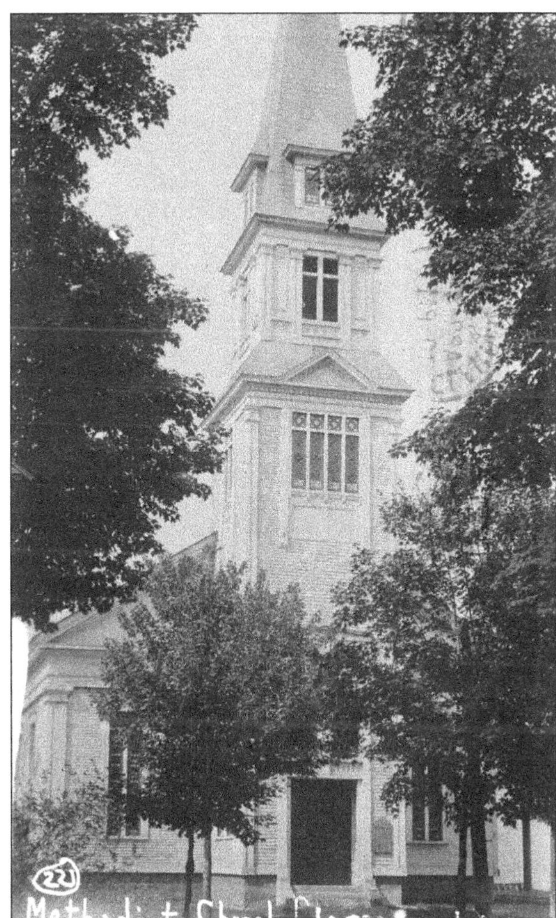

The Methodist church is seen here in 1912, when it was on Central Street. When a new, stone church was built on the corner of Sullivan and Franklin Streets, this site was used for the original St. Mary's gymnasium and then the Knights of Columbus Hall. The building is now a soup kitchen. (WLM.)

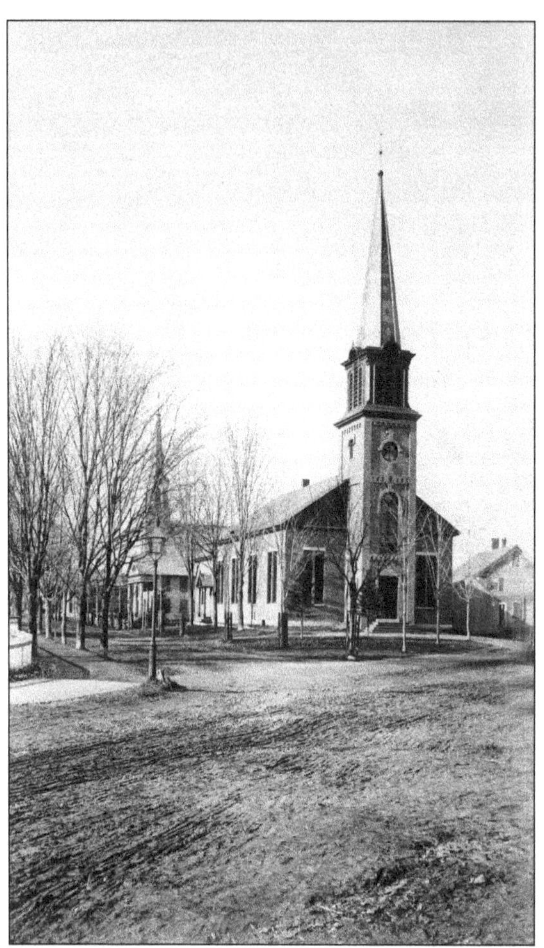

The Baptist church on the corner of Main and Central Streets was built in 1834, with major renovations and upgrades made in 1872. (WLM.)

The Congregational church on Pleasant Street is seen here around 1915. The church was dedicated on February 3, 1836, after the church sold the old meetinghouse to the town to be used exclusively as the town meetinghouse. (WLM.)

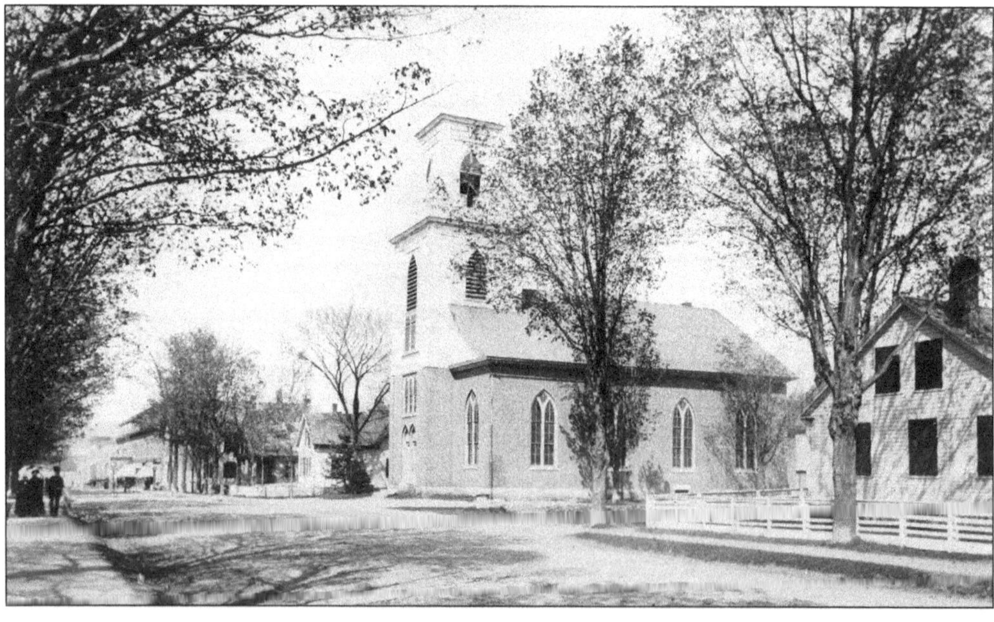

Five

Homes

Though many are long gone, the stately houses lining Broad and Pleasant Streets were once some of the better homes in the city.

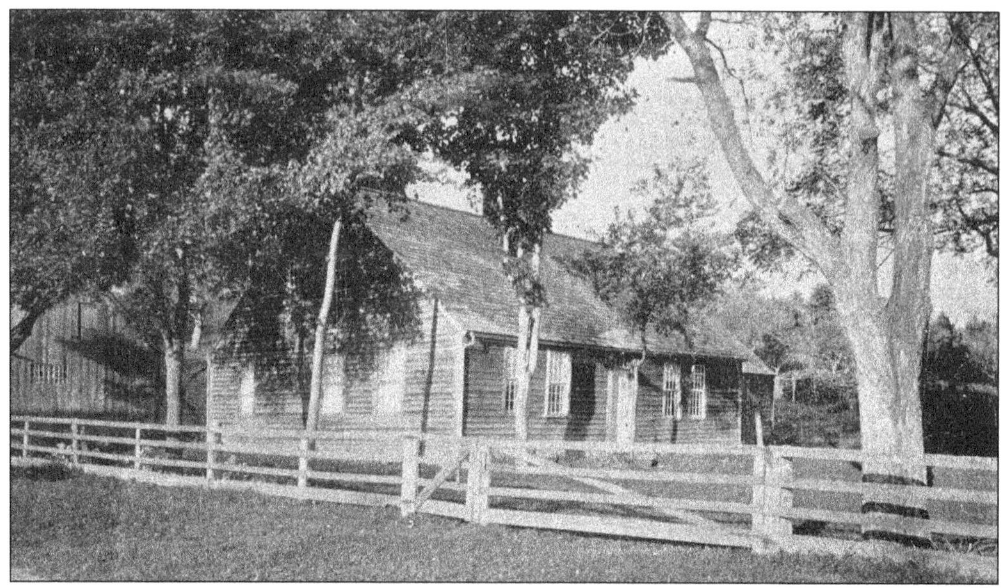

The John Tyler house on Clay Hill Road is the oldest house in Claremont. It is also sometimes called the Alden house. (CHS.)

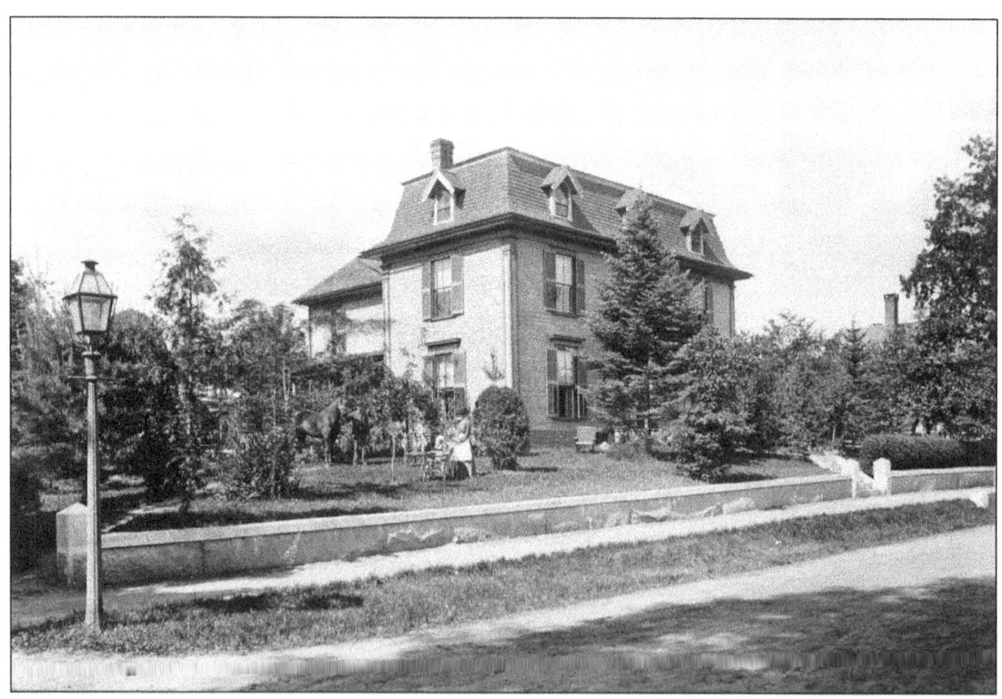

This home was originally on the River Road and was moved to Sullivan Street. It was later razed and the Del-E Motel was built on the site. (CHS.)

Noted Claremont builder Hira Beckwith built this Queen Anne–style home for himself on Summer Street. Among his best-known works are the town halls of Claremont, Newport, Windsor, Bellows Falls, and St. Johnsbury as well as the Hotel Claremont and Sunapee's Ben Mere Inn. (WLM.)

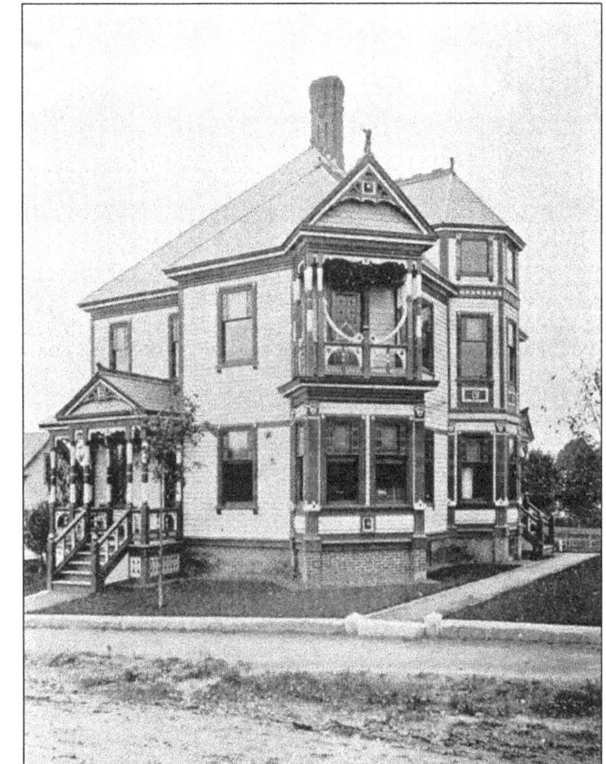

George Hale, a Claremont photographer who was active in the early 1900s and took a number of the photographs in this book, lived in this house on Central Street, seen here around 1910, between the Baptist church and St. Mary Church. (CHS.)

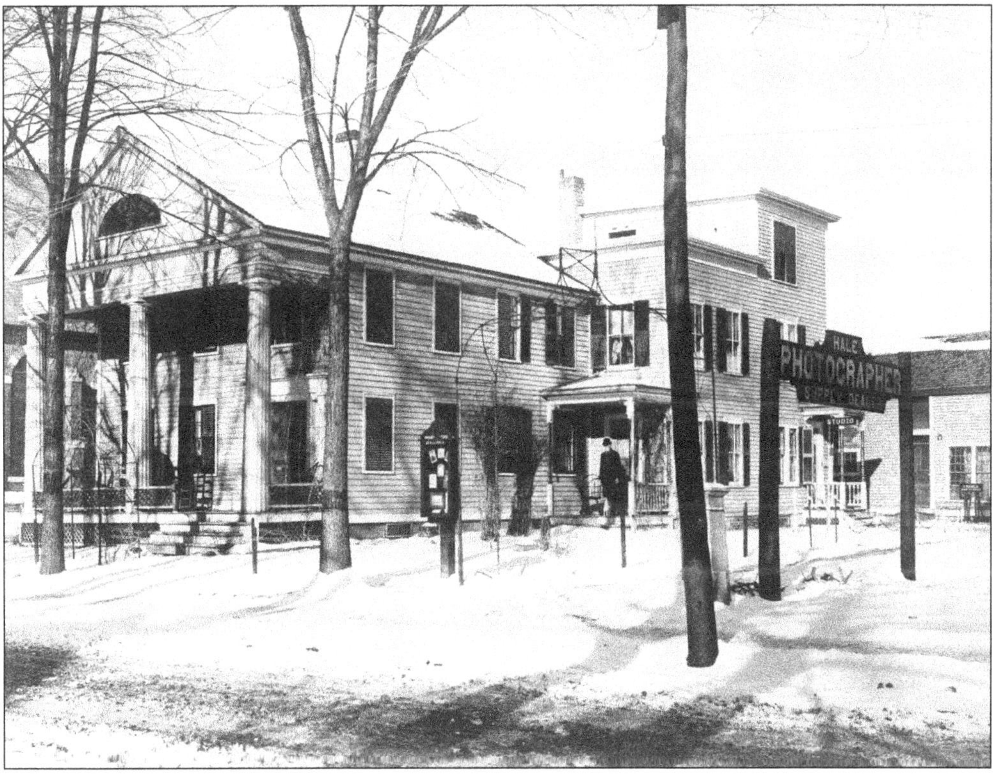

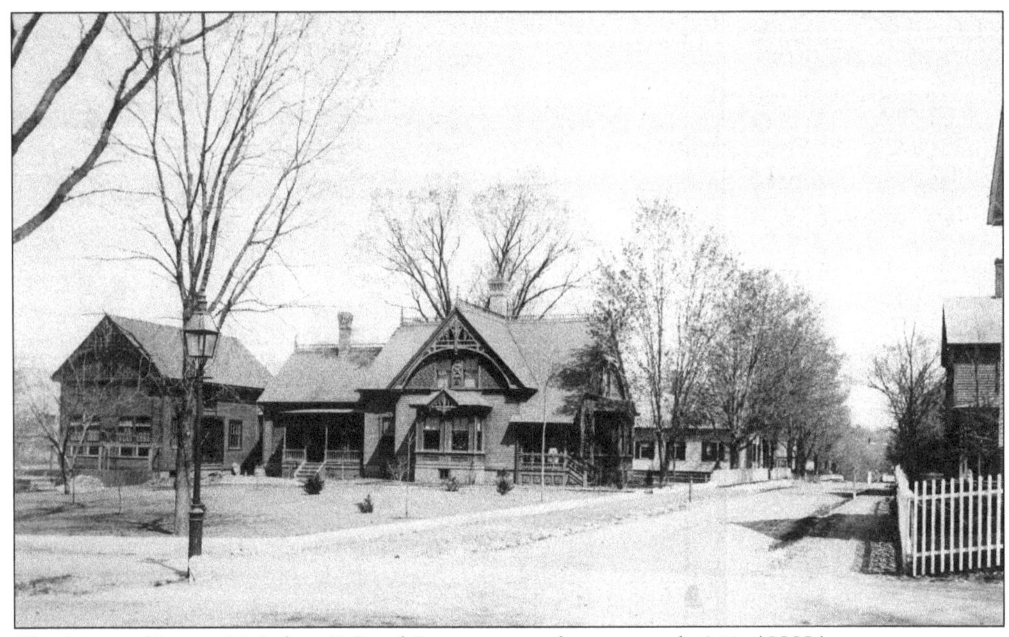

The home of James O'Neil at 43 Pearl Street is seen here around 1900. (CHS.)

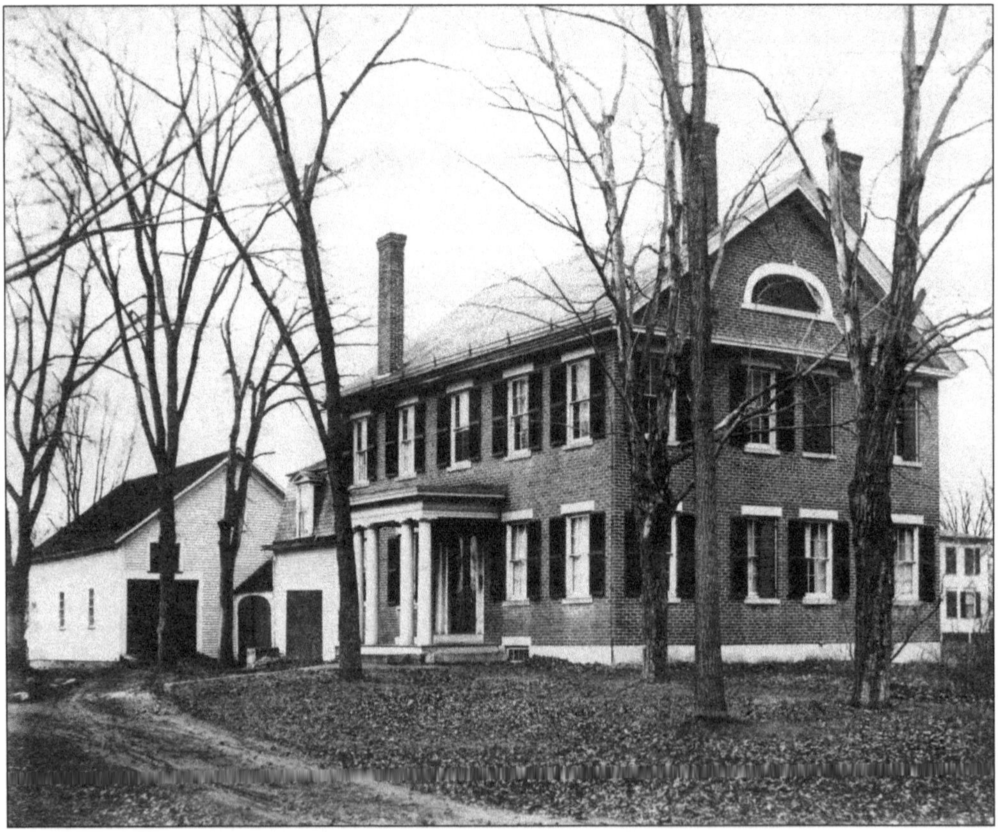

The Samuel Upham home on Broad Street is seen here. (CHS.)

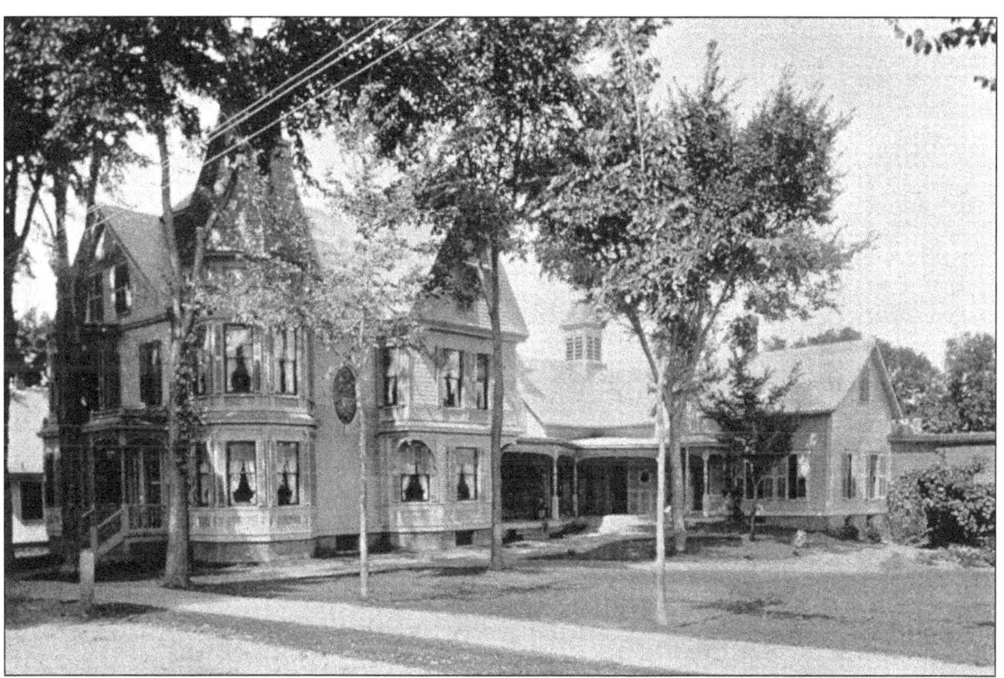

The home of Dr. Osmon Way on Sullivan Street is seen here around 1910. (CHS.)

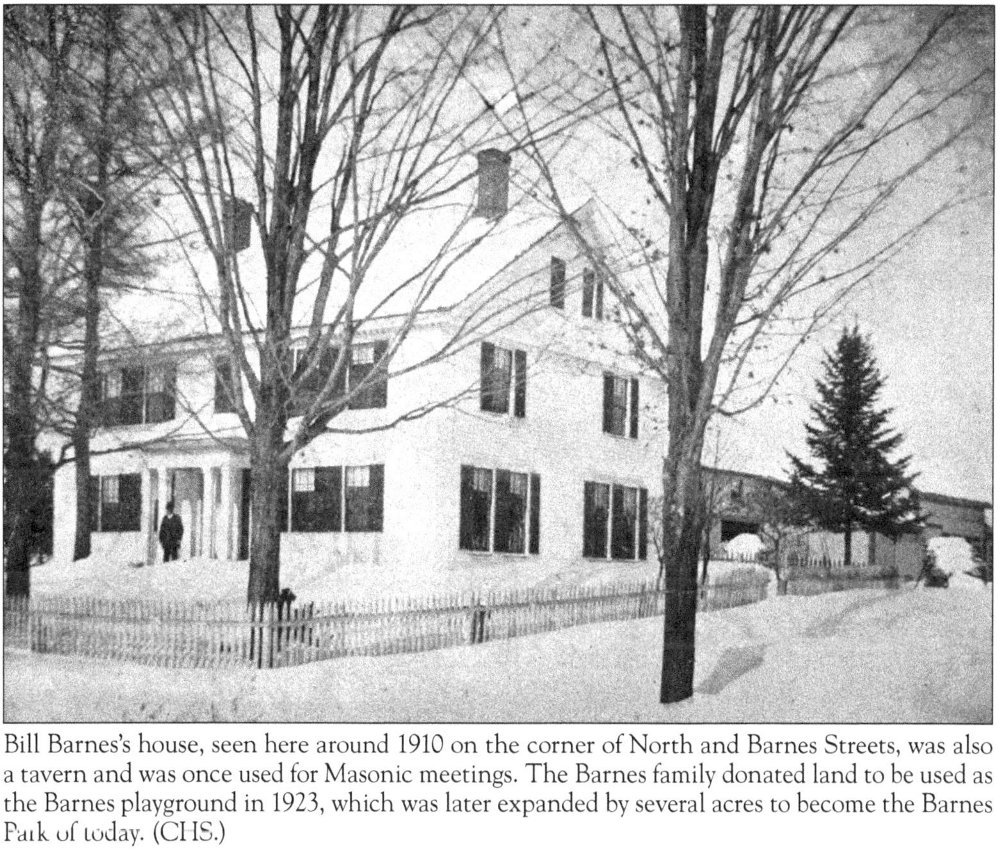

Bill Barnes's house, seen here around 1910 on the corner of North and Barnes Streets, was also a tavern and was once used for Masonic meetings. The Barnes family donated land to be used as the Barnes playground in 1923, which was later expanded by several acres to become the Barnes Park of today. (CHS.)

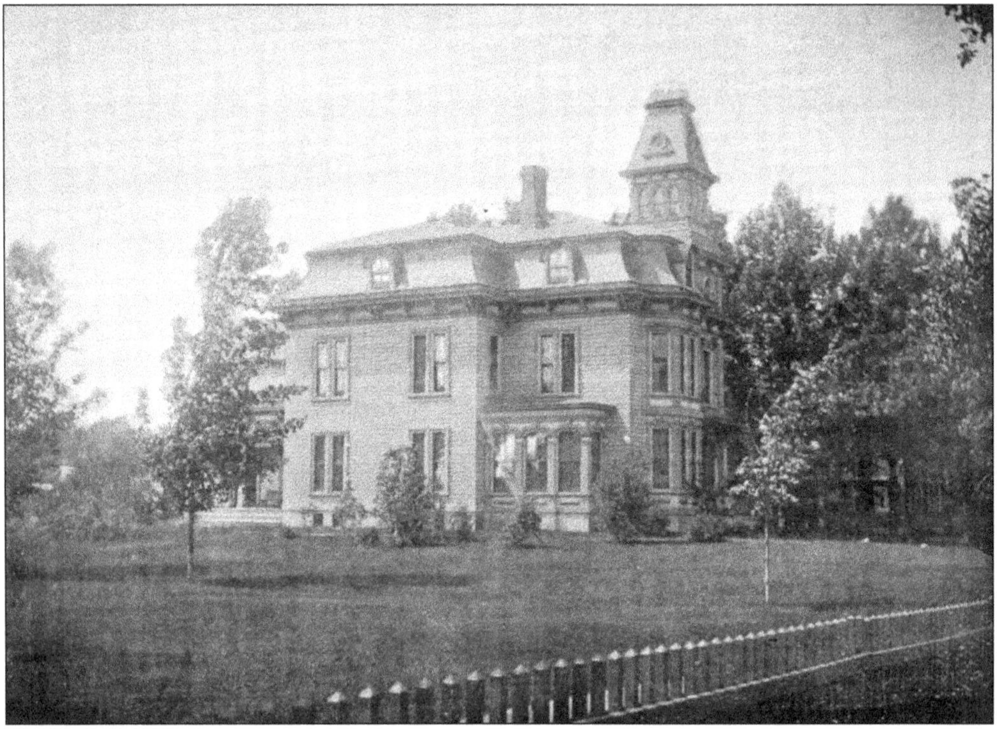

This Broad Street home, seen here around 1895, belonged to Hosea Parker, a lawyer and a member of the state legislature. The remains of the home are now part of the Moose lodge. (CHS.)

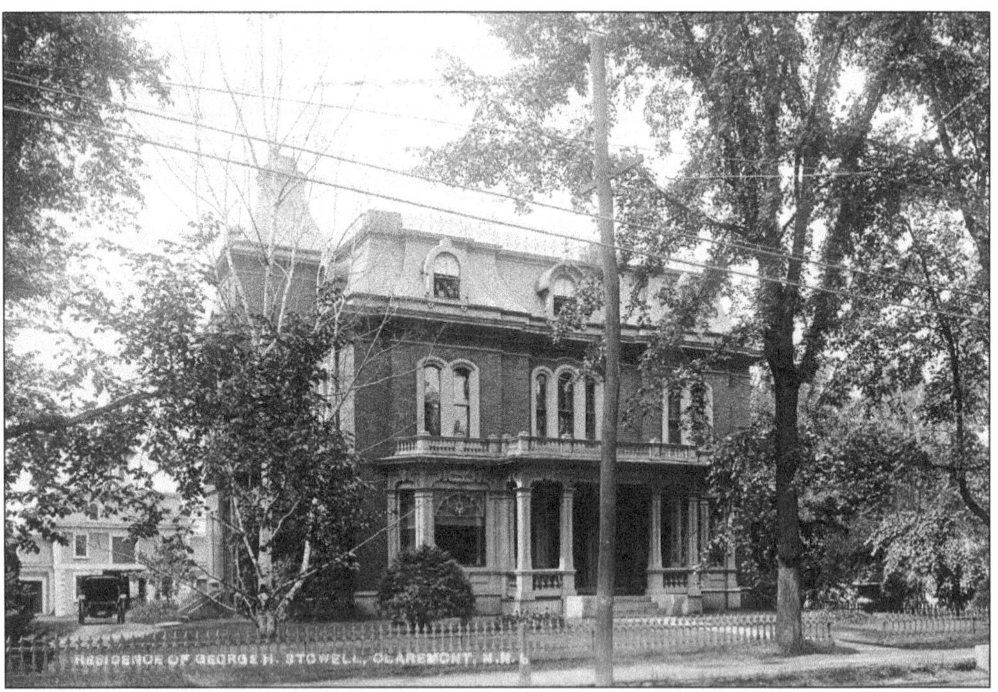

The home of George Stowell, on the corner of Pleasant and Summer Streets on the lot now occupied by Cumberland Farms, is seen here around 1915. (WLM.)

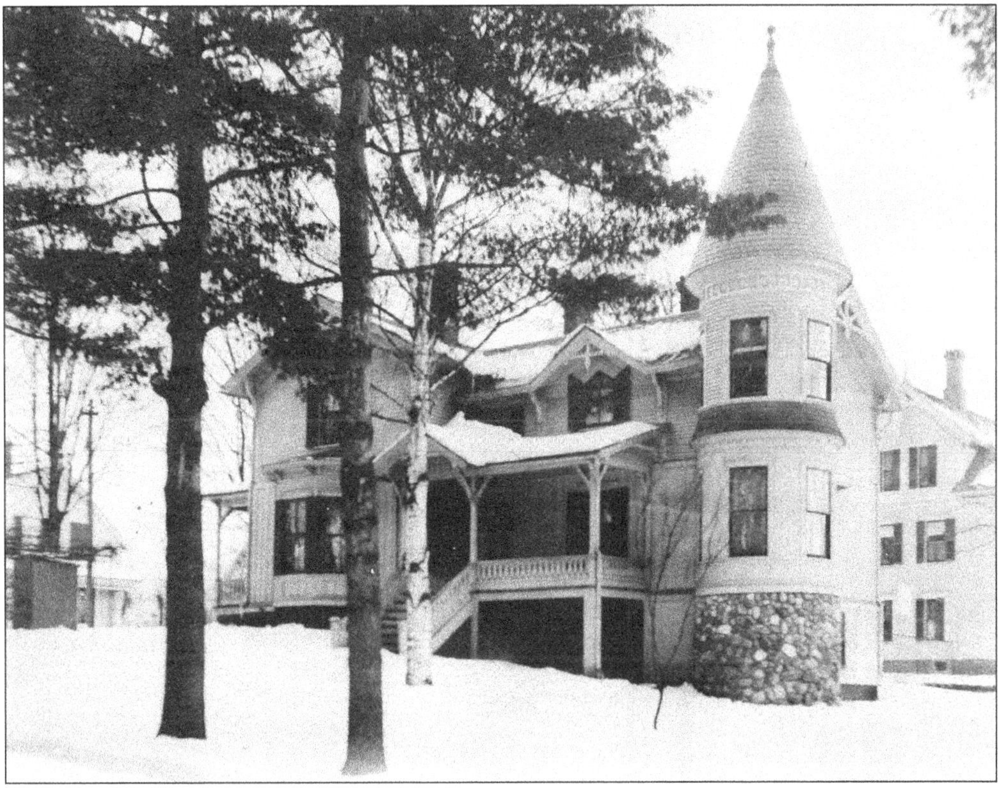

These two views show Frank Maynard's residence on Sullivan Street. Maynard lived here until 1903, when he moved into his new home, which is now known as the Goddard Mansion. (Both, WLM.)

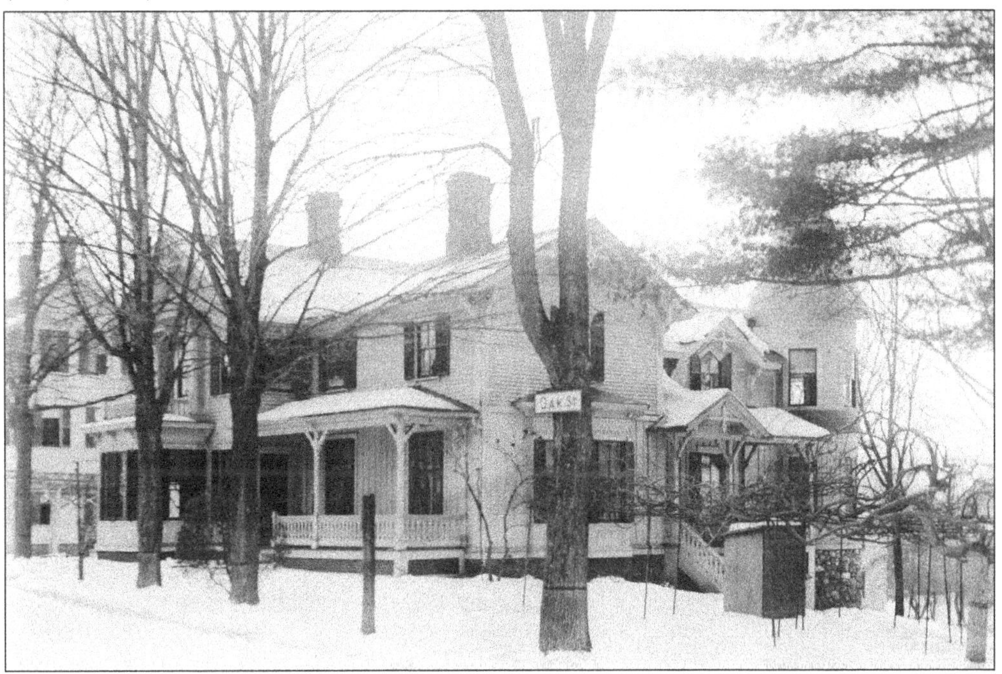

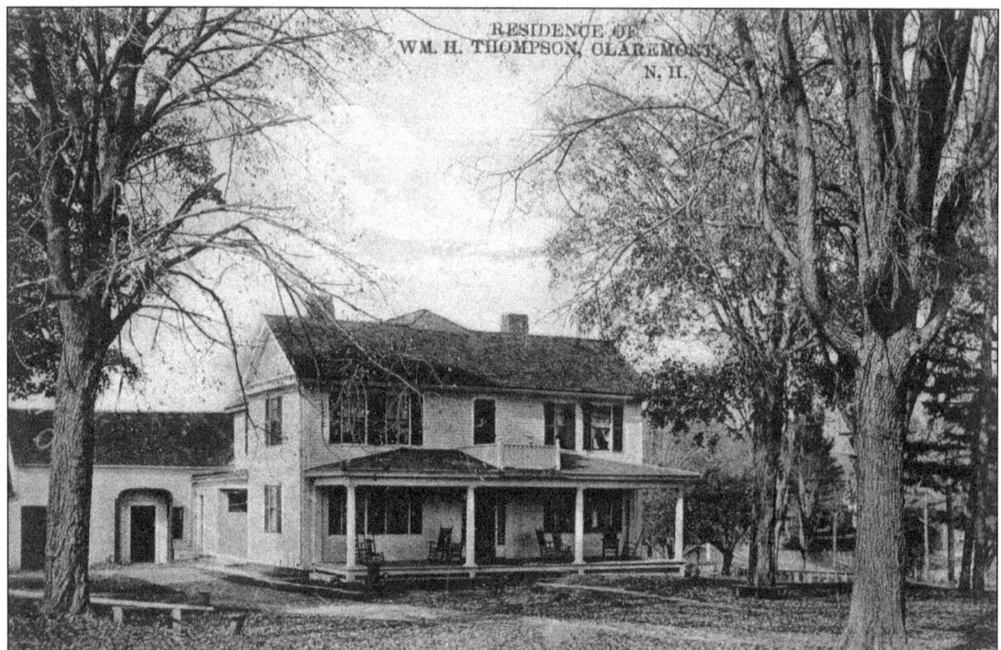

The home of William H. Thompson was at 56 Maple Avenue, just before Buena Vista Road. (WLM.)

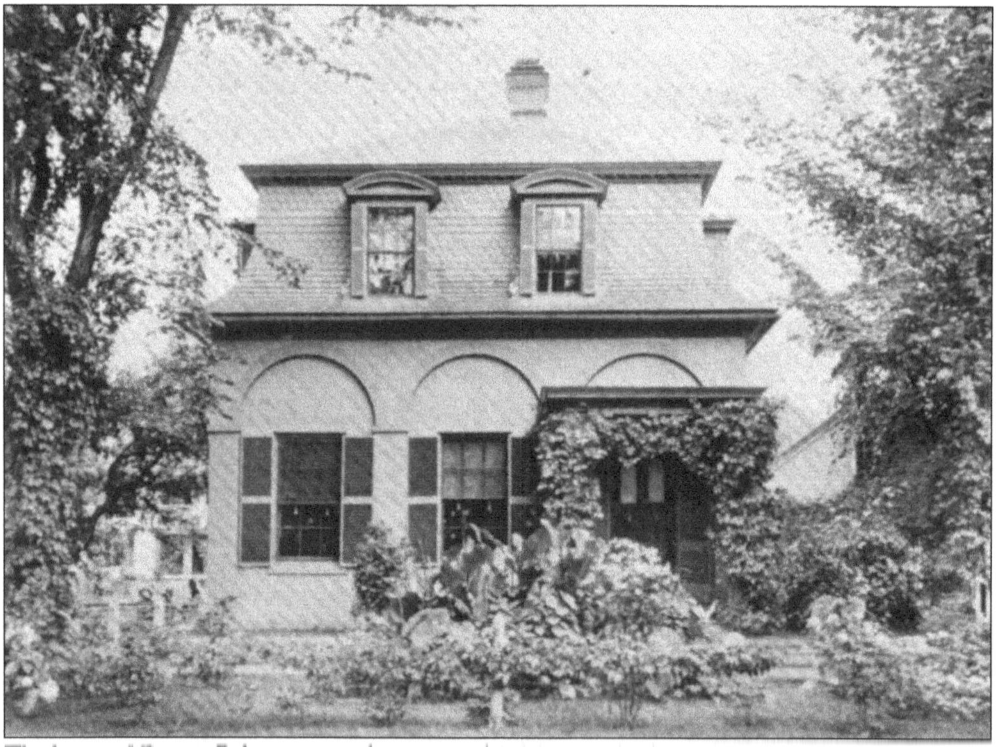

The home of George Balcom is seen here around 1895. It was built as a bank in 1826 and converted into a house in 1846. Balcom, who had one of the finest libraries of New Hampshire–related books in the state, purchased the home in the 1880s. (CHS.)

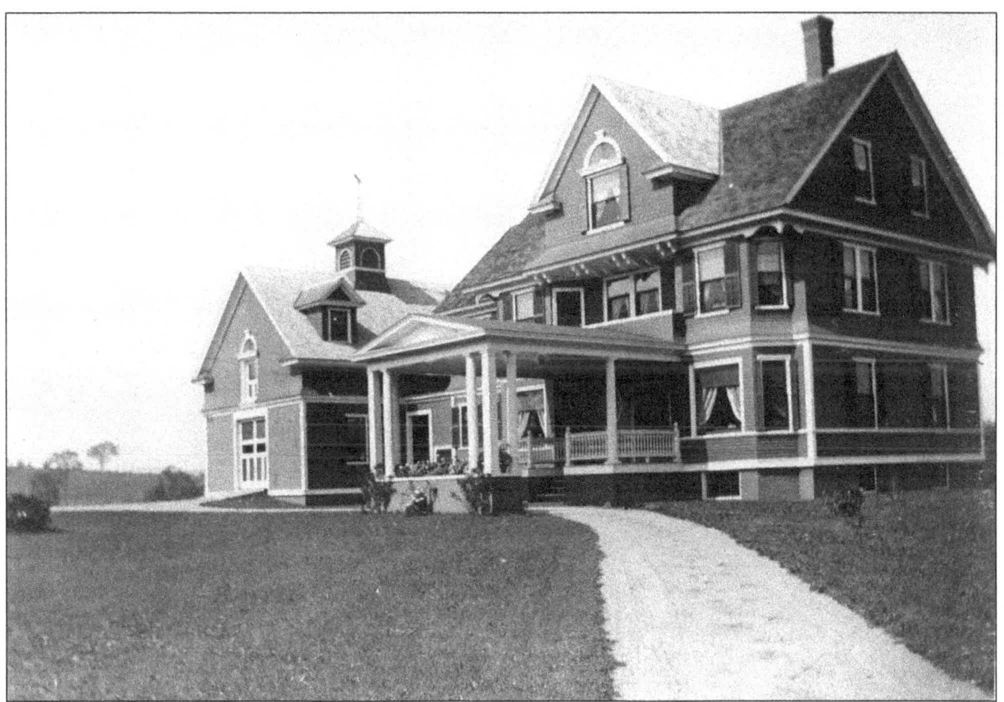

This is a front view of 21 Charlestown Road in 1907. The house is another example of the fine work of Claremont builder Hira Beckwith. (WLM.)

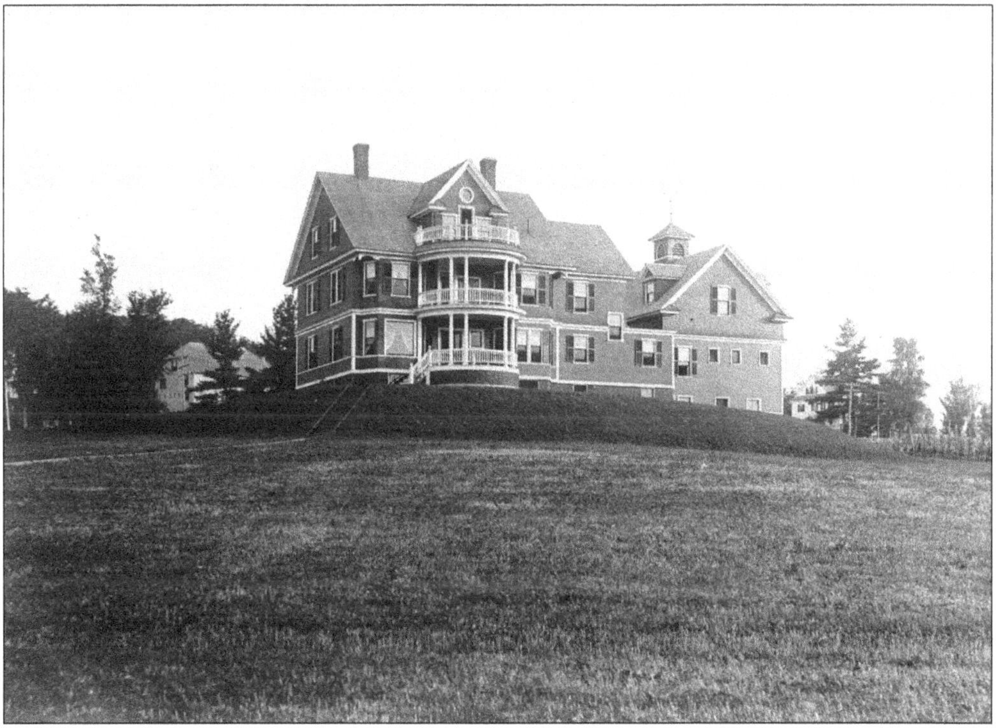

This is a 1907 view of the back of the home at 21 Charlestown Road. The open-air porches are now enclosed. (WLM.)

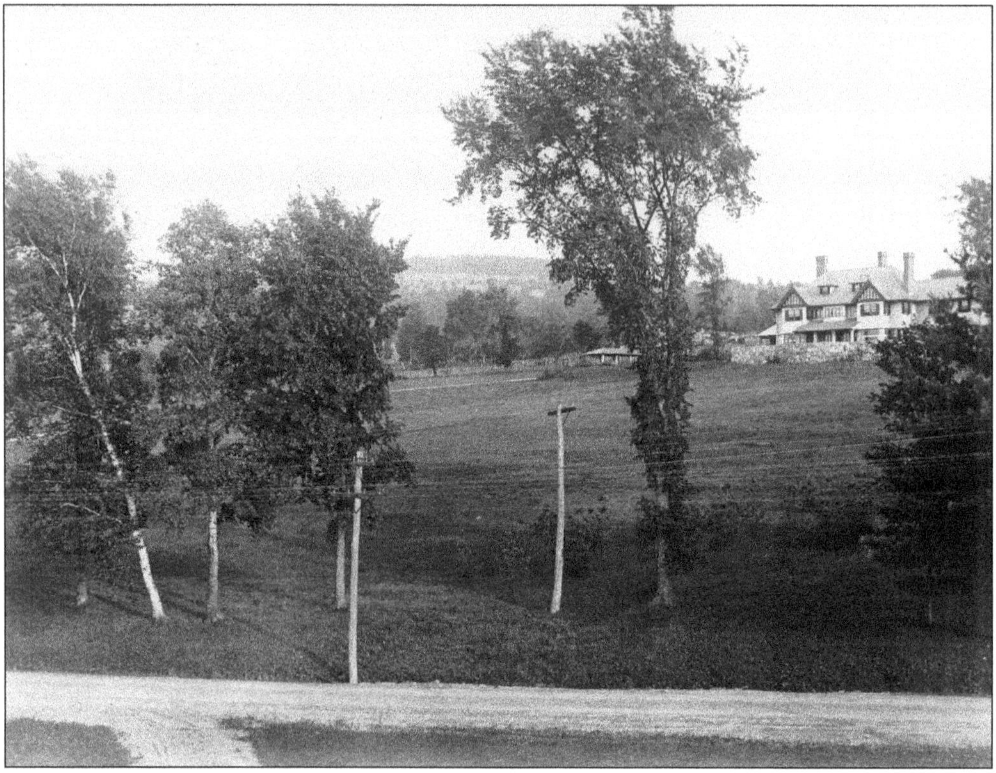

This view of Frank Maynard's residence, now known as the Goddard Mansion, was taken from the house at 21 Charlestown Road in 1907. (WLM.)

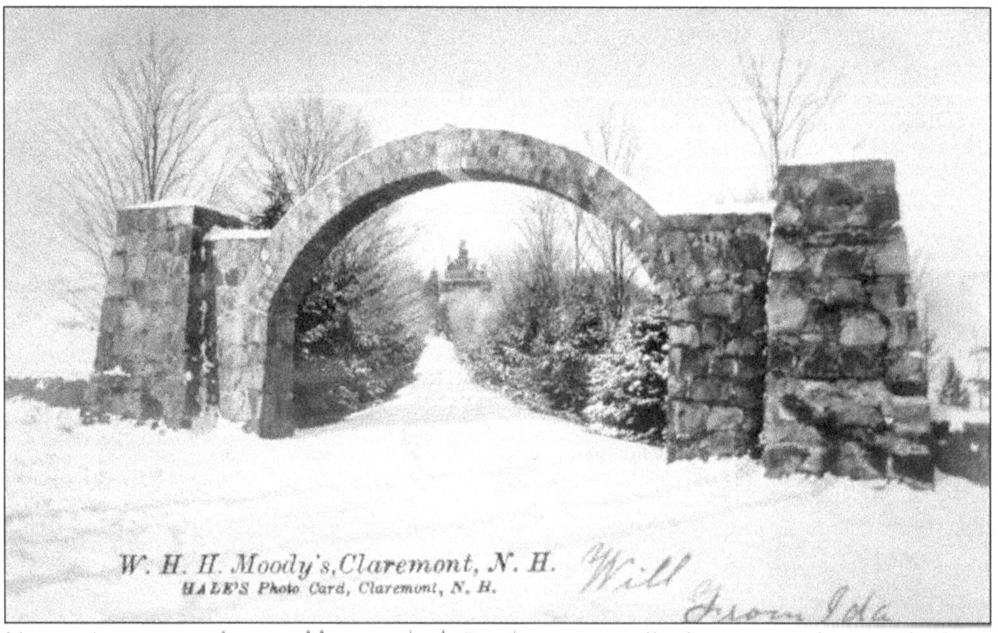

Now a city street with several homes, Arch Road was originally the carriage drive to the large estate of William H.H. Moody, whose mansion is seen here in 1910 at the top of the hill through the arch. (WLM.)

Six

Sports and Leisure

Claremont has always had a wide array of sports and leisure activities, from its theaters to its athletic facilities.

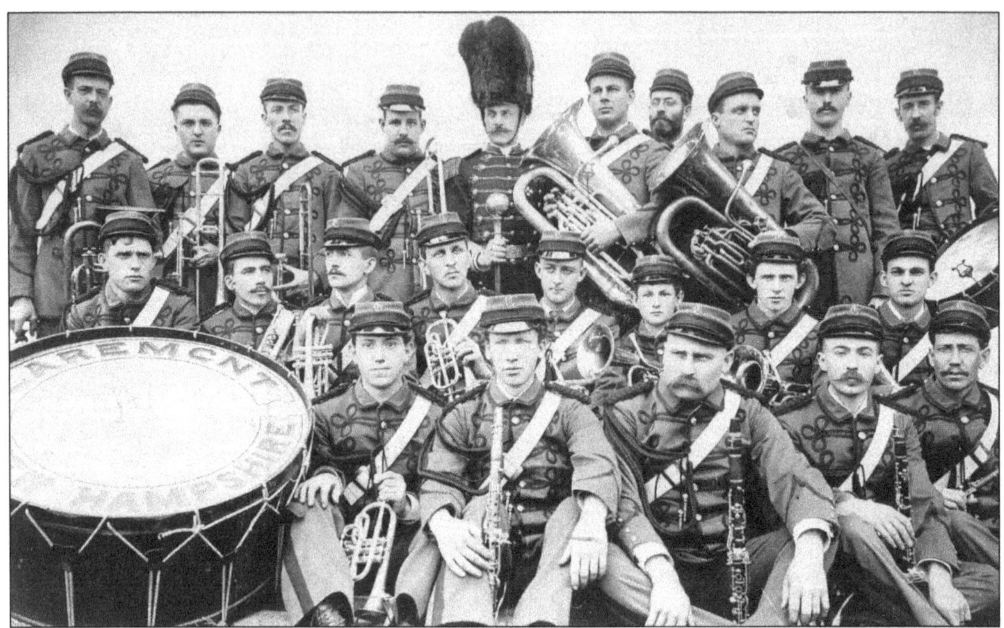

The Claremont American Band poses for a group photograph around 1890. The band was formed around 1880 and is still going today under the direction of Edward Evensen. (WLM.)

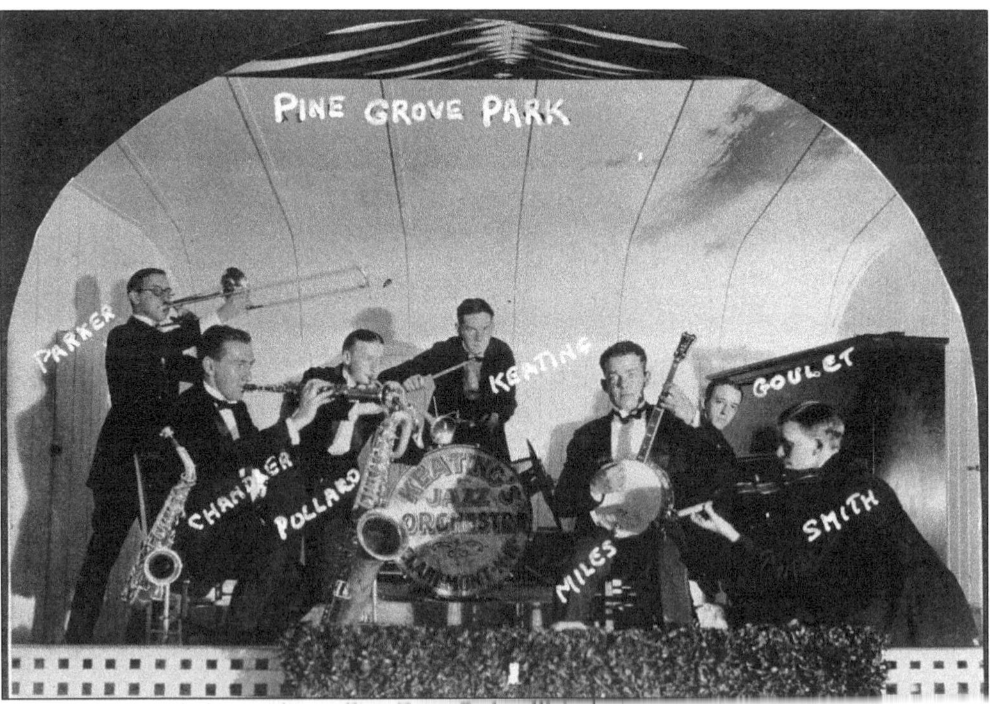

The Keating Jazz Orchestra plays at Pine Grove Park, off Maple Avenue, where the King's (later Ames) department store was located. The band included, from left to right, Bud Parker, John Chandler, Red Pollard, Buster Keating, Eddie Miles, Benny Goulet, and Addison Smith. (CHS.)

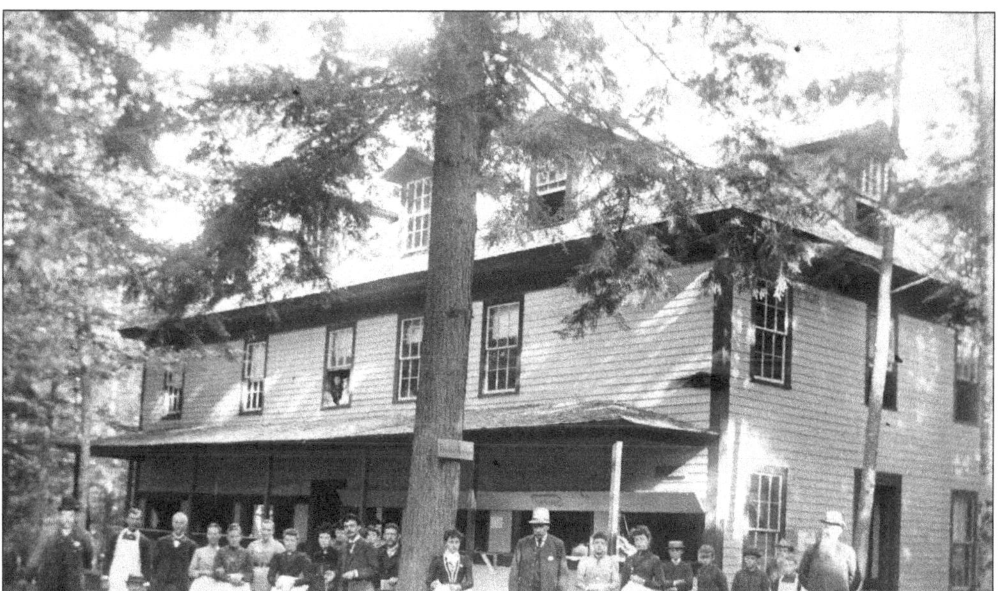

A campground area was built off River Road near the junction in 1872, and it continued to be used into the early 1900s. (CHS.)

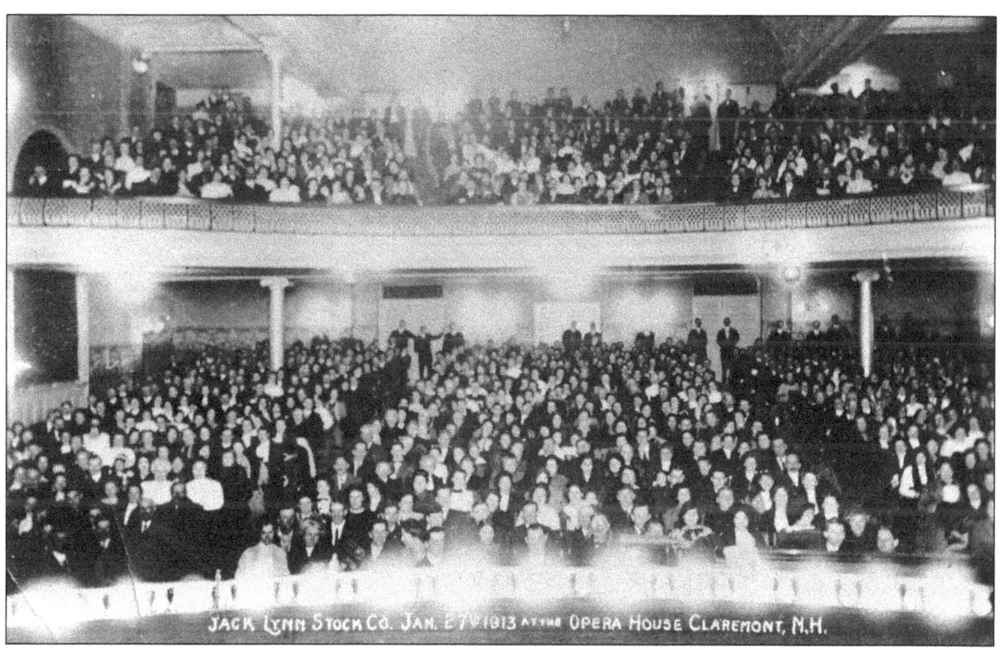

A packed Claremont Opera House is on hand to see the Jack Lynn Stock Company on January 27, 1913. (WLM.)

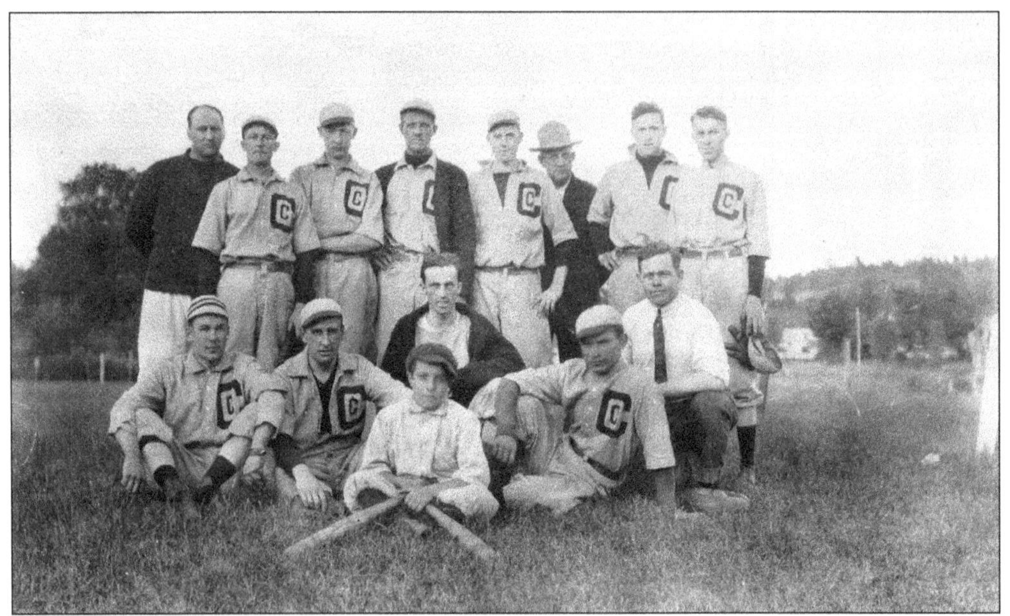

In addition to Claremont's long-standing entry in the semiprofessional Twin State League, a sunset league was formed in 1913. The league played near the southeast end of Broad Street on the Cossitt property. The Claremont Clerks, seen here, were the 1913 league champions. (WLM.)

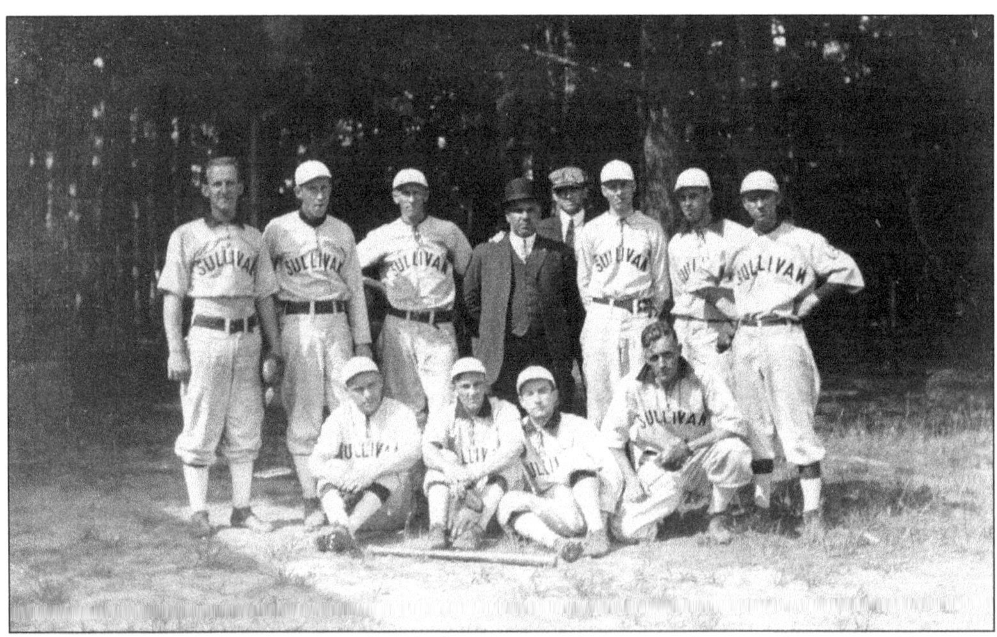

The Sullivan Machinery Company baseball team poses for a team photograph in 1913. This team was independent and was not part of the sunset league. (WLM.)

Eli Bourdon, a wrestler himself, was a promoter of area boxing and wrestling matches. Bobby Suber, one of his top fighters, is seen here around 1930. Promoters would mail these cards to each other to promote their fighters and arrange matches. (WLM.)

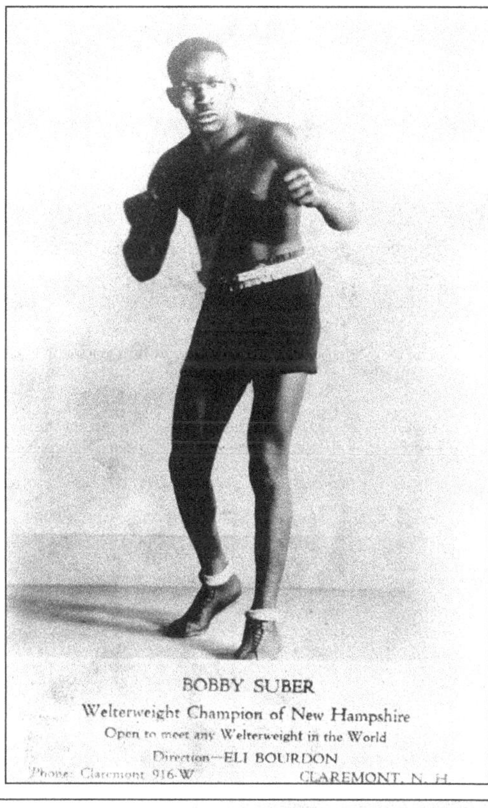

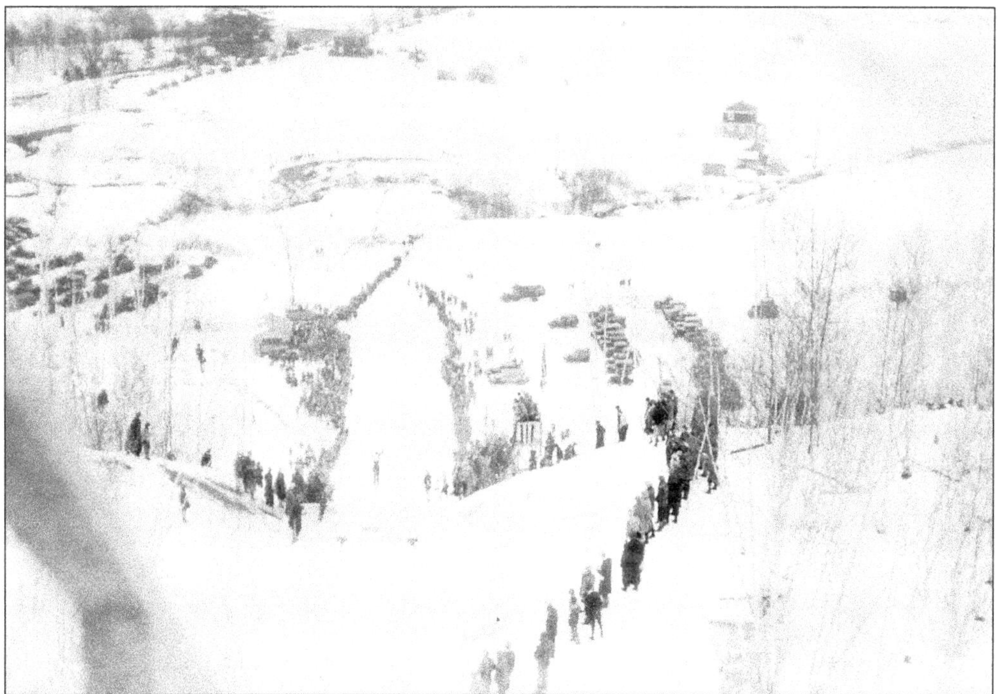

This ski jump was on the east end of the airport so jumpers could go down the steep hill toward Sullivan Flat. (Henry "Skip" Patten.)

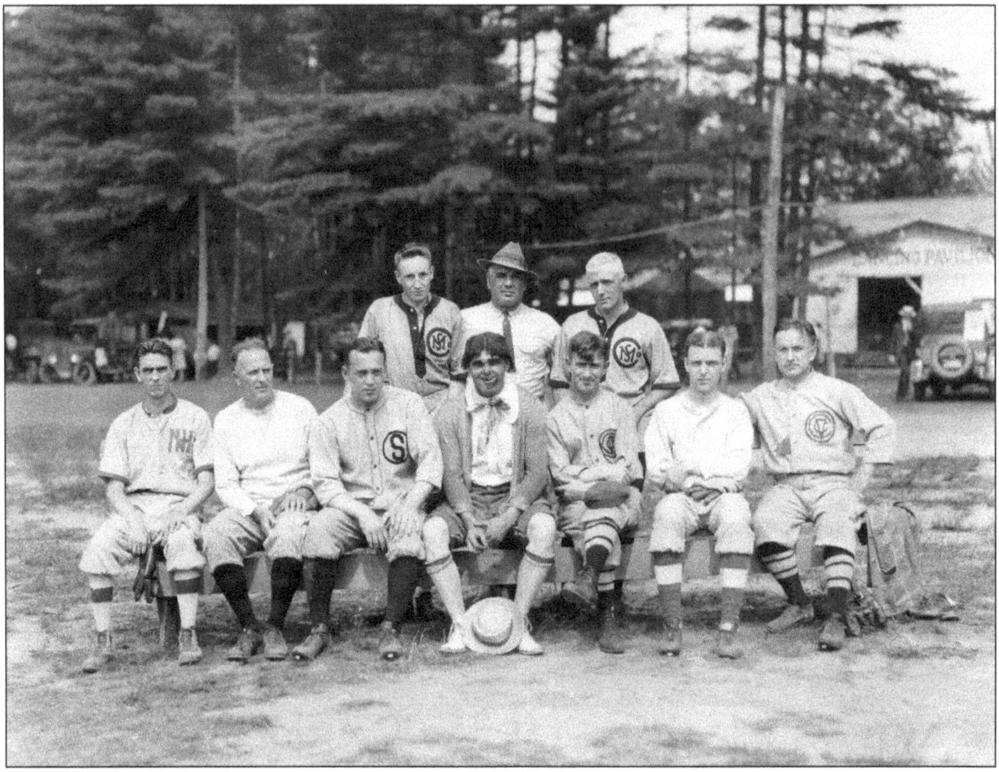

This group of baseball players at Pine Grove Park stops for a photograph around 1930. (CHS.)

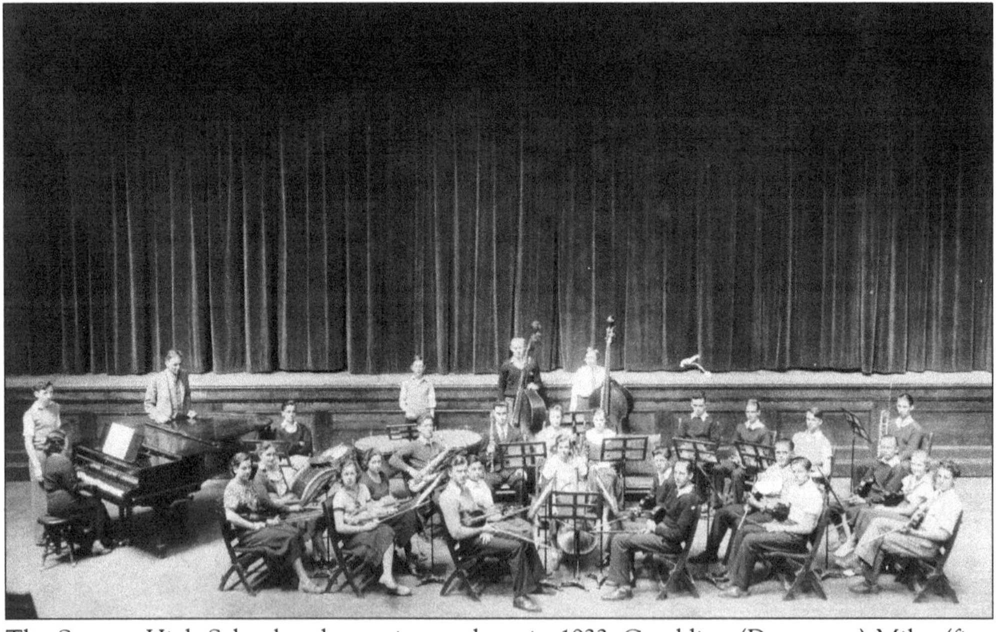

The Stevens High School orchestra is seen here in 1933. Geraldine (Dansereau) Miles (first row, second from left) was a longtime music teacher in the Claremont school district. Walter Paskevich (first row, third from left) was the music director at Stevens High School for many years. (WLM.)

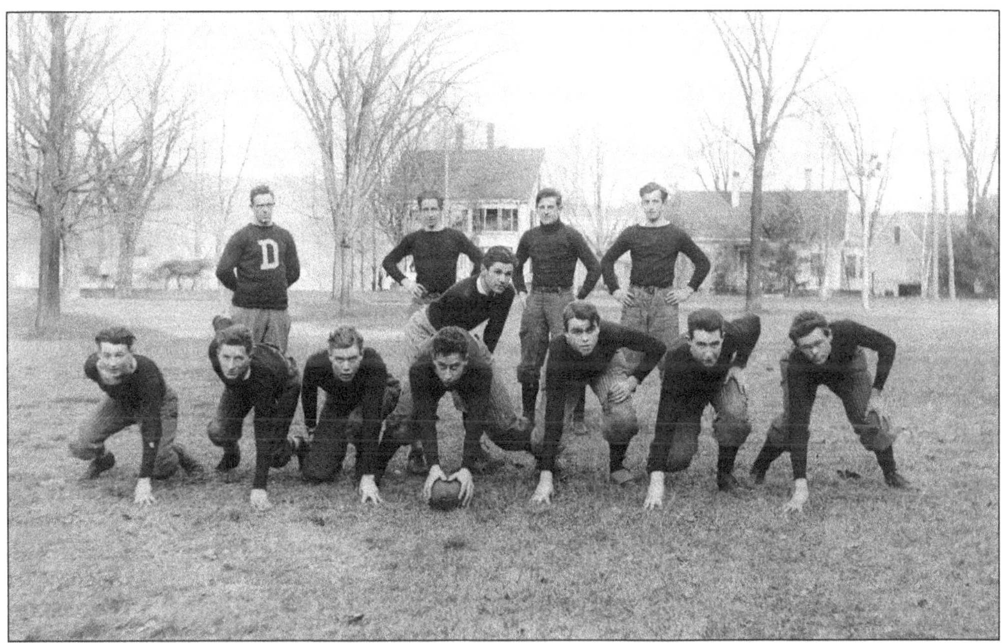

In the days before the creation of Monadnock and Barnes Parks, the school teams could not be choosy over practice space. The 1911 Stevens High School football team, co-state champions, lines up on the grass in front of Hosea Parker's house on Broad Street. (CHS.)

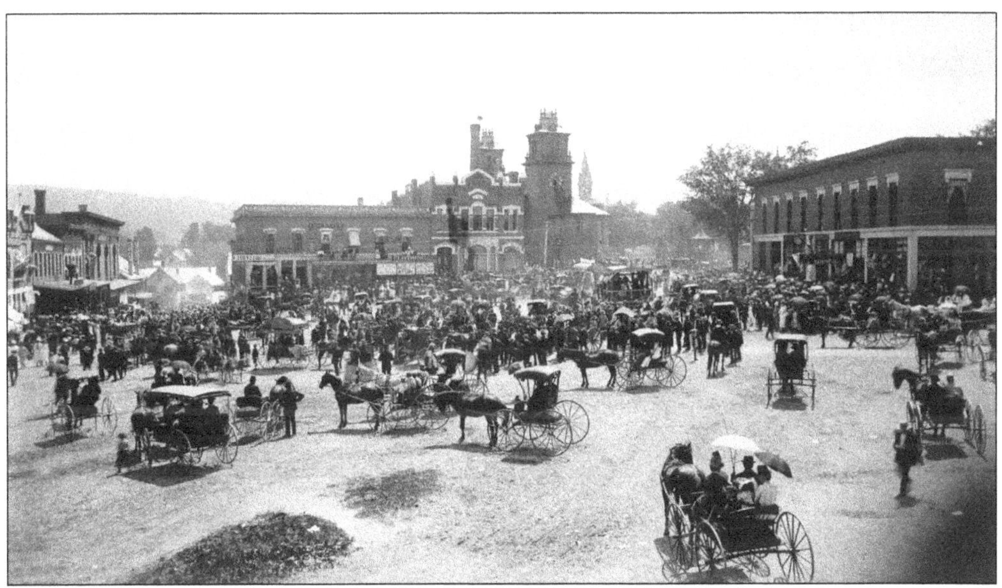

Townspeople celebrate the Fourth of July in the square in 1892. (CHS.)

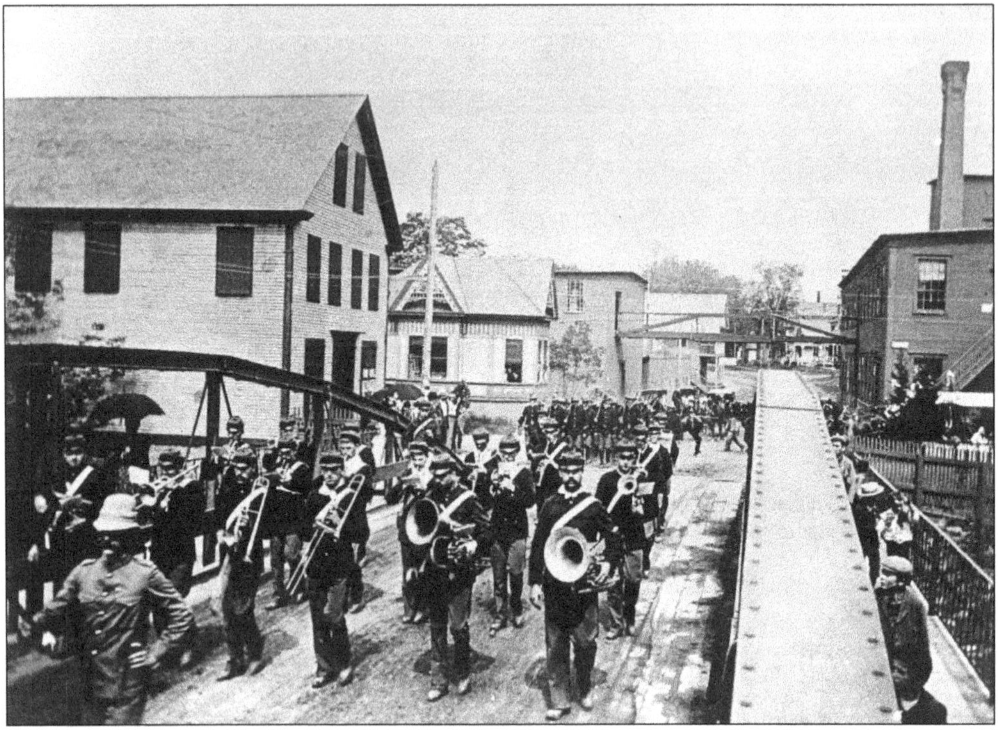

The Fourth of July parade marches over the Main Street Bridge in 1899. (CHS.)

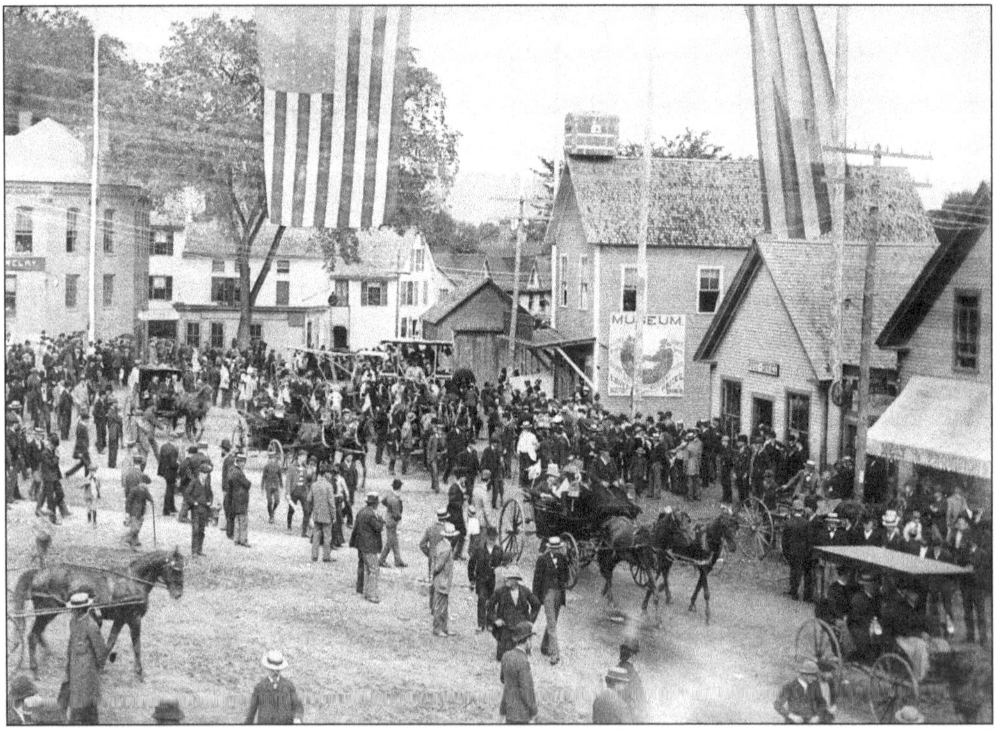

This Fourth of July celebration takes over the square around 1890. The rooftop trunk mentioned on page 34 is seen on top of the building at the center right.

Seven

1938 Hurricane

New England was hit by a Category 3 hurricane on Wednesday, September 21, 1938. It was the first hurricane of any significance to hit New England since 1869, and none have exceeded it since.

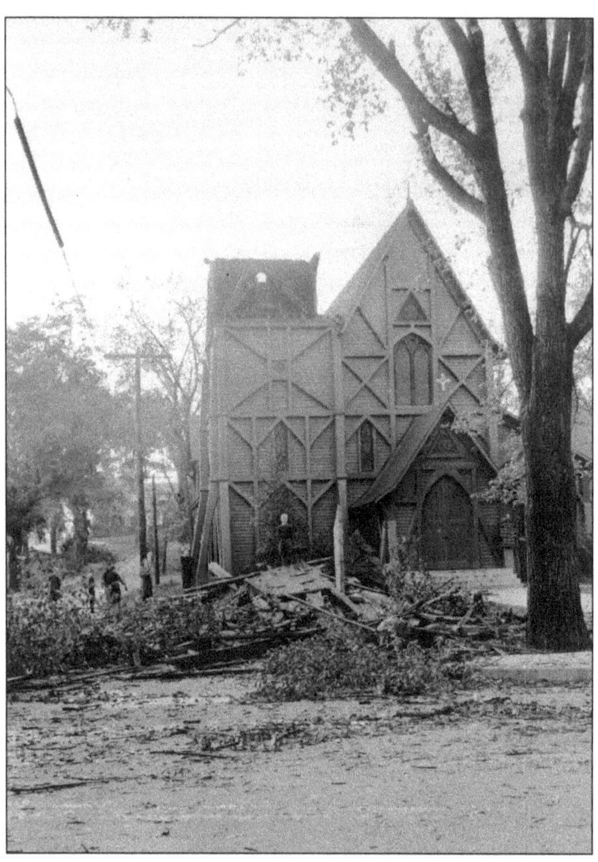

The Episcopal church on Broad Street had its spire blown off by the hurricane. (WLM.)

These trees were down on the corner of Myrtle and Mulberry. (CHS.)

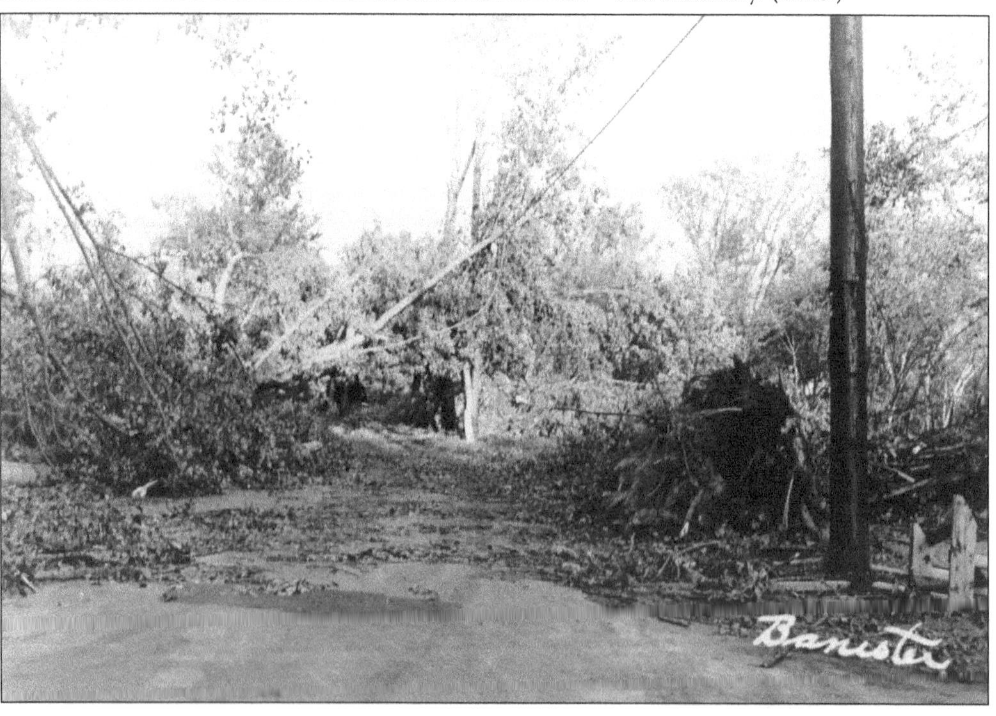

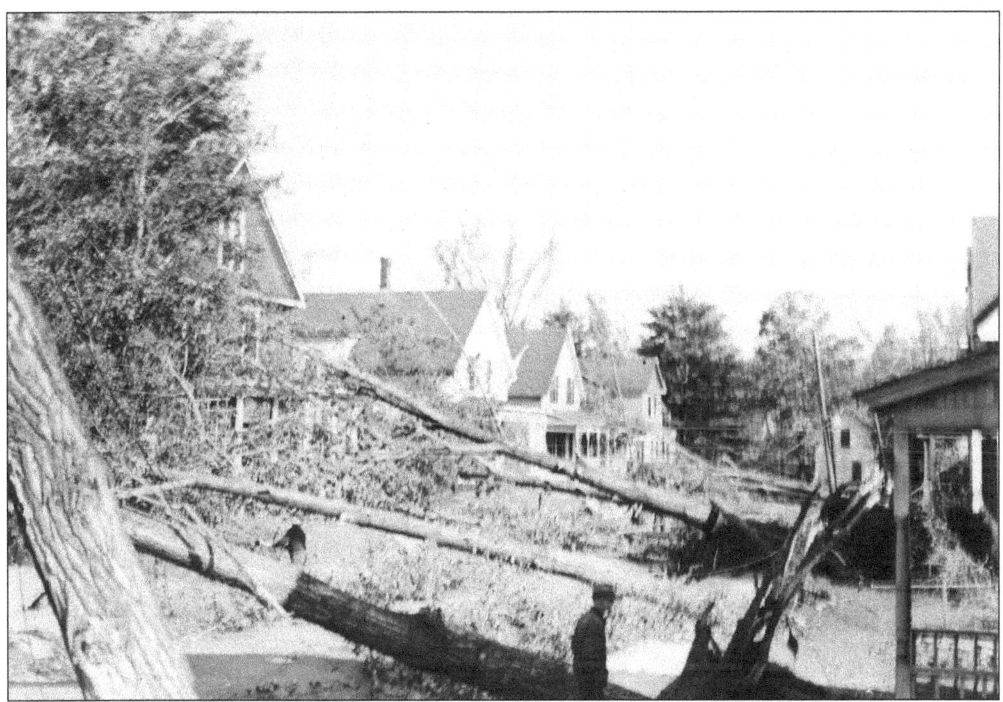

This photograph looks down Henry Street toward East Street through the wreckage of the hurricane. (WLM.)

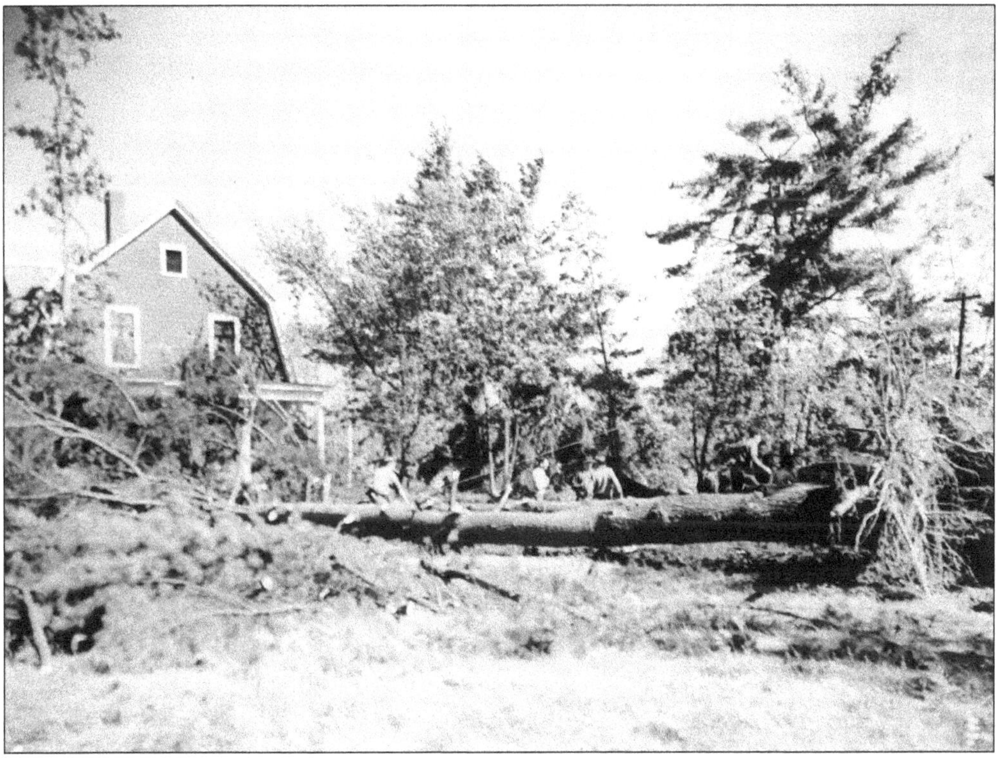

The Lloyd home at 61 Grove Street is behind these downed trees. (WLM.)

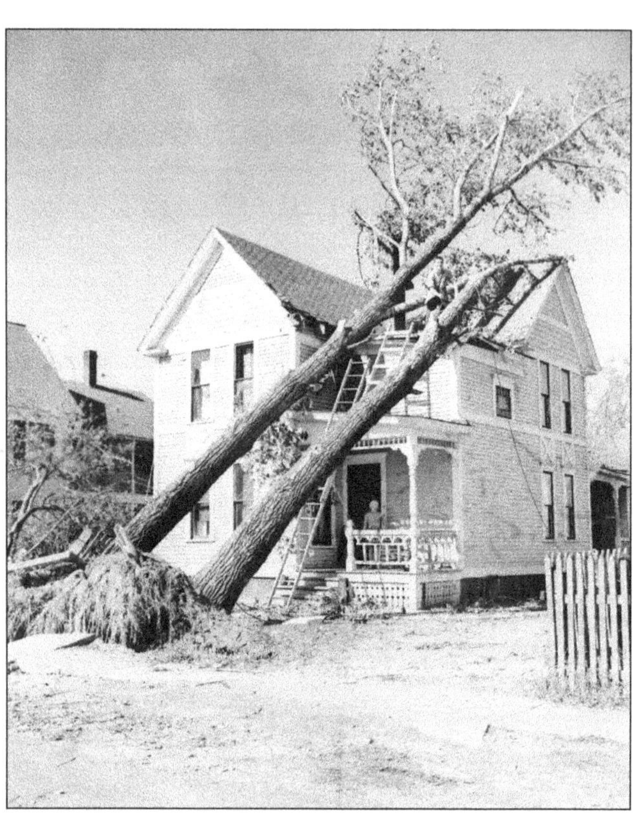

Trees rest on the roof of the Rzeczycki home on West Lafayette Street. (WLM.)

The Steinfield home at 31 Chestnut Street is surrounded by fallen trees. (WLM.)

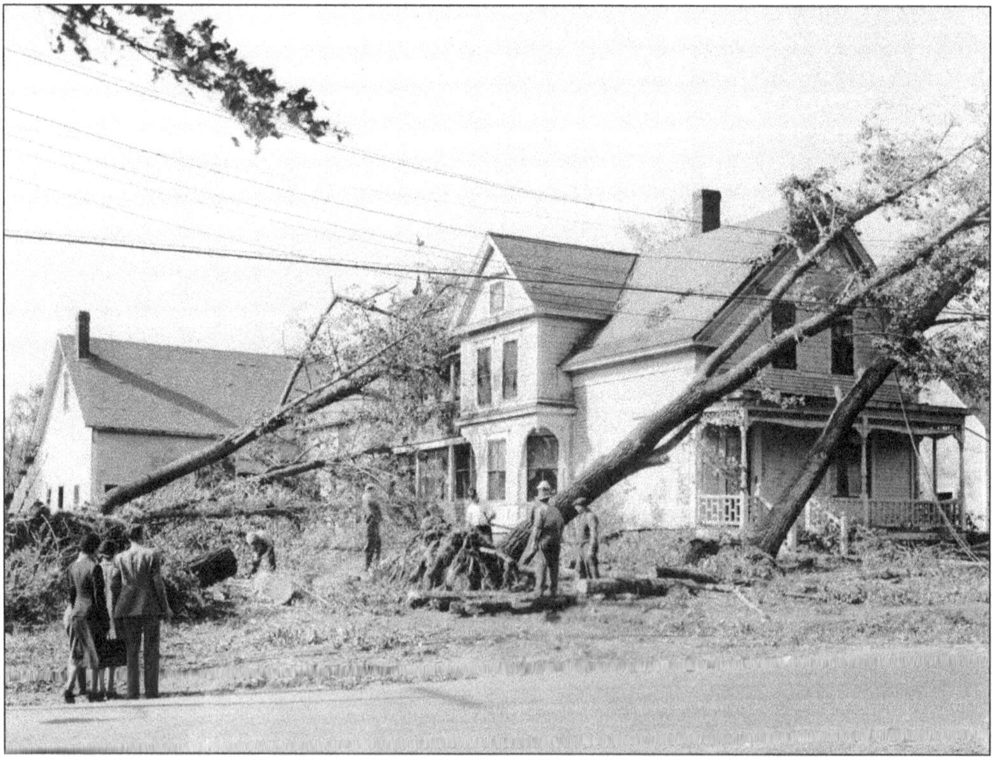

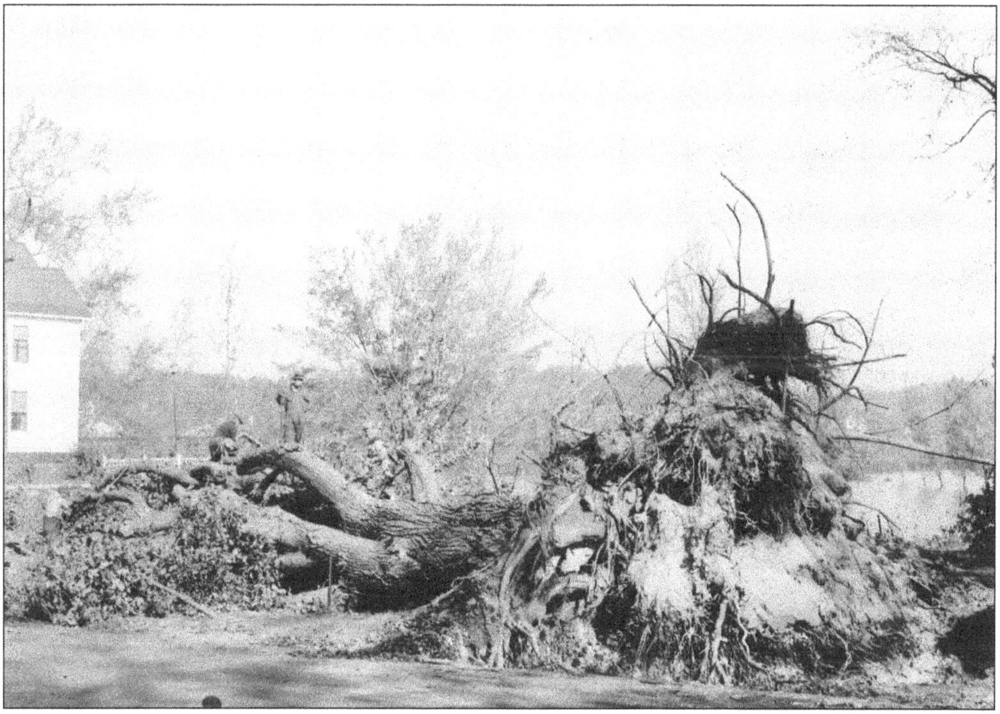

This photograph shows the largest tree that was downed in the storm lying across the railroad tracks on Chestnut Street. (WLM.)

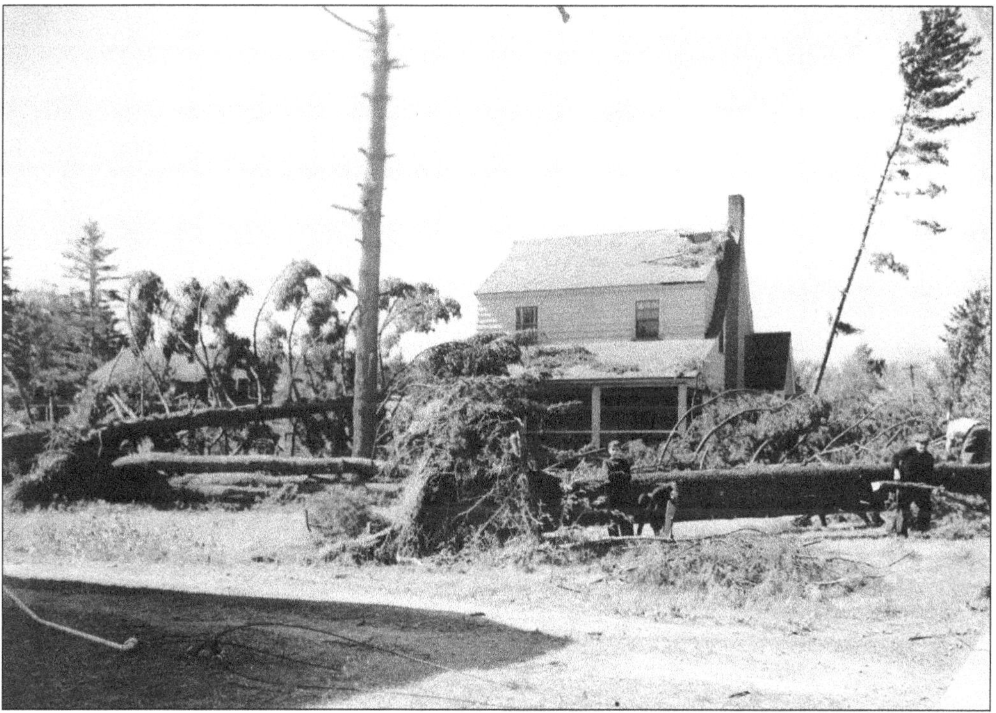

The Lyman Stoughton home on Grove Street had several downed trees. The Bluff area was hit particularly hard. (WLM.)

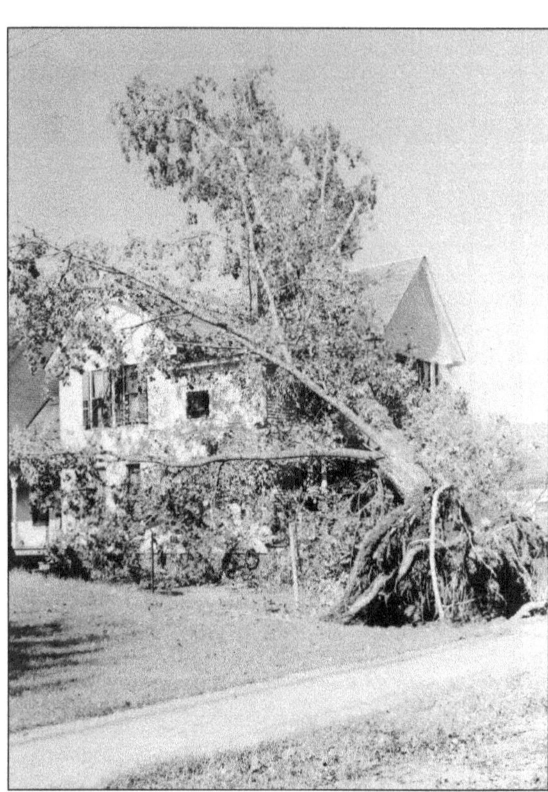

A large poplar tree fell on the Mason home on lower Main Street. (WLM.)

This view from the Claremont Paper Company looks downstream toward the old Dartmouth Woolen Mill on Sullivan Flat. (WLM.)

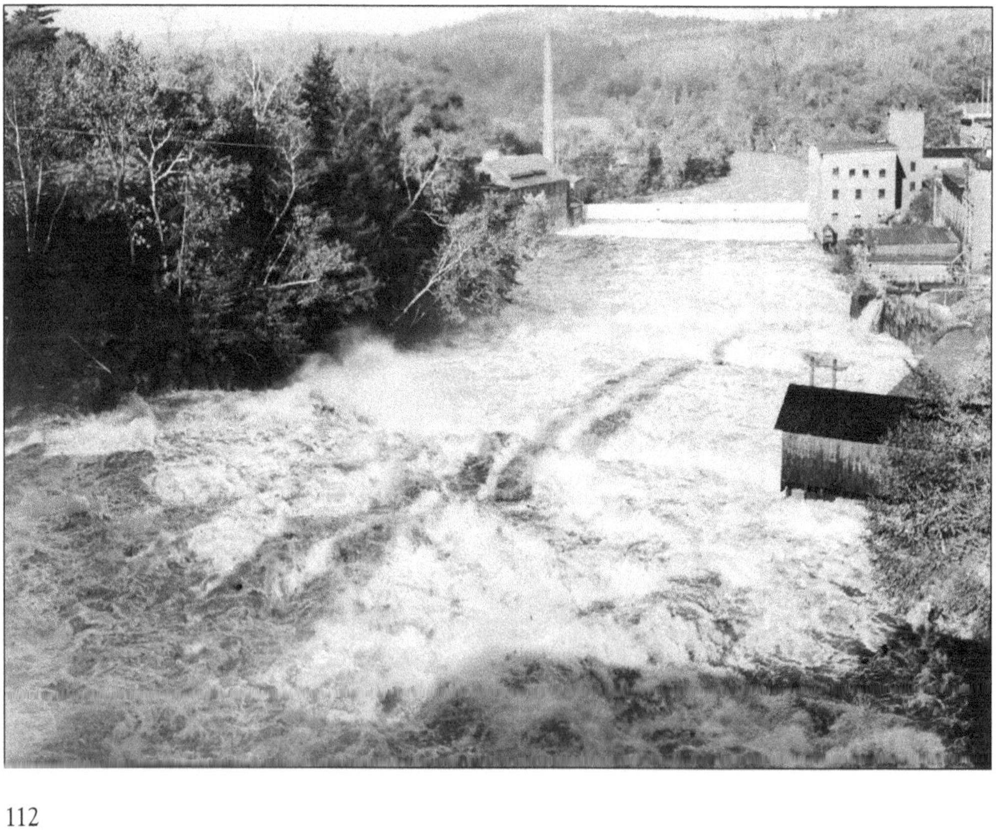

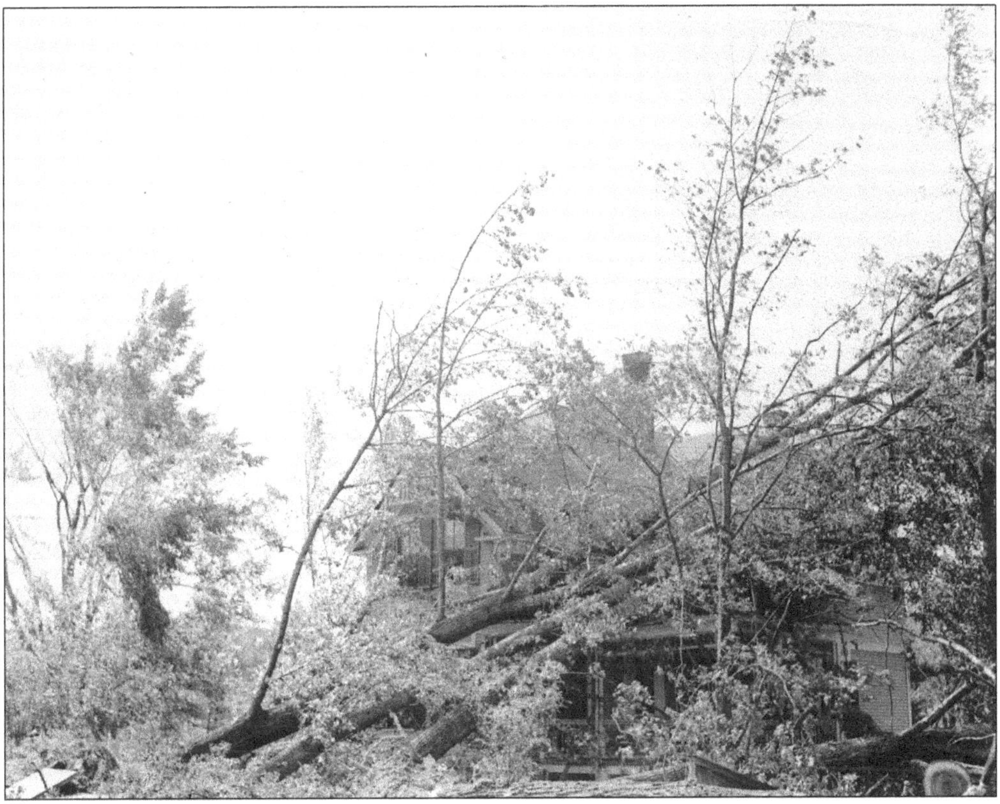

Trees fill the yard of the Wells home on Mulberry Street. (WLM.)

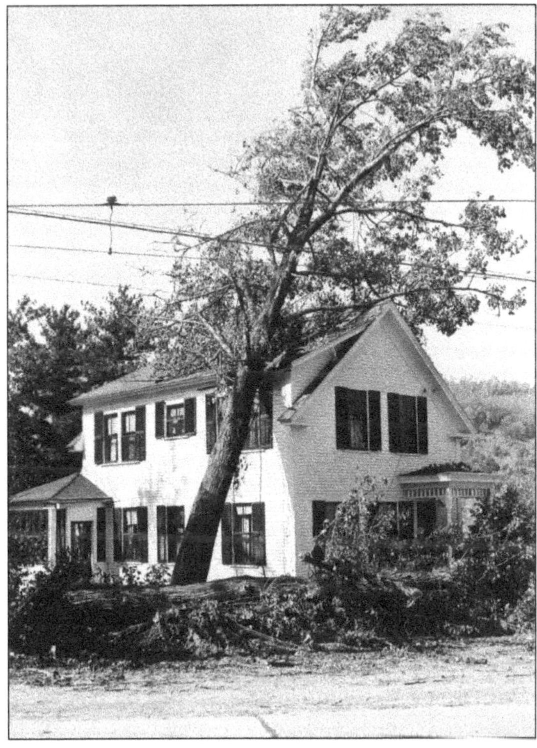

This tree nearly fell on the Carriel home at Joy's Crossing. (WLM.)

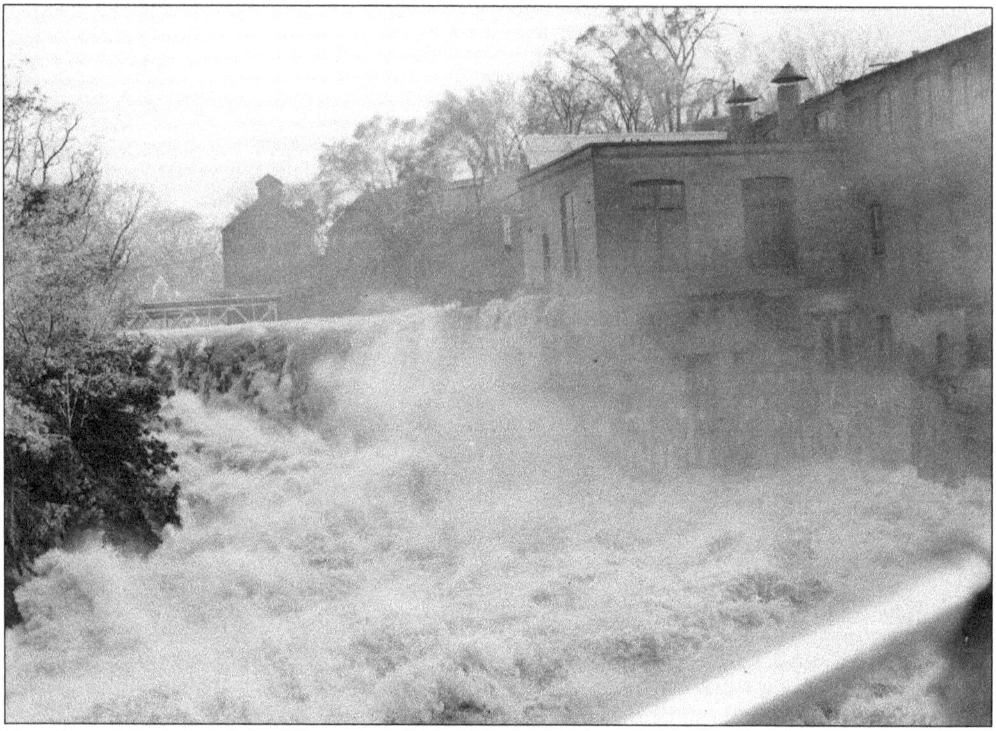

Seen here from behind the Claremont Paper Company, the river was rushing after the three days of rain that preceded the hurricane. (WLM.)

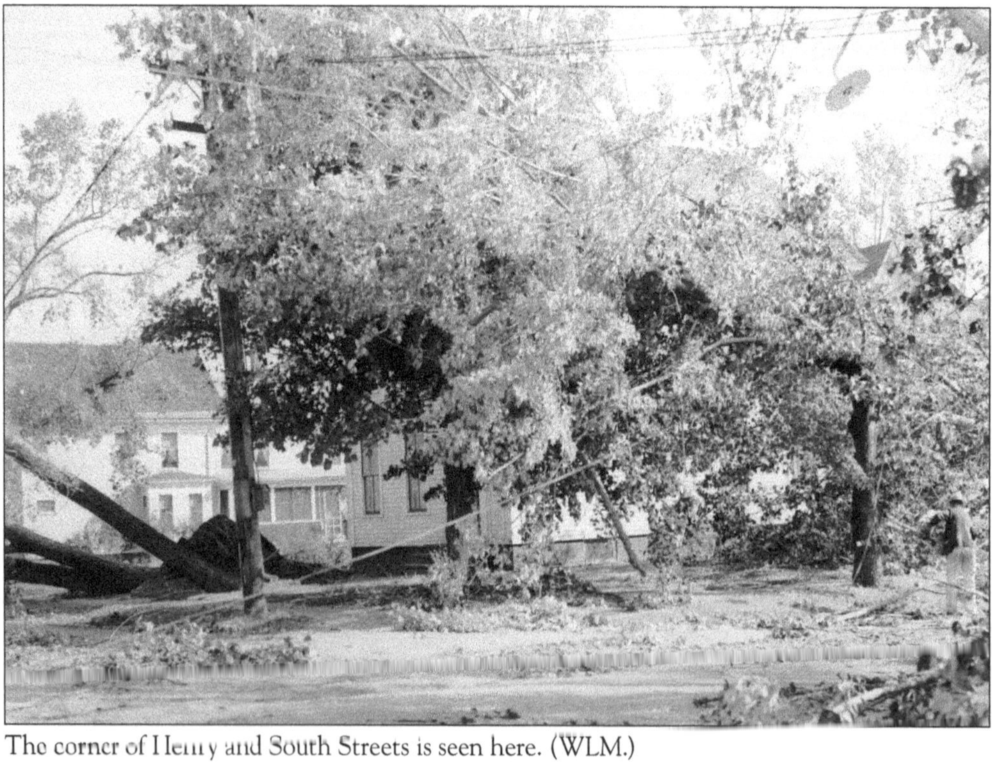

The corner of Henry and South Streets is seen here. (WLM.)

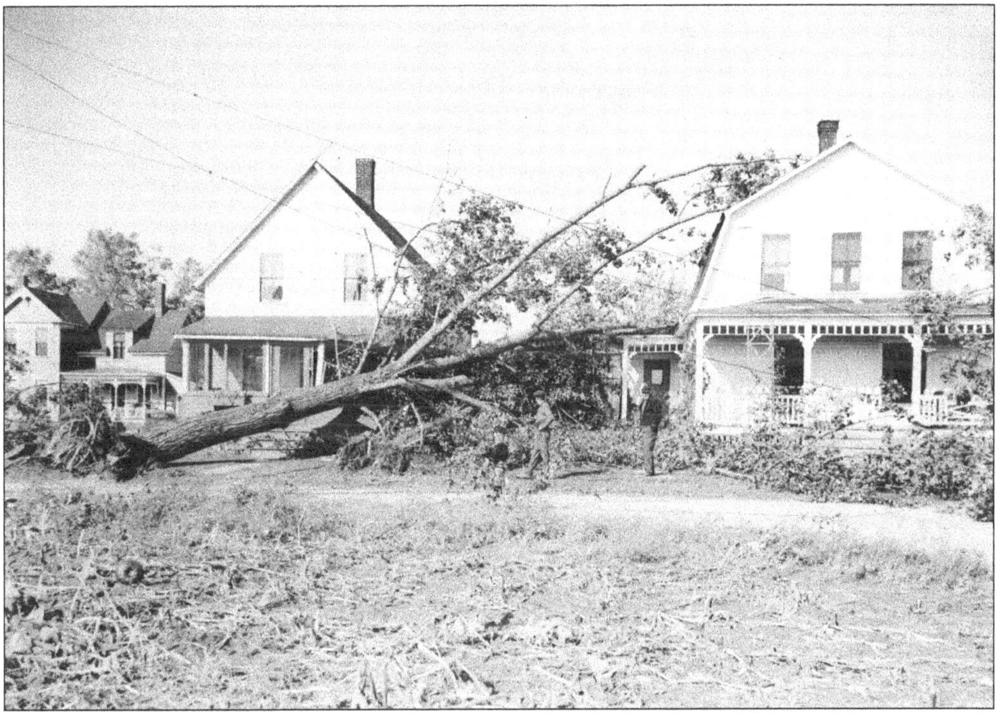

The Sawyer and Mayo homes on Maple Avenue are seen here. (WLM.)

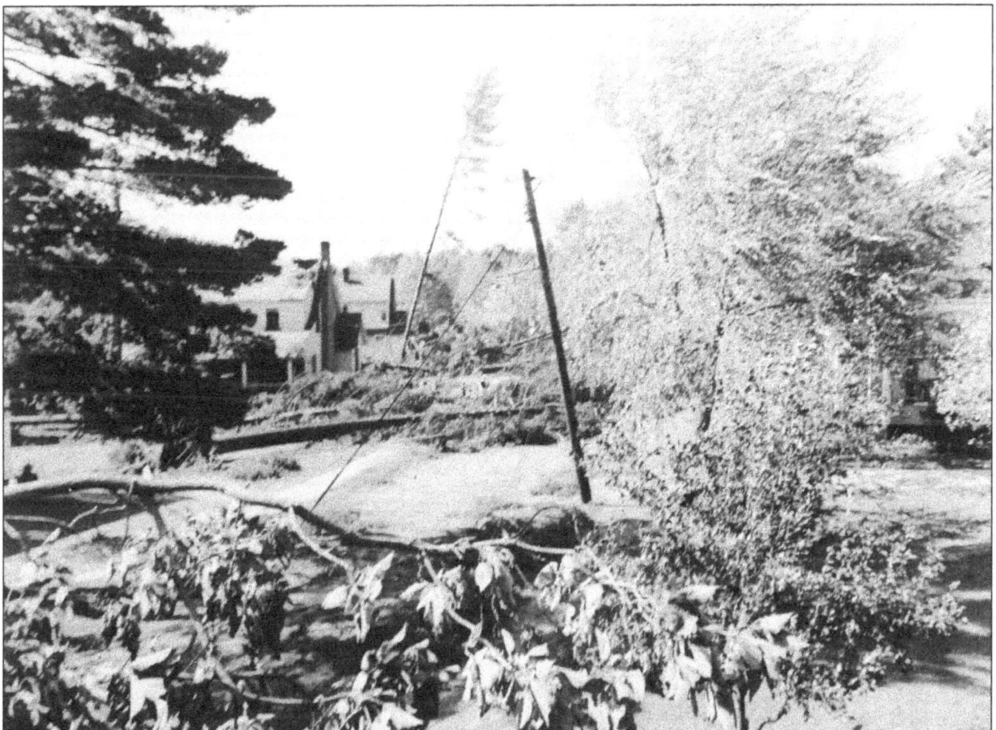

This is a view of the devastation on Grove Street. (WLM)

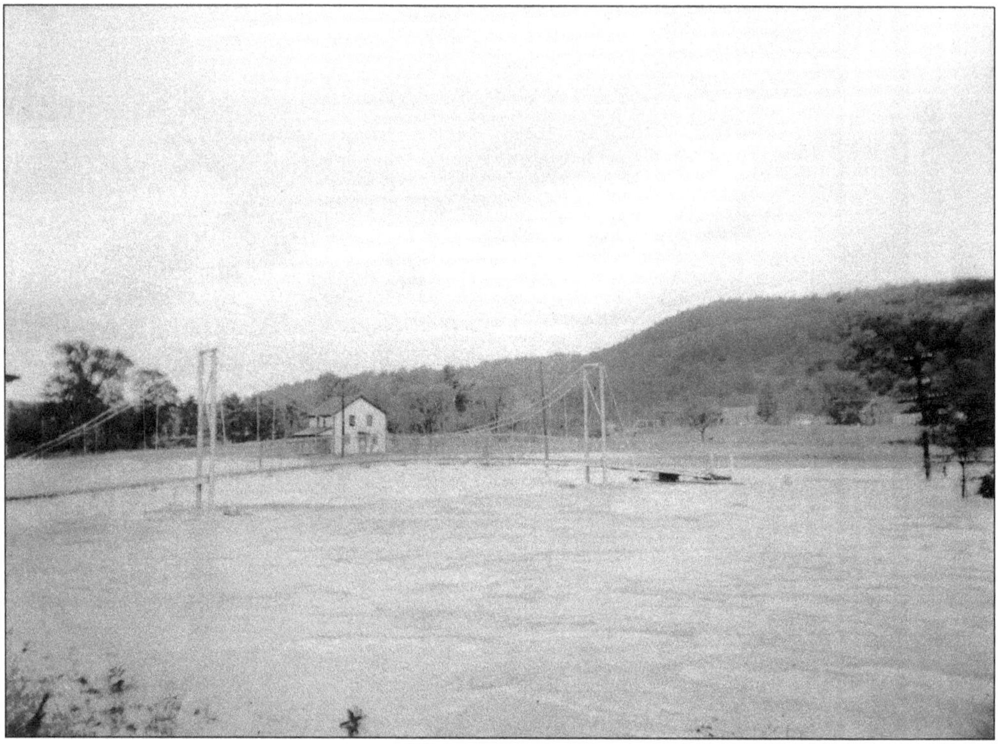

This photograph shows the suspension bridge, sometimes called "Claremont's Brooklyn Bridge," over the Sugar River at Beauregard Village. (WLM.)

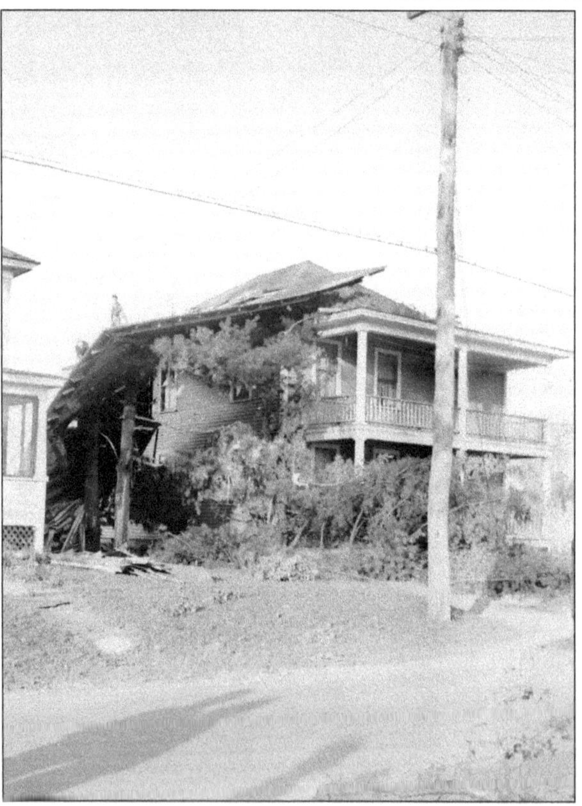

The roof of the home two houses down the street blew off, skipped over one house, and landed on top of the Marro home at 232 North Street. (WLM)

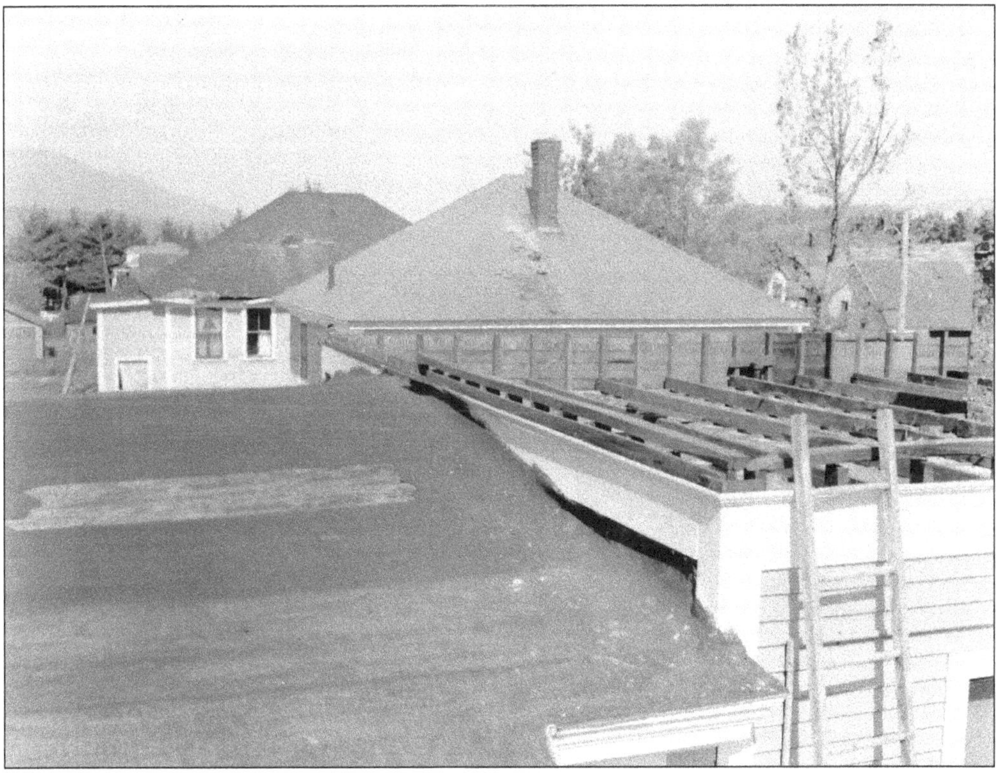

The roof blew off this house and flew over to the Marro house (pictured on the previous page). (CHS.)

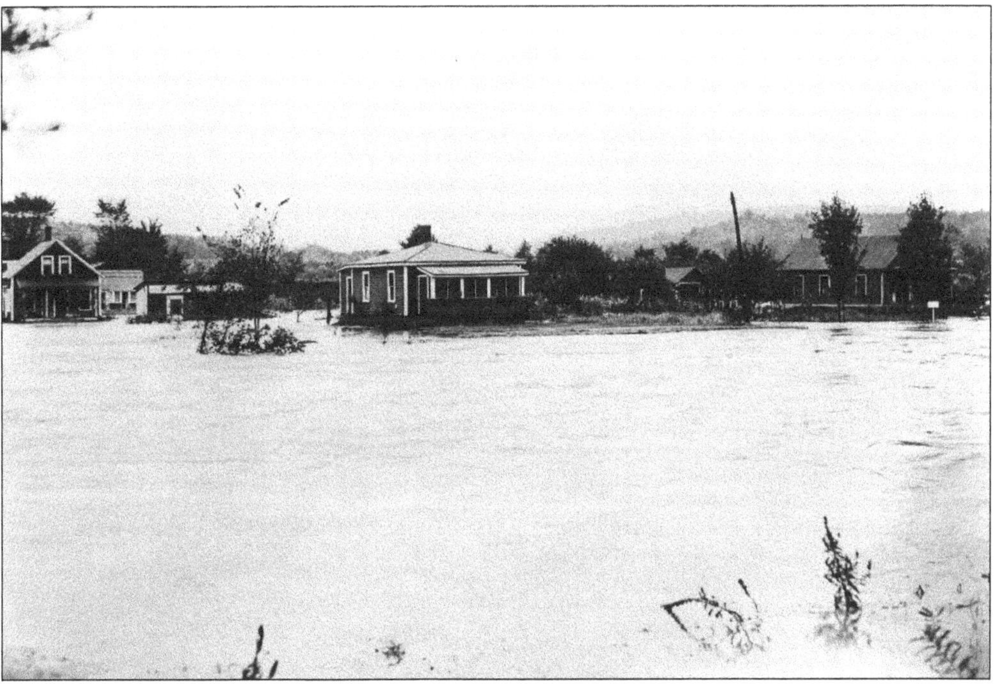

This photograph shows a flooded Beauregard Village. (WLM.)

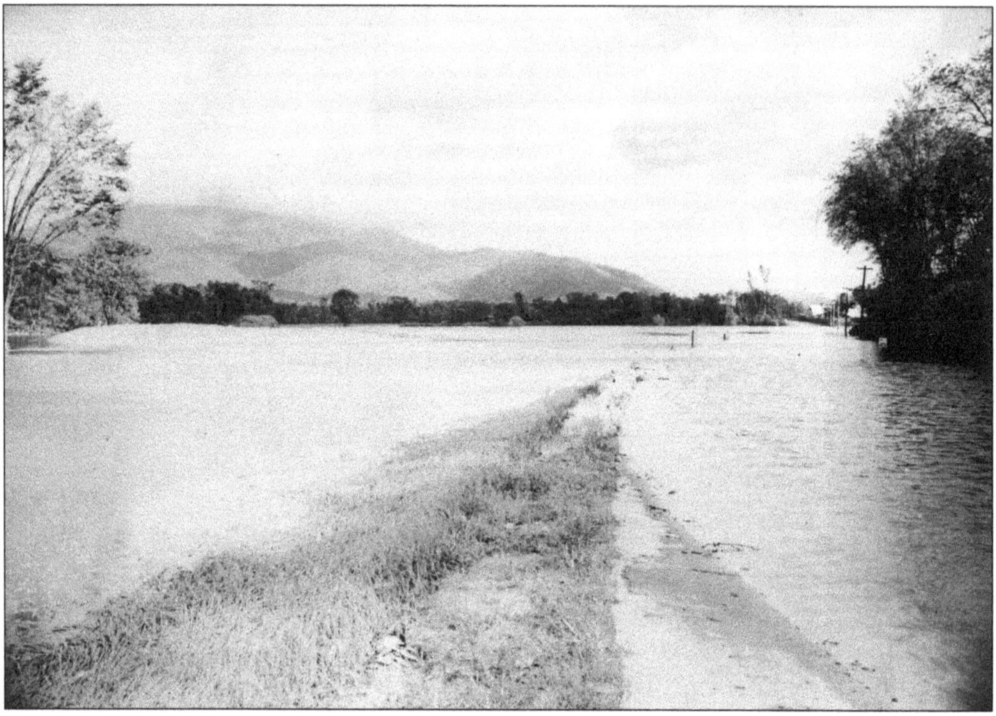

West Claremont is seen here below the high bridge. (CHS.)

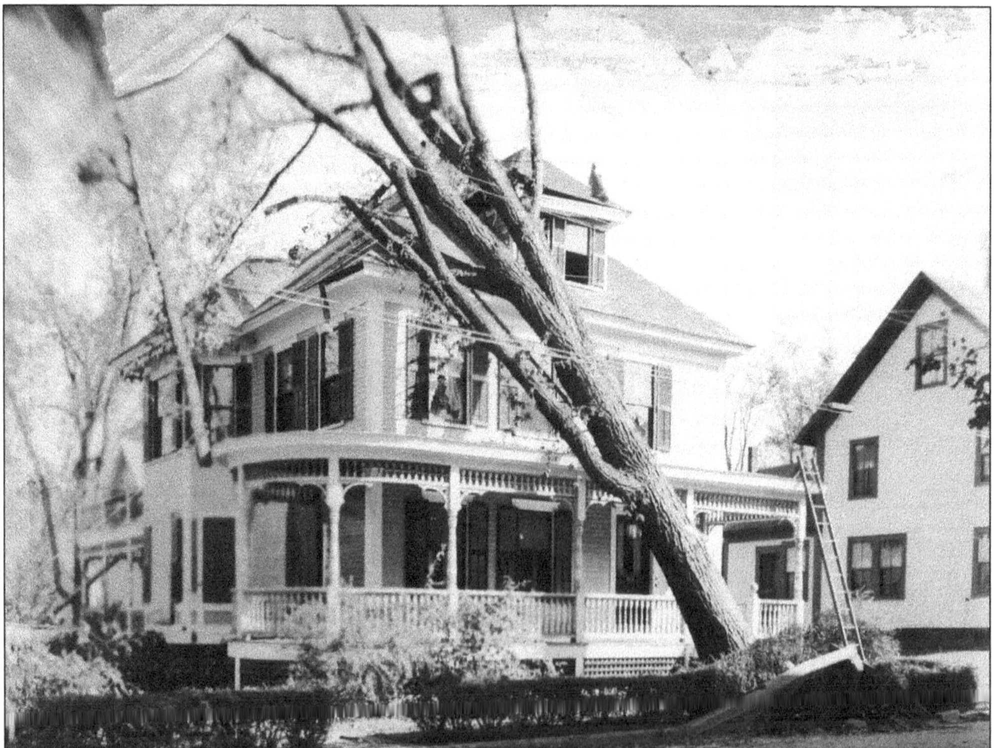

There was extensive damage on Putnam Street, with this tree falling on a house. (CHS.)

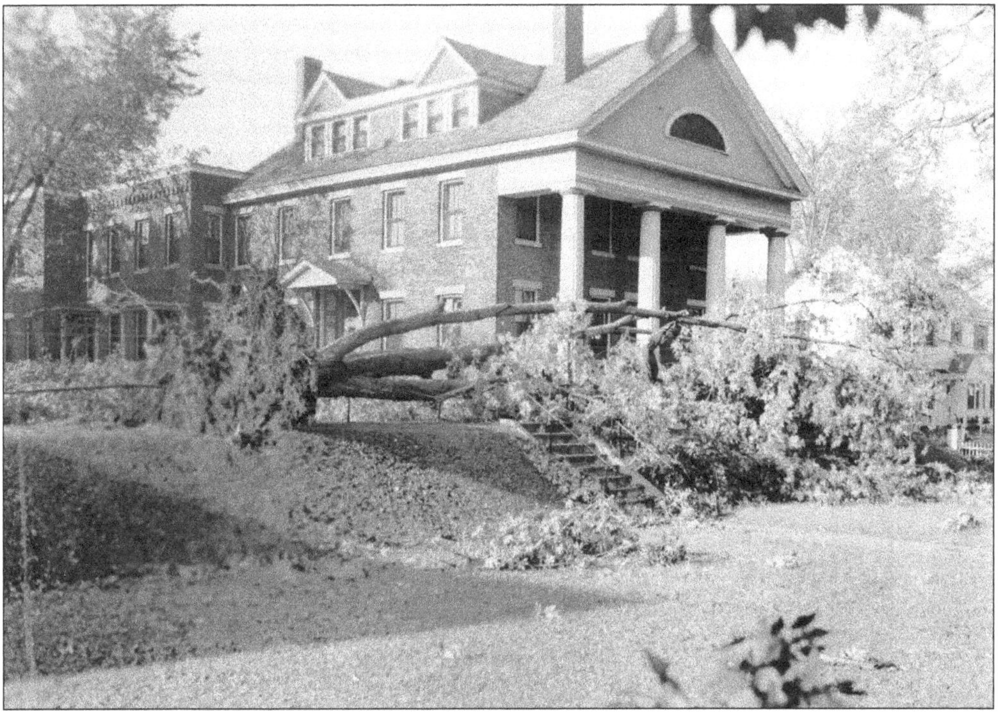

The St. Mary rectory is seen here after the damage. (WLM.)

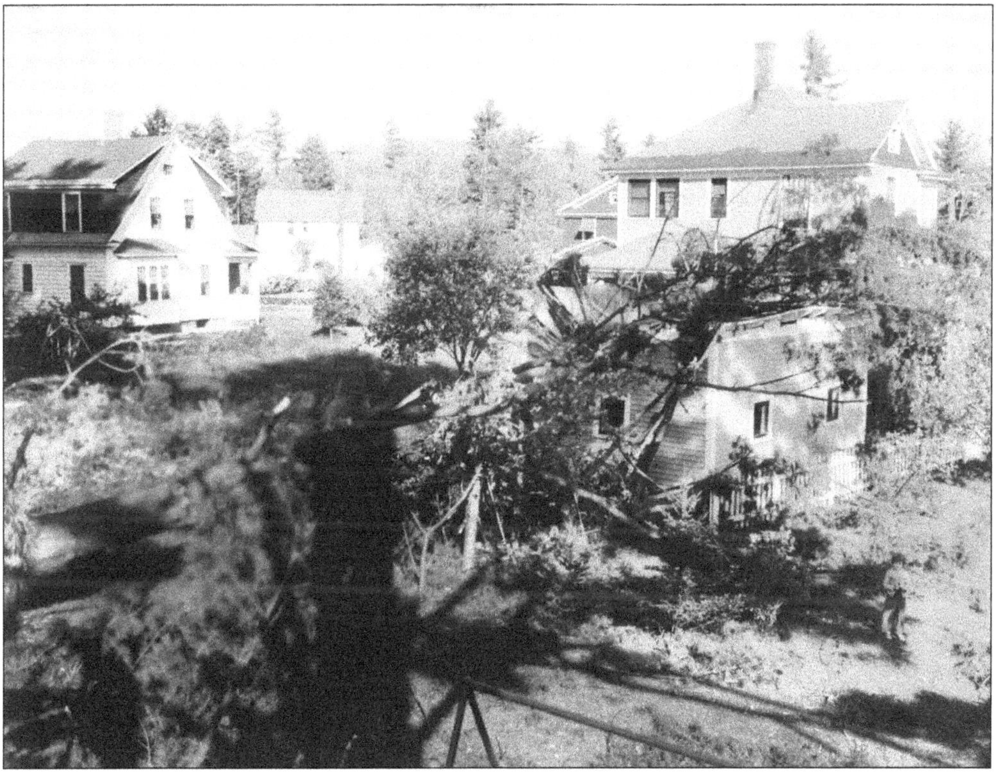

The McArdle home had several downed trees. (WLM.)

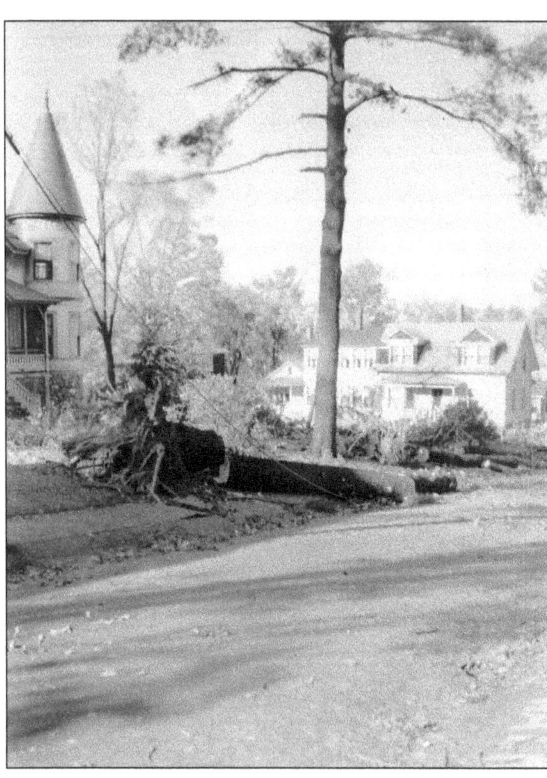

The Boynton home on School Street is seen here after the storm. (CHS.)

This tree fell in the Quimby family's yard. (CHS.)

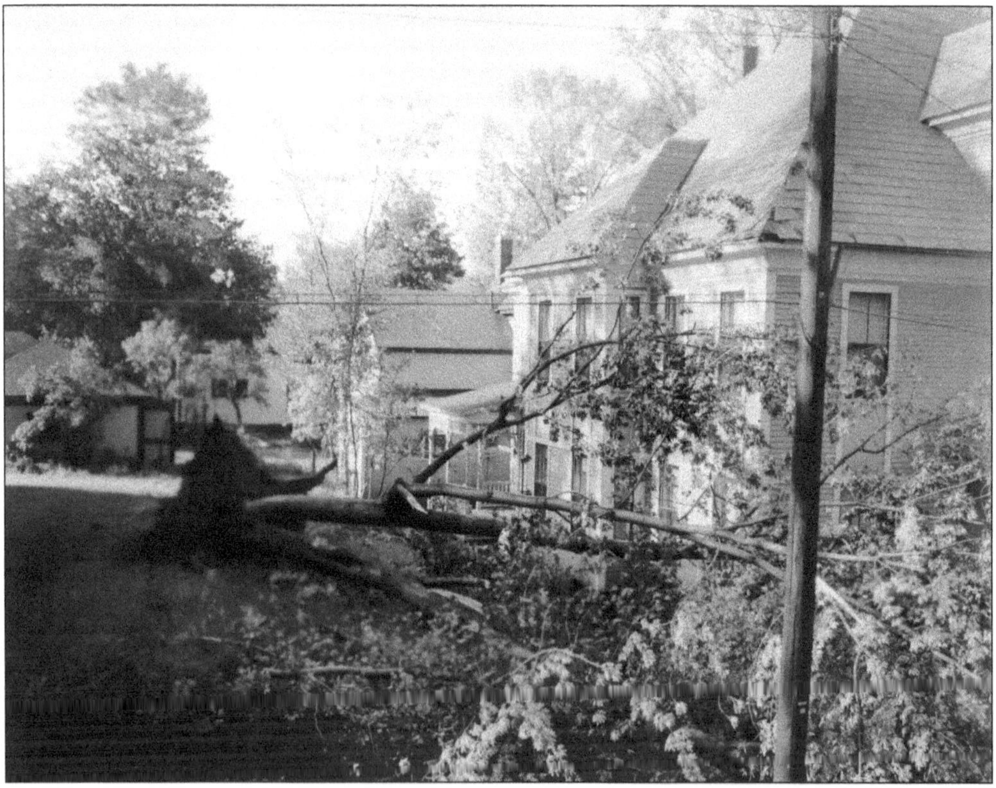

Eight

150th Anniversary

With plans for the city's 250th anniversary in the early stages, it is time to remember the biggest and longest celebration in Claremont's history: the three-day festivities surrounding the town's 150th anniversary in 1914.

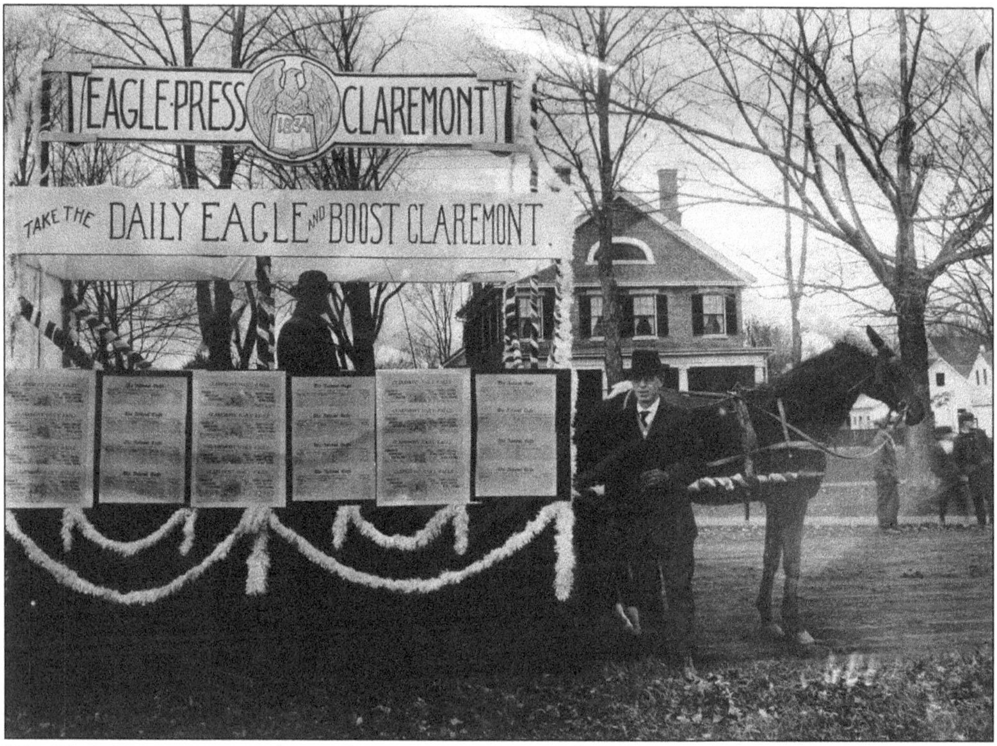

The *Eagle Press* was one of many businesses represented in the parade. There were actually two parades, one on October 26 and one on October 27. (WLM)

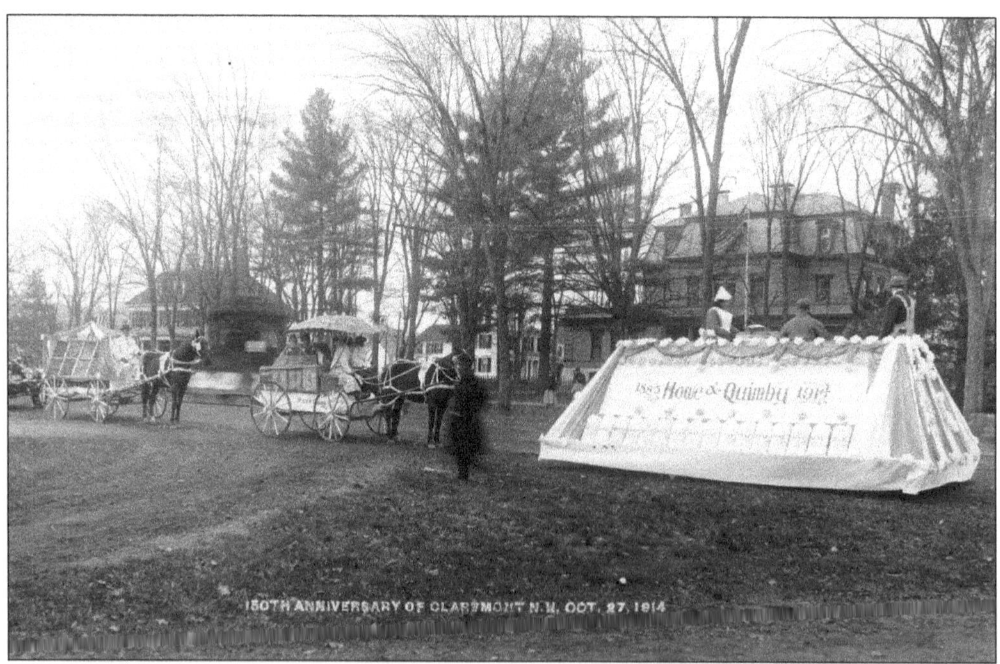

The Howe and Quimby grocery store had this float. The parade on October 27 contained 95 floats and was nearly two miles long. (WLM.)

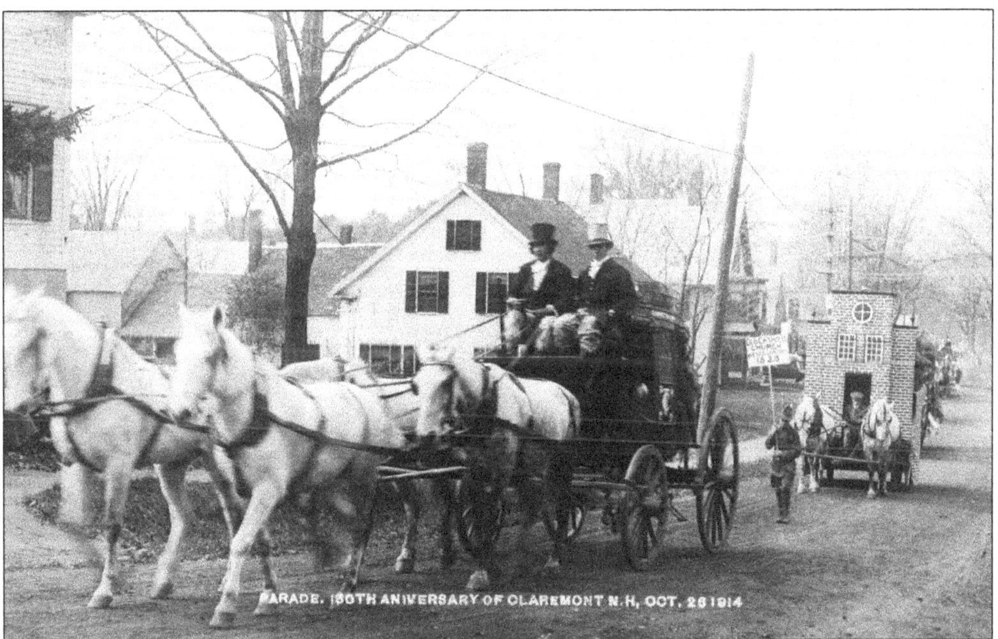

Adolf Emerson and a Mr. Dana (driving) are in this horse-pulled carriage. The parade on October 26 was for bands, the governor and staff, police, firemen, civic organizations, and 15 floats representing historical places and events around the town. (WLM.)

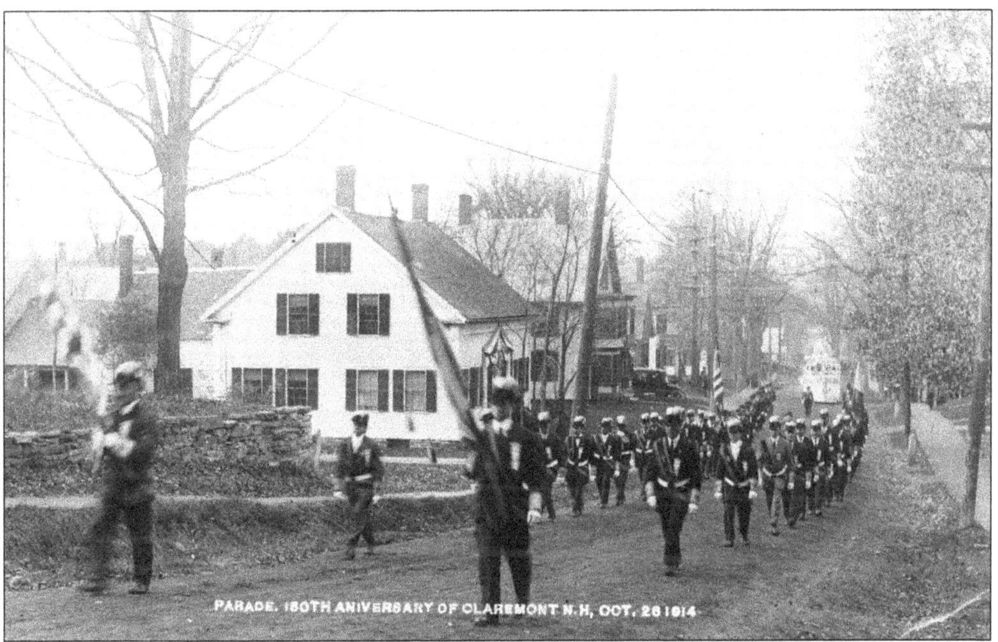

This parade marches down Sullivan Street. The parade route went from Broad Street to Summer Street to Mulberry Street to Sullivan Street to the square before going down Tremont Street to Broad Street to North Street, down Elm Street, up Main Street to Pleasant Street to Summer Street and then back to Broad Street where it started. (WLM.)

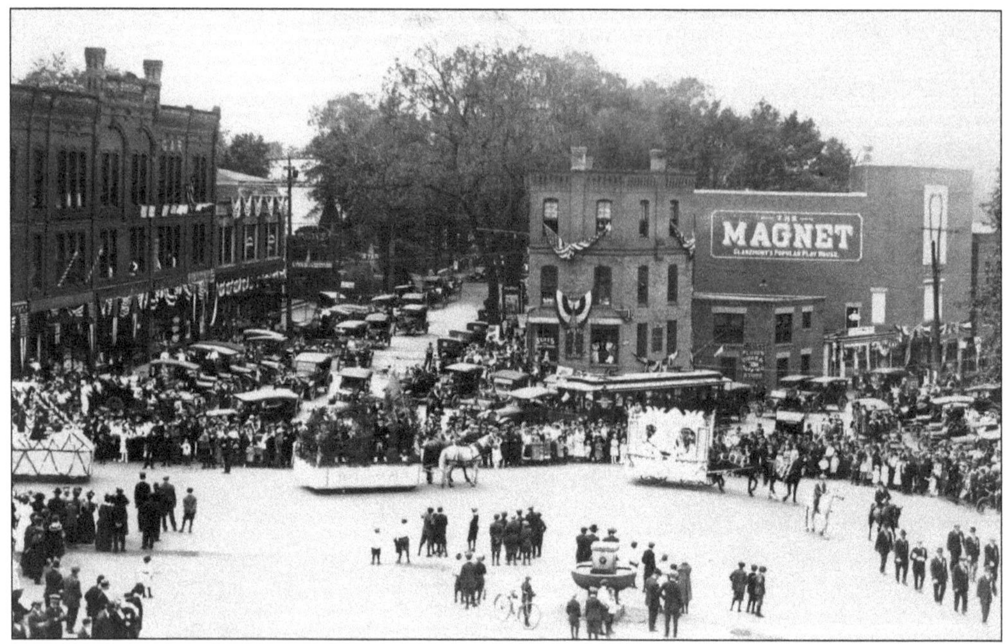

The 150th anniversary parade passes through the square. The back wall of the Magnet Theatre can be seen on Main Street. (WLM.)

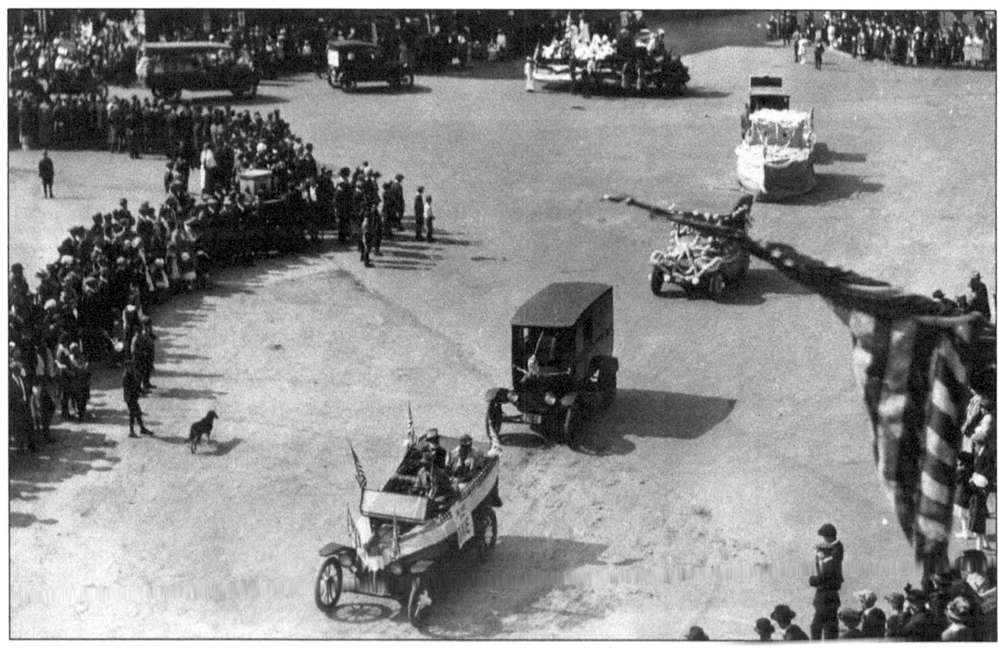

Cars pass through the square on the parade route. (WLM.)

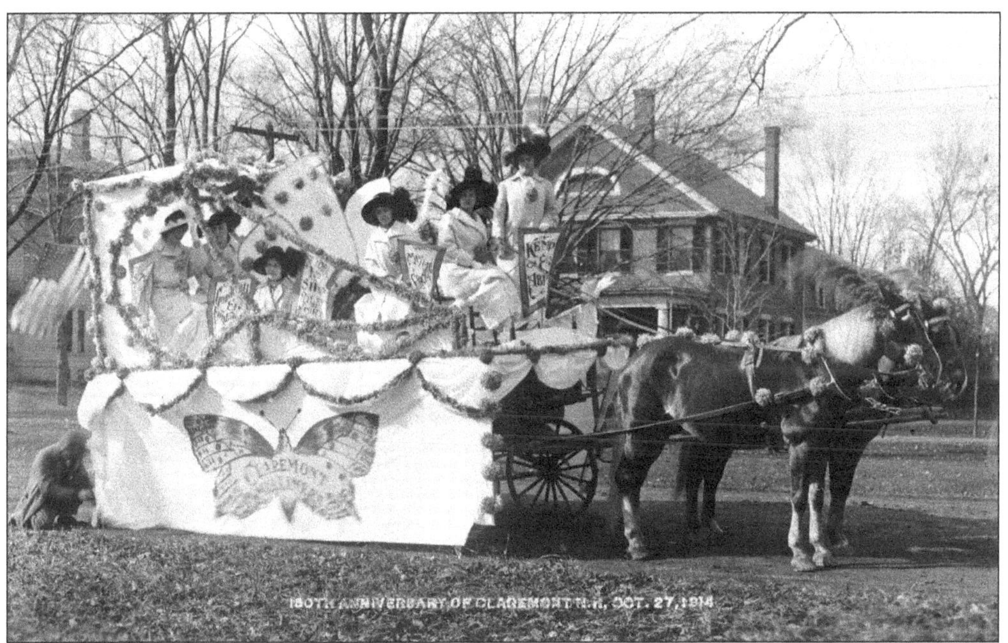
This float carries Claremont milliners down Broad Street. (WLM.)

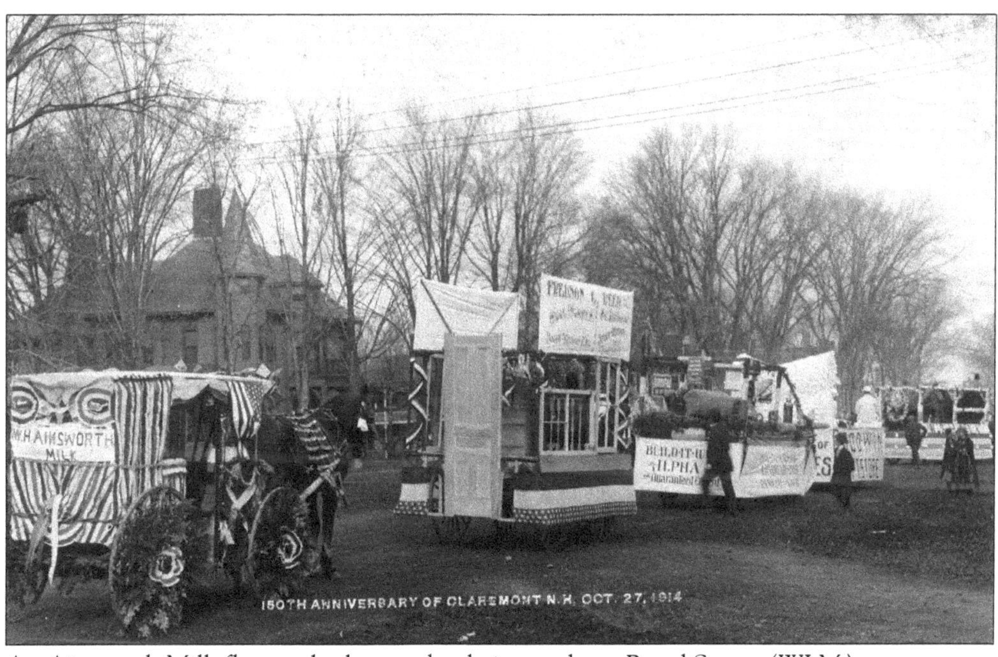

An Ainsworth Milk float and others make their way down Broad Street. (WLM.)

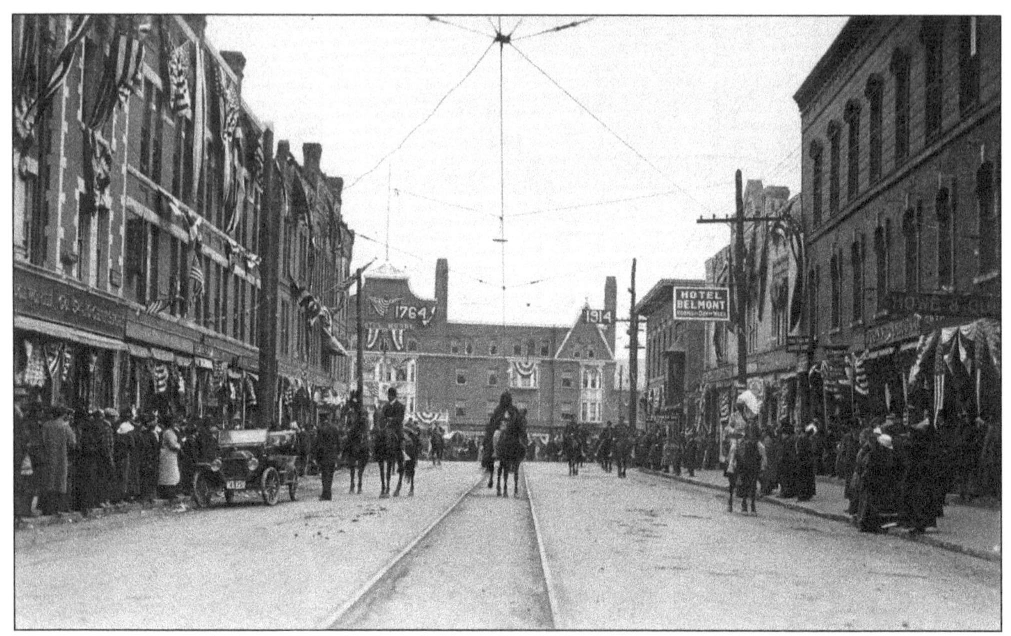

Men representing American Indians ride horseback down Pleasant Street. (WLM.)

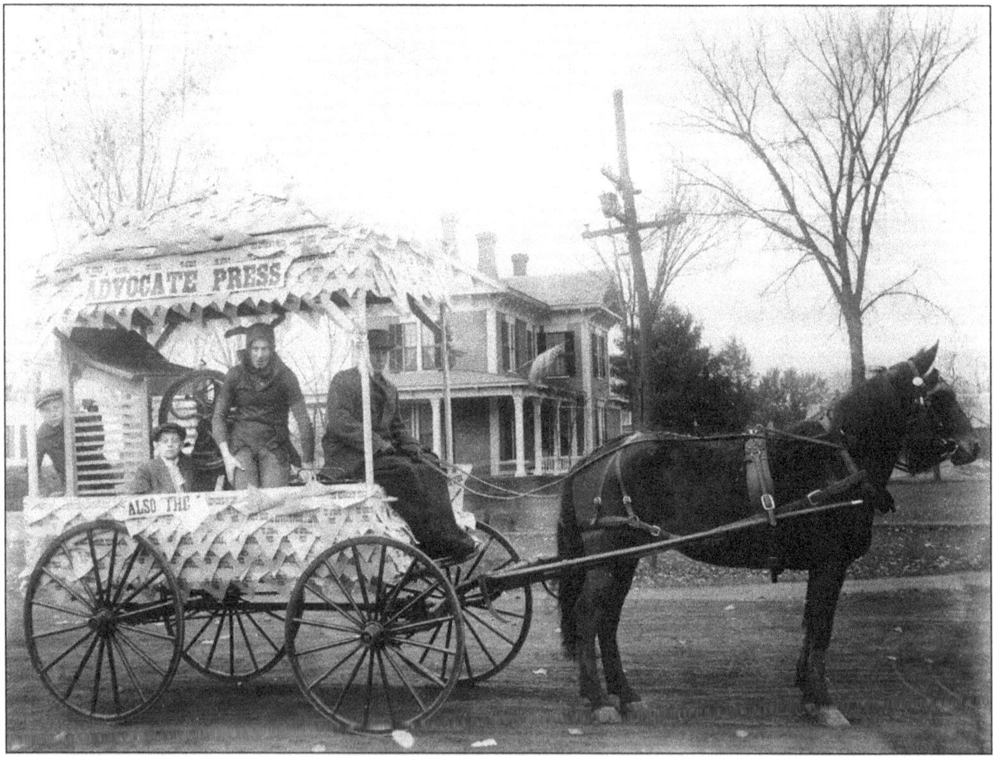

The *Advocate Press*, a longtime competitor of the *Eagle Press*, was represented in the parade. (CHS.)

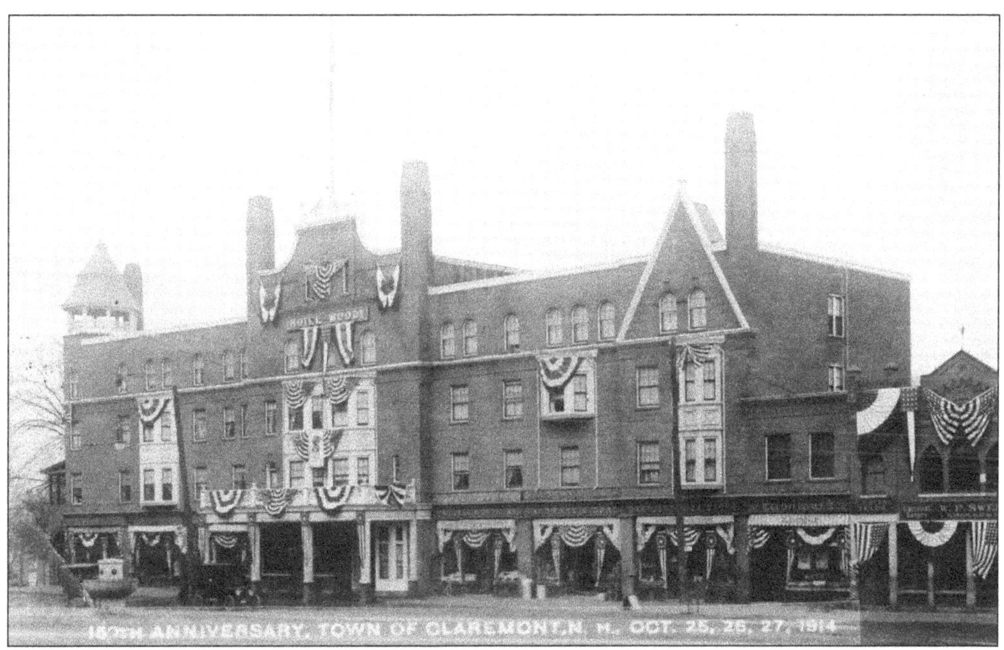

The Hotel Moody was decorated with bunting for the parade. (WLM.)

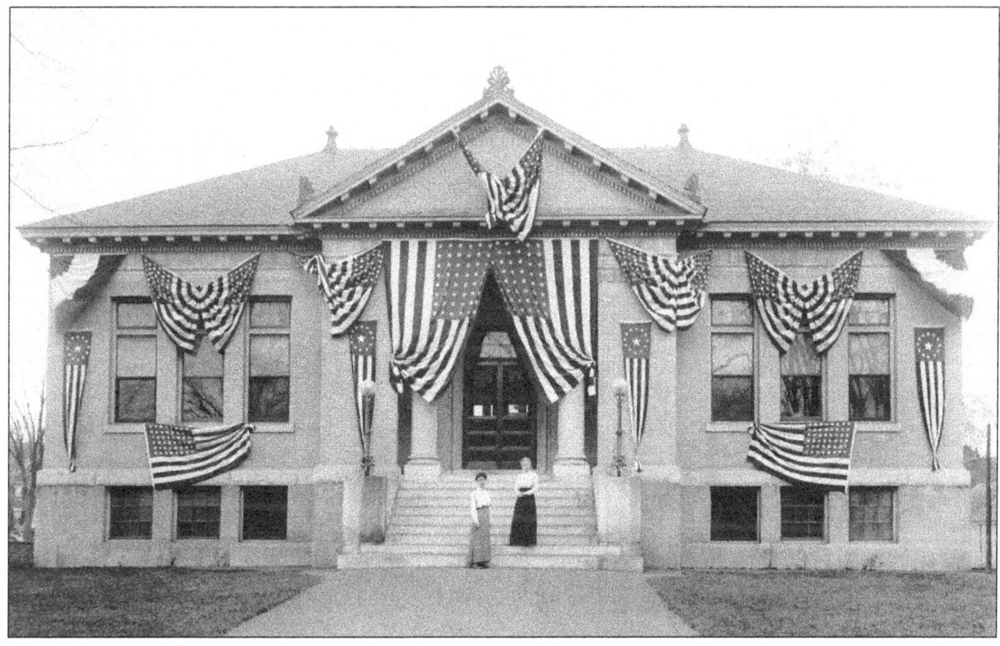

The Fiske Free Library was decorated in observance of the festivities. The only negative event during the celebration was when townspeople learned of the death of one of their most revered citizens. Dr. Osmon Way passed away on October 26, 1914, the town's 150th anniversary. (CHS.)

www.ingramcontent.com/pod-product-compliance
Lightning Source LLC
LaVergne TN
LVHW060624110826
845147LV00015B/933
* 9 7 8 0 7 3 8 5 9 2 9 7 8 *